The
TRANSGENDER
Teen

The
TRANSGENDER
Teen

A Handbook for Parents and Professionals Supporting Transgender and Non-Binary Teens

Stephanie Brill & Lisa Kenney

CLEiS
PRESS

Published in the United States by Cleis Press, an imprint of Start Midnight, LLC, 101 Hudson Street, Thirty-Seventh Floor, Suite 3705, Jersey City, NJ 07302.

Printed in the United States.
Cover design: Scott Idleman/Blink
Text design: Frank Wiedemann
First Edition.
10 9 8 7 6 5 4 3 2

Trade paper ISBN: 978-1-62778-174-9
E-book ISBN: 978-1-62778-175-6

Table of Contents

"This experience of parenting a trans kid has been such a wild ride, and one of the great gifts of my entire life. It's an amazing world, isn't it? So much richer and more complex than I knew."

"I still can't reconcile myself with the added hardship I gave my brave son. But I can say this: Finally embracing his reality, devoting myself to advocate for him and his right to be himself, while it is hard in the world we live in, it is much, much better than fighting the truth and being at odds with him."

Introduction

ARE ANY OF THESE SCENARIOS familiar to you?

- Your daughter just told you that she is transgender—and you had no inkling that this was coming.
- Your son recently asked you not to use gendered pronouns when referring to "him" anymore, preferring that you use "they."
- Your gay son announced to kids at school that he has always felt like he is a girl and now is going to transition to being female. He is not gay after all; *she* is actually straight.
- Your granddaughter has become seriously depressed and isolated, rarely going out of the house once she's home from school. You're not sure what's happening, but think it might be related to how different she is from other girls in how she expresses her gender.
- Your child used a term you have never heard of to describe themselves (neutrois, agender, non-binary, genderqueer,

androgyne…) and when you didn't know what they meant, they left the room and now won't speak to you about it.

- A student in your class has confided in you that they feel like they do not have a gender.
- Your school has informed you that transgender youth are now able to play on the sports team you coach and you're trying to figure out what that means regarding use of locker rooms and managing accommodations for tournaments and other away games that require overnight stays.
- Your transgender teen has been living in alignment with their gender identity since they were a child, but now puberty has hit, and you are conflicted about how to proceed medically.
- Your transgender teen wants to date, and you are nervous because no one at their high school knows they are transgender.
- A teen you work with came to their appointment and announced that they now understand why they didn't "feel right"—it's because they are genderqueer. You want to help and support them, but this is new territory for you.

You are not alone if there is a teen in your life who is feeling strongly that something about their gender does not feel right to them. We have written this book to help you, as the parent[1], caregiver, family member, or professional, to deepen your understanding of what may be happening with your teen and to support you in walking this unfamiliar path together with them.

There is a wide range of reactions that a parent or caregiver may have when their teen starts talking about exploring their gender identity. You may find yourself wondering if this is a stage or a way to get attention from you or from their peers. You may feel a strong desire to support your teen on their[2] gender path, but have no idea how to do that in practical, day-to-day ways. You may question if someone this young can really know this about themselves and fear that your child is setting off on a course where they will face discrimination and possible violence. It may be difficult right now to envision a happy future for your child.

For those of you who have a teen in your life who underwent a gender transition years ago, you may now be faced with new questions, concerns, and decisions. Perhaps they are once again questioning their gender, after you thought they were all done with that. You may find yourself at odds with your teen's other parent about choices your teen wants to make. Or you may be doing well and just want to be sure you're able to support your teen as they enter new developmental stages.

Some of you may be concerned for your teen's psychological health and well-being as they are exhibiting troubling warning signs such as eating disorders, cutting, or not wanting to leave the house. Perhaps your gender-neutral child is about to enter puberty, and you are faced with the tough decision of deciding what is right for them since neither male or female puberty is a match for who they experience themselves to be.

Perhaps your own upbringing, religious beliefs, or cultural expectations are at odds with your teen's sense of gender. You are concerned about how you and your family will be perceived by others in your family and community. Or perhaps you are worried that this is your fault, and if you simply begin parenting differently, this will go away.

Raising a teenager is challenging; when the teen is transgender or non-binary, the task becomes that much more difficult. Yet, as you already know, parenting is an improvisation; we figure it out the best we can as we go along, and what seems initially difficult and overwhelming ultimately becomes manageable. This parenting challenge is no different in that regard. Parenting is an undertaking that requires growth, compassion, and courage. Having walked thousands through this journey, we can help you get a better understanding of what may be happening with your teen, how to best respond, and what steps to take next. Although there are no simple, one-size-fits-all answers, there are strategies you can use on the journey. You are not alone. We will help clarify the issues at hand so that you are able to refocus your attention on the whole of your child, and not just their gender. We will help you move from a place of concern, disbelief, fear, confusion, or wariness to a place where you can become an effective ally for your child—no matter where they may lie on the gender spectrum. We want to help you move to or return to a place where your teen knows they can count on you to support them, to love them, and to help them through the rough patches of life, both in these years and the years to come. Nothing you did created your child's gender and you can't control it, but you can and will make a tremendous difference (positively or negatively) in how their gender affects their sense of themselves as a person of value who is worthy of love.

This book is for all adults who want to better understand teens and gender. This book is for you.

Understandings of Gender Are Continuously Evolving

We often think of gender as fixed and immutable, yet each of us in our own lifetimes can think of many ways that ideas about gender have changed. Notions of gender are continuously expanding in our society and vary throughout the world.

As our understanding of both gender itself and the developmental processes that shape it deepen, the landscape of gender becomes much more beautiful and varied. We can see that the two categories of male and female, based exclusively on the presence of a penis or a vulva, are inadequate. We also know that the associated gender stereotypes do not work for most of us. The exploration of gender can be tricky territory as the issues involved are some of the most personal aspects of our social and emotional existences.

And yet our society is indeed expanding our understanding of this core aspect of who we are. At the time of this writing, there are movies and television shows with prominent transgender and other gender-diverse characters; the U.S. military has announced its intention to allow openly transgender people to serve; and the U.S. Department of Education has unequivocally stated that transgender and gender-expansive youth have significant protections under federal law. It's not unusual to see musicians, actors, and other celebrities in clothing that doesn't conform to "traditional" gender norms, including those who identify as males wearing dresses and skirts. When Facebook announced in the U.S. that they were giving users fifty-one gender identities to choose from, many wondered how they could possibly have identified fifty-one options (the number of gender options Facebook offers varies by country—an interesting discussion topic for another time). It wasn't long after they rolled out these options that they announced they had underestimated the range of gender identities and provided users with the ability to customize their gender identity. When Fusion released the results of their 2015 Millennial poll, in which they surveyed one thousand people aged eighteen to thirty-four and asked them whether they believed there are only two genders (male and female) or whether they believed gender is on a spectrum, 50 percent said they believed gender is on a spectrum, 46 percent said they believed there are two genders, and 4 percent said they didn't know.

Your teen is not alone in seeing and experiencing gender in a broader way, and their peers are likely to have greater understanding and acceptance of gender identity and gender expression than the adults around them. While this book may not immediately get you on the same page as your teen or their peers, we hope that it will give you new perspectives to broaden your understanding of gender and ultimately help you sleep better at night.

Gender Is Personal

As more and more people resist ill-fitting gender categories and choose, instead, to express their own authentic gender identities, they are opening up a world where we understand that gender is personal. This is leading to an ever-greater range of variability than was once thought. Gender variability is a natural part of humanity. We have evidence of this across cultures, species, and recorded history. The diversity of gender, including transgender identities, is nothing new. Certainly there are new ways this may be expressed, as well as new language, terminology, medical options, and an ever-evolving set of responses to gender diversity—but gender variability is not new.

As gender diversity becomes more visible and rigidly defined gender roles become less compulsory, an increasing number of people feel more comfortable expressing themselves authentically. As we are exposed to a wider variety of gender expressions and gender identities, our assumptions about gender understandably come into question. Is it really true that biology dictates so much about our physical, psychological, and cognitive abilities and inclinations? How much of gender is actually culturally influenced or prescribed? How do our personal cultures (family, religion, ethnicity, race, sexual orientation, etc.) exert influence, and what is the impact of the intersections of these cultures? Where does the physical influence begin and societal influence end? If gender is "inborn," then why is it expressed so differently around the world? What if our genitals do not dictate gender at all? What is gender anyway? Why do we feel so scared (uncomfortable, unsettled, anxious…) by the thought that it may be bigger than we realized? And what does all this mean for the way in which we try to raise our teenagers to be safe, happy, and healthy?

Although gender diversity may be more visible than ever before, we don't believe that's because the percentage of transgender and non-binary people has increased in recent years. Rather, as the times become more accepting of overall cultural diversity, an increasing number of people are exploring gender and more openly expressing their gender in ways that challenge societal expectations. More people are choosing authenticity over repression, and we hope that more people are choosing authenticity over self-harm. As more people are openly being themselves, it becomes the challenge of our society to afford everyone a place at a table that values diversity over conscious or conditioned conformity.

Unfortunately, we have ample evidence that the alternative is dismal. The rates of violence toward those who express their gender in ways that don't conform to society's expectations are appalling, and the rates of suicide and attempted suicide of transgender and non-binary teenagers are as high as 40 percent or more. We all must move out of our comfort zones and learn to understand and embrace gender diversity for the sake of our children and the health of our society at large.

Some teens experience an untenable level of discomfort with the constraints of the outdated and restrictive binary assumption of gender, and all youth are impacted by it. The problem with the simplistic, binary, male/female, either/or gender roles and expectations is that they inherently discourage expression outside of the two options presented. The boxes, though perhaps larger than in times past, still remain. The societal pressure to conform to gender expectations dictates consciously and unconsciously how each member of society should look and act in order to be accepted. The binary notion of gender is taught and learned, with the policing of gender beginning in infancy.

These notions of gender inhibit all of us from knowing what our true expression would be in the absence of such limited options and serve to prevent people from exploring their gender and expressing themselves in the ways that are most natural to them. Everyone has difficulty fitting into these boxes of male and female in some way or another; for some, the fit is so uncomfortable that they simply cannot make it work. There is nothing wrong with them—the current gender system is simply too limiting. For the non-binary and transgender teen, there can be a large and painful divide between what is expected of them and how they experience themself.

It can be difficult, at first, to imagine gender as something complex rather than binary. It can be challenging to move away from the long-held understanding of two fixed genders assigned at birth and inherently linked to genitalia. Those notions have worked well enough for many people for a very long time. Your child has now become a catalyst to evolve your thinking. It may be difficult to understand and accept your child's struggle with their gender if your gender isn't something you've spent much time thinking about before now.

Language is evolving to describe the varied experiences of people who do not identify with traditional gender identities and roles. We use a number of terms that may be unfamiliar to you. Please keep in mind that there is a glossary at the end of the book. Getting a handle on some of the words used to describe gender is very helpful when it comes to being able to effectively understand this topic. To communicate more effectively with your teen and other people in your teen's life, you may find it helpful to ask questions such as "What language would you like me to use when referring to your gender?" or "What does this word mean to you?" It is important to recognize that transgender, non-binary, and other individuals who are gender-expansive do not all share the same experience of gender or language. Curiosity and openness will go a long way toward understanding your child's gender without trying to put their identity into a box. In the process, you may discover that you begin to think about your own gender in ways that you have not before.

Like all of us, transgender and non-binary teens want to be seen and recognized for all of who they are, not just one single aspect of their identity. As fundamental as gender is, we are all more than our gender. In fact, our understanding of gender is inextricably linked to our communities and experiences—race, ethnicity, religion, and class—making it even more complex and rich.

We are not proposing or seeking a genderless society. Far from it! Gender is a fundamental part of who people are. If you have a child or teen who identifies and is comfortable with a "traditional" understanding of gender, that's great; it should be valued and respected. We simply believe that value, respect, and support should be available to all. We want a world where everyone, including the children and teens in your life, can be safe in expressing themselves. Simply put, we believe gender identity and gender expression are human rights matters.

Your Role

You're reading this book because you love your child or care about a teen in your life. The challenge to consider is how that love and care translate into support for your teen around their gender. As parents and caregivers, there are so many questions, fears, and concerns that you balance with your responsibility as caretaker for your child. Our goal is to assist you in identifying your fears so that they don't drive your interactions with your child, and to answer your questions and address your concerns so that that you can parent with clarity and compassion.

Being a gender non-binary or transgender person is not a choice. Regardless of whether a young person has supportive peers and adults in their life, there is a cost to living outside a family's, community's, and society's expectations of who they should be and how they should express themselves. Our experience, however, is that by the time a teen discusses their gender identity with a parent, they have decided that the costs of trying to conform are much greater for them than the costs associated with living authentically, which makes it all the more important for them to be able to rely on a parent's love and support. These teens are often confronted by serious risks for living outside of the social expectations of gender conformity.

Choosing to be one's self should not lead to discrimination or violence. Nor should it mean having to face disrespect or ridicule at home. Your role is to help your child be safe. While you cannot ensure their safety in the world, you can help create conditions in which their safety will be more likely, and you can certainly ensure it in your own home. Research shows that family support is the single most important factor in shaping transgender and non-binary youths' lives. This juncture is a critical time in your child's life and in your relationship with your teen. If you are unable to support your teen effectively at this time in their life, the chances of harm—to them and your relationship with them—are significantly increased. Staying connected through these years is critical, and it is our aim to help you do just that.

We hope that *The Transgender Teen* will be a great resource and source of support for any adult with a transgender or non-binary youth in their lives. Although written primarily for adults raising transgender and non-binary teens, it will be useful for professionals working with them as well. We hope to be able to provide you with the tools and support you need to focus your attention on the love you hold for your child—regardless of their gender.

----

1   We use the word "parent" in the book as shorthand to broadly encompass any and all adults responsible for raising a child. This includes, but is not limited to, immediate and extended family members, foster parents, step-parents, guardians, and chosen family.

2   We use "they/their/them/themself" in the book as a gender-neutral singular pronoun. We know this may be less familiar for you at first but it will soon become natural. In fact, the American Dialect Society voted for "they" used this way as the word of the year in 2015.

Chapter 1

Being a Parent of a Transgender or Non-Binary Teen

"What I first learned about trans teens terrified me. I have to be honest, I was falling apart. But then I realized—this is not my issue—my losing it will not keep my kid safe. It was a cop-out. I snapped out of it and started to educate myself and everyone around me.… I know that I can make a difference. I have to make a difference. My kid, your kid, all of our kids need to know they are loved and valued and that their existence has value."

"The hardest thing [about talking to my parents about my gender identity] was knowing that they wouldn't be able to relate to how I felt."

WHAT IS YOUR STORY? How did you hear that your child is trying to understand and grapple with issues related to their gender? We've heard thousands of stories over the years and while some themes emerge, what is always moving is a child's desire to be seen and accepted by the people they love and need most—their family.

Some of you heard from your children when they were young. While having a younger child tell you that their gender is different from what you thought it was has its own challenges, there is a simplicity that can also make it a little more straightforward (at least at the time). The developmental issues younger children experience are commonly less unnerving to parents, and there is a sense that there's enough time to work it all through together. With teens, it's more complicated. Their understanding often takes into consideration gender identities outside the binary—and they want to find the one that best encompasses who they are. On top of this gender exploration, they are going through the developmental challenges of adolescence. With teens, time feels very short, like a ticking clock counting down the time until they leave home, when working through things with the convenience of a shared roof over your heads will no longer be possible. Finally, time also has an urgency because teens don't depend on their parents to take actions on their behalf in the same way that young children do. As a parent of a teen you are well aware that if you do not act fast enough, your child will take matters into their own hands. Because of this, the risks feel greater when dealing with a teen's gender issues.

How did your child raise the issue of their gender with you? Did they talk to you in person? Some parents we know received a letter (in a couple of cases on top of cookies or brownies that their child made—love that!). We know parents who were told in the car on the way to school, in an email, while on Skype/FaceTime, by one of their other kids, as a "by the way" as they left the house to go out, and even by text. Regardless of how you heard, your teen had given it a lot of thought before they told you. It wasn't done on a whim. It was a courageous act to make themself vulnerable to you, whose love and acceptance they most desperately want and need.

If you just found out that your child is transgender, non-binary, or questioning their gender, we know how much your world is probably whirling around you right now. Understanding your teen's gender identity can be challenging; it is potentially confusing and stressful for teens and their families alike. We will help you understand what is most important in this initial period after learning about your teen's gender identity. All parents who have teens sorting through issues related to their gender have questions (and have been questioned by others) about what all of this gender stuff means, why it's coming up for their child, and what to do about it. Since this is the place where everyone starts, we thought we'd start here too. So whether you've been talking with your child about gender for a day or a decade, this is a good place to look at the issues, concerns, and questions likely to be a part of your process.

More than anything else, your goal as a parent of a transgender, non-binary, or questioning teen is to reassure your child that you love them and to keep the communication between you open. Reassure your teen that while you may have some things to learn, you are committed to doing so. Let them know that they are not alone and you want to help and support them. Your child will be paying particular attention to what you *do* after this disclosure, not only to what you say. Be mindful that they are observing you—and interpreting your actions—in a much more careful way than usual. Be sure to check in with your teen to ensure that they know you understood the importance of what they told you, that you are working to understand related information, and that they are not coming to incorrect conclusions based on their own fears or concerns about how you might react after they shared with you who they are.

If you feel knocked off-balance, confused, afraid, or even angry about this news, realize that many parents have felt the same way. You may feel many things all at once, including a certain numbness of emotion in response to your child's disclosure, and these emotions can change rapidly. This is normal. It will be best to find ways to express these feelings with people other than your child—for example, with supportive friends, family members, and mental healthcare providers. Try as hard as you can to stay patient and nonjudgmental with your teen. Remember, they are probably scared too and are looking to you for support.

There are usually a lot of feelings, including fear, on all sides, especially in the early days of conversation. Your teen is likely afraid that you will no longer love them, or will reject them in some fundamental way because of their gender identity. They are concerned that you will be disappointed in them or disapprove of who they are. They may also be afraid that you will not support them in the changes they want to make in order to feel congruent and that postponing these changes until they are eighteen and can decide on their own may seem an impossible delay. You, of course, have your own complex set of reactions.

It is ideal if you can stay in a patient, supportive, and nonjudgmental place when engaging in conversations with your teen and family around issues of gender. If you feel like your initial response to your teen was negative, poorly received, or simply didn't sufficiently communicate your love and commitment to your child, you can change your approach to one that feels better for you and also supports your teen. **It is never too late to make that shift.**

Taking in the Information

You may have learned about your teen's gender identity anywhere along their journey of self-discovery—from before they were aware of it themselves to after they have been working with this understanding of themself for a few years. Perhaps the school called you in for a meeting to discuss their thoughts on your teen or share observations about what they see as gender-related issues. Or perhaps when you dropped your son off at school and they casually announced while leaving the car, "Bye mom. By the way, I am really a girl. Will you pay for surgery over vacation so I can come back to school as a girl?" Maybe the therapist of your severely depressed child has just told you that they suspect your child has a non-binary gender and that the physical changes of puberty are triggering their depression. The therapist is recommending hormonal suppression immediately as a potentially life-saving measure. Or maybe your child left you a long letter on the table when they went away to camp describing how they feel about their gender, recommending this book, a conference, or other resources so you can get up to speed, and be able to fully support their gender transition when they return home.

Depending on the circumstances in your family, you may need some time to catch up with your teen. One strategy that is particularly helpful during this time is to simply listen and ask questions. You may be tempted to talk more than listen, to tell your teen all the reasons why things may be different from what they think they are, how they couldn't really know this about themselves at this age, or that you know them better than they know themself. This is not surprising as you seek to try and slow down what feels like a runaway train. However, even if the information your child shared regarding their gender comes as a total shock to you, it is critical that you truly listen and resist the temptation to discount what they are telling you.

Others Will Follow Your Lead

This initial period of communication is a crucial time. Even as you grapple with your own emotions, it is an opportunity for you to set the tone for the type of discussions that you will be having going forward. We have frequently found that others—your teen, others in your family and community—will follow your lead. When you appear frantic and highly distraught, others will respond in kind. If you can present a centered, thoughtful stance, others will feed off this as well.

We fully recognize that this is no simple task; but if necessary, this is one of those times as a parent when you should try to fake it 'til you make it.

Be sure to take the time to acknowledge what your teen is saying about their identity—even if you are afraid, confused, worried, and even doubtful. You can begin by listening and validating what you hear them saying. For example:

"I hear that you feel your gender is different than what we assumed and this has been very difficult for you. I want you to know that I am here for you and will do everything I can to educate myself so you will no longer be alone with this. Thank you for sharing this with me. It may take me some time to adjust and I may make mistakes along the way—but I want you to hear that from this moment on it is my intention to listen to you and support you. I love you and want you to never forget that."

Make a specific point to make affirming statements to your teen as often as you can, not couched concerns or judgments, but simple statements of support and reassurance:

"I love you no matter what."

"We will get through this."

"I am here for you; you are not alone in this. I will help you."

By making it clear that you are on their side, you are actively building and reinforcing the bridge of connection with your teen. This keeps them anchored to you at a very vulnerable time of their life.

Common Adult Fears About Non-Binary and Transgender Teens

There are so many feelings that arise when you are just learning that your teen is transgender or non-binary. It can be a destabilizing time for the entire family, and you may feel as though there will never again be a time when gender isn't your family's entire focus.

The following section will cover some of the most common fears and concerns that adults feel when they discover their teen is non-binary or transgender. However, before we go on, please know that while your new awareness regarding gender will never go away (thankfully), the amount of time and space it takes up in your family will change with time—you *will* find a new normal that feels comfortable.

The following are not only the hesitations and concerns that parents and caregivers experience, but the worries and apprehensions that will be expressed by all well-meaning adults in your life. You may find it useful to communicate the following information as part of the initial disclosures you will be having with others about your teen's gender.

Most parents experience numerous fears and concerns when they are coming to terms with the possibility that their child may be transgender or non-binary. The period when teens are sorting out their gender can be a time of distress for the entire family. It can put a strain on every relationship, as each member of the family sorts things out in their own way. In order to continue to provide your teen with the love and support that they need and deserve, try to contain your worries, concerns, and beliefs in order to maintain a stable bond with your child. If you are having a difficult time, it is best to try to address your struggles apart from your child. See a counselor yourself, do research online, and get the support that you require in order to be able to be fully present for your child. This does not mean that you can't have feelings or disagree with the approach your child wants to take (or is already taking), but continue actively loving your child through it all. Prioritize your intact relationship over everything else. Try to refrain from criticism and judgment in order to not alienate your teen. Home should be the safest place for your child. If this isn't the case, they will go elsewhere for support, and you may find yourself without information about what they are doing or the connection to them needed to influence their actions.

Later in the book, we share the specific parenting practices that have been shown to create the most positive outcomes for transgender and non-binary teens. But for now, this chapter will explore the questions, fears, and concerns that parents commonly have when hearing their child has a gender other than the one they had always assumed.

How Common Are Transgender and Non-Binary Teens?

In truth, there is no way of knowing or even estimating how many transgender and non-binary people there are. Gender variability is real. It is now being tracked in different ways in a number of societies around the world. Doing so remains a complicated task, as there are so many points of variability. However, we can safely say that in every school, there are youth who either do not identify with their assumed gender or who feel that the gender options available need to be expanded. What is critical for you to know as a parent is that your child's experience is part of the amazing variation that exists in human beings everywhere.

Is My Child Really Transgender or Non-Binary?

"Isn't my child just gay?"

"I was really hoping she'd be gay instead, because it would be safer."

"I had no idea."

"My head was swimming and it felt like all the air had left the room."

Because transgender and non-binary identities are not well understood in our society, it is common for parents to assume that their
child is gay or lesbian rather than transgender. This is especially true
for parents who recognized early on that their child's gender didn't
neatly conform. In our culture, individuals with a gender expression
outside of typical norms are often stereotyped as being gay, lesbian,
or bisexual. Of course in reality, Lesbian/Gay/Bisexual/Queer (LGBQ)
people are like everyone else; some fit into traditional ideas of gender
and some don't. But given the prevailing stereotypes, it is natural to
have assumed that your child with a nontraditional gender expression
would be LGBQ.

Sometimes when a teen insists that their gender identity is not
what was assumed at birth, parents try to tell their child that they
are actually gay or lesbian. At this point in time, the path of an LGBQ
person is often less stigmatized than that of a transgender person.
Thus, many parents find themselves hoping that their teen is gay
and not transgender or non-binary, believing their teen will face
less discrimination and be more widely understood and accepted.

Further complicating this, some transgender and non-binary
people initially confuse their internal state with sexual orientation,
and then realize over time that gender identity, not sexual orientation, is the issue. There are many reasons for this. Teens are not
immune from the general confusion about gender and sexual orientation. Discussions about sexual orientation have been increasingly
common over the last several decades, so the teen's sense that they
are somehow "different" may have been associated with sexual orientation. However, it is much less common for someone to feel they are
transgender, only to discover that they are really gay or lesbian. Of
course, some youth are both transgender and LGBQ.

Having your child tell you they are transgender or non-binary can
be a much bigger shock when it comes from a child who has always
appeared to be traditional in their gender expression. Your disbelief

may be much greater than the disbelief of families with a child who has always been a bit outside of their prescribed gender box. If this is the case in your family, be particularly mindful that you may need some additional time to process this new information. Let your teen know that you need some time to take in what they have shared with you, but it doesn't mean you don't love and support them—you just need to catch up to them.

If someone in your child's life has shared with you that they think your child is transgender or non-binary, don't discount it. Try to remain open-minded. Seriously consider their observations and listen to their reasoning. They may be onto something you were not aware of or have been unwilling to see.

Is Being Transgender or Non-Binary a Choice?

> *"Some people hate me for something I cannot change and I just don't understand. I'm smart and beautiful and human and they treat me like dirt."*[1]

People don't choose their genders.

Many parents find greater compassion for their teen once they understand and accept this critical idea. People are who they are. Your teen didn't choose their gender any more than you chose your gender. While it is true that your teen is deciding to communicate about their gender identity with you, it is not a choice as to what that identity is.

There Are Choices Involved

The issue of "choice" is an important one.

Your child had a choice to share their gender identity and address the issues in their life that this will bring up, rather than deny it to themself and to others. They had a choice to share with you who they are, rather than hide it; to be vulnerable and risk intimacy and connection with you in the hope that you would see them and love them as they are. They have made a choice to live authentically despite all the pressures not to.

You have a choice about how you will respond to what your teen has had the courage to share with you. You have a choice about how you will expect others to treat your teen. You have a choice about whether or not you will support your child in relation to their gender identity. You can choose how you express your care, love, and support for your child.

For many reasons—religious convictions, upbringing, cultural customs, family traditions—parents feel that it is their responsibility to tell their child that it is wrong to live as their authentic self, or that they will not "allow" it. Viewing your teen's gender as a choice may allow you to feel more comfortable trying to mandate conformity, but trying to control how your teen expresses who they are will not change their fundamental gender identity. We have worked with many families who have pursued such an approach, and unfortunately they've created great damage along the way, requiring significant healing once they come to realize that this was never a "choice" their child was making. Parents of all cultures and faiths have found ways to reconcile gender issues with their traditions—we are confident that you can as well. You are not alone in trying to find ways to reconcile your child's gender identity with other important parts of their identity—your child is trying to do the same. Talk with your teen about any conflicts they perceive with different aspects of themselves. Together you can brainstorm ways to resolve them.

Why Is a Child Transgender or Non-Binary?

We will next explore some of the commonly held ideas about why a child might identify with a gender different from the one they've been raised as. While many of the questions we address might be on your mind, try to bear in mind that what's most important is not *why* your child is "the way they are," but rather that they simply *are* who they are. What truly matters is what you are going to do next.

What Caused This?

Many parents wonder if they "caused" their child's transgender or non-binary gender identity. Having a transgender or non-binary child is not related to poor parenting, divorce, neglect, or abuse. It appears to be an innate characteristic of an individual. It is neither a choice nor a lifestyle. And when it comes to gender identity, it is not something that can truly be changed. It can be repressed and hidden, but not without great harm.

Gender is part of who we are. Being transgender or non-binary is simply part of the human experience.

Was It Our Parenting?

Parents often blame themselves or each other for the issues their children experience. When a child expresses their gender in a nontraditional fashion, with a less common gender identity or an unexpected gender expression, parents frequently feel that they are to blame. Fears that perhaps your parenting style caused this are common. You may fear that you were too restrictive or too permissive in what your child was allowed to wear, what toys they were allowed to play with, or what activities they were encouraged to participate in. Some parents feel that having an absentee parent, an overly present parent, or a parent with different values caused their child to become transgender or non-binary. There is absolutely no evidence linking these things together. It's important while you are working through your feelings to avoid statements to your child, partner, spouse (or everyone, actually) that try to place blame. They will not serve you as you seek to support your teen.

Is This a Sign of Mental Illness?

Adults in a transgender or non-binary teen's life can be concerned that their teen's expressed gender identity is actually a sign of mental illness. This is an easy mistake to make especially if your teen has been exhibiting signs of serious depression or anxiety, an unfortunately common experience. A well-meaning parent or uninformed therapist can assume that the real issue is the depression or anxiety and that the gender issue is more of a side effect or a cry for help. Generally, it is the reverse; the depression and/or anxiety are usually the result of a struggle with a gender identity or gender expression that is less common and frequently met with disapproval and scorn. Sometimes it is the internal shame around being "different" that triggers the depression. Depression and anxiety do not trigger someone to think that they are transgender or otherwise gender-expansive. Rather, depression and anxiety can be a response to how that person feels about their gender and/or a response to how others are treating them.

Was This Caused by Trauma or Loss?

Some adults in a transgender or non-binary teen's life perceive their gender identity or nonconforming gender expression to be related to past trauma, loss, or even sexual abuse. This is not the case. Although people respond to traumatic events in different ways, many people experience traumas at various points in life that do not result in gender identity shifts. It is definitely important to process traumatic events in one's life. But resolution of such traumas does not result in a person no longer being transgender or non-binary.

Is This a Ploy to Get Attention?

"My dad keeps telling me I am faking it for attention. Why would
I fake how I feel about myself? He just doesn't get it."

Being transgender or non-binary in one's gender identity is a difficult
road to walk. The potential costs are extremely high, and your teen
knows this. If your teen simply wanted to annoy you or try to get your
undivided attention with their gender, they would likely do what teens
have done for generations and use gender expression to assert their
individuality and independence (think hair, makeup, clothing styles).
Gender identity is internal and therefore far less likely to provoke a
response from others than how they present their gender publicly. We
will explore these elements of gender in the following chapter.

Aren't They Too Young to Know?

One of the most common responses that parents and others have
to a child expressing that they are transgender or non-binary is the
fear that they are too young to know this about themself. There is a
fear that they will be making choices that have permanent implications and that they are not prepared for this level of decision-making.
Although the concern is understandable, it is based on a lack of information. According to the American Academy of Pediatrics, "Before
their third birthday, most children are easily able to label themselves
as either a boy or a girl. By age four, most children have a stable sense
of their gender identity."

Adults are having the wrong debate when they are concerned
whether or not a thirteen, sixteen, or nineteen-year-old is mature
enough to know their gender. We don't question if all teens are too
young to know their gender; it is only when a teen asserts a gender
identity other than their assumed one that we question their ability to
know themself.

Being "Sure"

"When people ask if I'm sure—of course I am, why else would I be I telling you?!"

It is important to break down the looming question about being "sure" into smaller pieces. Clarify what you are specifically questioning. Are you wondering whether your teen is sure that something about their gender does not feel right? Are you questioning if your teen is sure that they experience discomfort in their gender? Are you wondering if they are sure about the language they are using to self-identify and if they will always want to use that term? Are you questioning if they are sure that they would like to share with others how they feel about themself? Or are you nervous about how sure they are about making more permanent medical decisions about their body?

It is easier for the adult mind to simplify concerns by breaking them down into manageable pieces. We encourage you to begin by separating your new awareness about your child's gender from your thoughts and concerns about permanent medical decisions and your fears for their future. When you separate their gender identity from their desire for body modification, you may discover that it becomes easier for you. Most of us can recognize suffering and empathize with struggle. Focusing on and honoring your teen's lived experience better positions you to think clearly about any complex lifelong decisions.

Your teen is not deciding what gender to be; they are sharing with you what their gender is. Very rarely is anyone 100 percent sure about anything in life, and to expect your teen to have such certainty is unrealistic. Asking them if they are *sure* they are transgender or non-binary puts them on the spot. Just the question itself can feel undermining and rejecting. Try to be understanding and open-minded in your explorations so that your child does not feel like they need to defend themselves to you. By needing them to be 100 percent sure in order for you to take them seriously, you may inadvertently push them into a corner that they would otherwise not feel the need to occupy.

What if This Is Just a Phase?

"When my daughter came out to us, I held her and talked to her, told her I loved and supported her, and then left her room and broke down out of fear and shock. While I was supportive of whoever she was, I held on to the hope that it was just a phase for some time. That she was simply "confused." That it would pass and I would get my son back. Having a trans child terrified me."

The most common concern that the adults in your child's life will express is that your teen is probably just going through a phase. It is worthwhile to take a moment to note that teenagers are well aware that living authentically as someone with a less common gender identity or expression brings with it marginalization, possible bullying, and other conflicts, along with a seemingly insurmountable amount of logistics involved in order to publicly change genders. Again, people don't decide to undergo a gender transition on a whim.

But for a moment, let's suppose that this is a phase; even if it is, it is still real and valid to your teen at this point in time, and thus they remain worthy of your love, support, and acceptance. We can never really know what will and won't change in our lives or in our teen's life.

Given notions about the static, lifelong nature of gender with which we have all grown up, a teen's revelation about their understanding of their own gender can seem monumental. It is natural to have difficulty staying in the present. On one hand, you want to be able to look back in time to see if this pattern has been there over the long term; seeing some signs leading up to this moment can make it seem more valid. On the other hand you may try and jump forward, wishing for a crystal ball to know how your child will feel about themself five, ten, twenty, and thirty years from now.

You may fear that you will support your teen to make "wrong" decisions. But let's step back for a second. If we proceed on the premise that gender identity is not a choice or a sudden decision we make about ourselves, but rather an internal understanding and naming of who we are, then there is truly no way that supporting your teen could possibly be wrong. Whether you view it as a phase, or as something permanent, your teen needs your support. They have been courageous in coming forth with this part of themself; now it is your turn to be courageous and respond with love rather than fear.

Desire for Your Child to Wait

> "My dad just doesn't get it. He says I need to wait until I am eighteen and get in to a good college. Then I can transition. He doesn't realize I won't make it to eighteen."

Many parents we encounter believe that gender-related changes, including name/pronoun, medical, surgical, legal, and other congruence-related requests should be put on hold until their child becomes an adult. They consider this a neutral approach because they are not changing anything. Further, parents sometimes pronounce that they will no longer discuss the matter; their minds are made up. Please know that this is not a neutral decision. Doing "nothing" is most definitely a decision—one with potentially very serious consequences.

While parents often focus on the risks of moving forward, the risks are often greater in not doing so. There is a tremendous cost in living a lie, in not being your authentic self. You cannot have true connections with others because intimacy in relationships relies on authenticity. Asking your teen to wait until they are eighteen to seek congruence may be asking them to accept isolation, deception, and a lack of intimacy and connection with others. Refusing to even explore possible options may leave your teen feeling desperately and hopelessly trapped. There is a tremendous psychological price to be paid for that. Just what are you purchasing at that price?

If you are asking your teen to wait to authentically express their gender so that you can say it was their legal decision and not yours, you need to accept the risks associated with waiting. The internal desperation for transgender and non-binary teens can run at unbearably high levels. The risks in waiting can be catastrophic: your child may leave home to gain independence and a level of control in their life, or they might harm themself. Even if they wait until they are eighteen, there will likely be significant damage done to your relationship with them, as well as damage to their overall mental health and well-being.

It is a very important step to accept that the necessary interventions needed for your child to thrive may involve moving at a faster pace than you are initially ready for.

Consider too that there may be no better time to go through the difficulties of making decisions about what changes are right for your teen, weathering other people's initial reactions to their changes, or undergoing awkward or painful medical treatments and procedures than when they are still at home in your safety net.

If you are feeling overwhelmed by the enormity of the decisions before you, there is one approach for you to consider that will allow you a bit of time to work things out while demonstrating your support in the meantime. There are medical options available that allow your teen's adolescent body to effectively push a pause button on pubertal changes. These hormone suppressants (your teen might refer to them as "blockers") are fully reversible and do not lead to permanent changes. These medications can be used while you and your teen have the discussions that you need in order to feel comfortable with their gender.

Fear of Harm

> *"I remember a conversation I had with another father who has a transgender teenager. I told him how worried I was about keeping my child safe and his response stuck with me. He said, 'Sure, we have some specific new worries now that we know we have transgender kids. That's real, but aren't we always going to worry about our kids in one way or another? It goes with being a parent.' That conversation hasn't made me worry any less, but at least I don't feel like the only one with these fears."*

Gender Spectrum holds conferences for transgender, non-binary, and other gender-expansive youth, their families, and the professionals who support them. Every year, one of the best-attended workshops is entitled "What Keeps Me Up at Night?" As parents, grandparents, and other family and friends name the fears that live within them when raising a transgender or non-binary child, there are a couple of recurring themes, one of which is: Will my child be harmed—by someone else or by their own hand—because of their gender?

It is no wonder that these fears exist. We hear countless stories about both teens and adults who have experienced violence or harassment due to their gender. How can you feel safe sending your child out into a world that does not understand them? How can you protect your child from harm? This is such an overwhelming concern that it touches your heart directly. How can you allow your child to be who they are and express themself freely when you are also tasked with the sacred job of keeping them safe?

We also hear about the staggering rates of self-harm and suicide in this population. You may think that your teen will be able to avoid these risks if you simply do not allow them to express their gender openly. That is not the case. In fact, when a teen is unable to express their gender authentically, there is a significant increase in the risks of depression, suicide, self-harm, and substance abuse. Research has shown that parental rejection or lack of parental support increases these risks significantly. Your support and affirmation of your teen's gender is the single most important thing you can do to reduce their risk of self-harm.

Your support is paramount in decreasing your teen's risk and in increasing their ability to weather the challenges their life provides for them. You have the power to make things significantly better for them. None of us can control as many things as we'd like for our children and loved ones, and your actions alone will not be able to control whether harm comes to your child; that is the awful truth. However, there is a lot that you can do to positively affect your teen's safety, health, and well-being. We will be sharing these throughout the rest of the book.

Fear Your Child Will Not Find Someone to Love Them

"I just want to know that love is still possible, that they won't be alone."

The second most common fear we hear is that parents are afraid that as an adult their child will be alone. They fear that their child will not find someone who will love them, that they will miss out on some of the aspects of life that give many of us joy and meaning, like our partners and children.

The world is filled with transgender and non-binary adults who have partners who love them. Marriage and family can absolutely be a part of their life, if that is what they want. Many transgender and non-binary people choose to have children, both biologically and through adoption. Transgender and non-binary people have the same lives, loves, careers, friends, and community as people with other gender identities. Your child's gender identity will not close off their future; there is still a full life to be lived.

What Does This Mean for Me?

"When someone in a family unit comes out, everyone is affected.
That one person's transition becomes a family's transition."

Some of your fears and anxieties around your teen's gender have more to do with how your child's gender affects you on a personal level, rather than concerns about your teen. This is natural. It can feel like your entire life is being overhauled, as though everything you held to be true is no longer so. If the gender of your child is in question, what can you count on in life? It can trigger a pretty major personal crisis. These can be powerful feelings, and they are important to acknowledge.

But these are your personal issues; as difficult and real as they are, it is best if you can find places to process your feelings away from your teen. This does not mean you cannot express your need to become informed and to better understand some of the issues being raised. As we have said, demonstrating that you are seeking to learn and understand their experience is a powerful testament to your being "in it" with your teen. But this is different from doing your work of emotional healing with them.

The situation may seem overwhelming and even unbearable now, but stick with it. Resist the urge to run away from your family, to check out with substances, or to reject your child. Please know that few parents are able to accept everything about their child's "new" gender immediately—no matter how they respond to their child outwardly. It is perfectly normal to need time to fully accept that your child is not going to live the life you had envisioned for them. It takes time to adjust to a new and different reality in your life. There is great support out there—reach out for it in order to ease and quicken your adjustment period. It may be hard to believe now, but you can emerge from this with a much deeper and stronger relationship with your child than you experienced previously—and with new insights into yourself.

We are not going to try to tell you that this is an easy journey; it may not be. We all have assumptions of what lies in store for our children throughout their life based on their gender. This can burst that bubble. Every parent's pace of adjustment to this change is unique to them. Many people go through a process that is very similar to the stages of grief: shock, anger, denial, guilt, and loss. It is perfectly understandable if these are the feelings that you are experiencing. But along with these, there may be others in store for you as well. Surprise, understanding, acceptance, celebration, and advocacy may also be on your horizon if you can hang in there. You may see in your child (and in yourself), a courage, strength, and resolve to live life authentically that wasn't there in the same way before.

Shame and Embarrassment

It is very common, before moving into acceptance of your child and their gender, for you to be ashamed of your child and/or feel personal embarrassment. You may feel that having a child with a less common gender somehow reflects poorly on your own character. Perhaps you no longer want to be seen in public with your visibly nonconforming child. Or you worry about bumping into someone you know who asks about your child. How will you explain that your son is no longer on the soccer team at school because *she* wants to use the girl's locker room and the school won't allow it? No parent wants to feel this way about their own child, and yet here you are.

Of course, your child is worthy of your love and affection; your feelings are not actually about them. Your reaction has to do with you; it reflects your fears, discomforts, biases, prejudices, and the ways you were socialized around gender. You may be having feelings of transphobia, insecurities about your parenting or other parts of yourself, as well as fear of rejection—in other words, there are a thousand different things, none of which really has to do with your child. You may need to begin moving through these feelings before you again feel your love flowing freely toward your child. Although these difficult and uncomfortable feelings may be very real for you, do yourself, your child, and your family the honor of actively addressing them so that you can move through to the other side. Don't think that your teen cannot see or feel what your reaction is even if you are trying to hide it. It will take time, but the more you dedicate yourself to sorting through your feelings, the closer your relationship will be with your child.

Resentment, Anger, and Loss

"I just couldn't reconcile this overwhelming sadness and feeling that my child had died while I was standing right in front of him."

"Doesn't matter to me. I love you no matter what. Let's figure it all out together. I'll cry as I mourn the loss of my daughter. It doesn't mean I don't love you as my son. I just have to mourn losing my dreams for my little girl."

Some parents resent the disruption to their life that this issue presents. They may even be angry with their child for messing things up for them or for putting so much pressure on the family. Many parents feel that they are losing their child. They feel sadness and grief as if their child has died. It can take time to realize that the only thing you have lost is your own image of your child, the dreams you created about them. Take the time to mourn the loss—but also move as quickly as you can into embracing what is. In actuality, no one has died; in fact your child still has the same favorite color, the same tastes in food, the same shared experiences, and the same favorite jokes. They are who they have been; they're just continuing to understand and name who that is—and share who they are with you along the way. Over time, you will replace your image of the child you had created with a new and clearer one.

What Will Others Think?

Parents feel worried that their child's gender will have a negative impact on their lives. They do not want to be talked about behind their backs. They fear they may lose their social circle or their respect within the community. They are afraid of being discriminated against. They are also afraid of how to tell people and what to tell them. These are understandable discomforts. The early days of addressing your child's gender needs affect so many parts of your day-to-day life; it can feel overwhelming to figure out how to navigate this new world. You will find your way in time.

For many parents, having a transgender or non-binary child helps them to stop caring so much what other people think. They develop a thicker skin in their knowledge that they are doing the right thing for their child regardless of what anyone else thinks. They become more confident in their parenting and in themselves through this experience.

As we said before, people will follow your lead. If you share with them about your child from a place of love and compassion, and comfort with the topic, the people you are speaking to are more likely to respond in kind. It can even help if you directly ask for their support. Practice the specific words you will use to make this request. Explain that you are coming to understand more about gender now than you ever knew there was to know. You'll be surprised how many people will tell you their own gender stories, or the story of someone in their life. Your disclosure may be just the opportunity they needed. Parents have shared with us that when they started speaking out on the issue of gender diversity at their school board and PTA meetings, they were shocked by some of the responses. Sure, some reactions are hurtful and difficult to take. But as one mom said, "I thought I was the only mother in Lincoln, Nebraska, with a transgender child. But once I spoke out on the issue, other parents started coming forward about their children too. Now I have people contacting me from all around the country, friends of friends wanting to talk about their child."

Get Support for Yourself

"LOVE your child no matter what. It is the most difficult process for a parent to go through, but share your fears, your heartache, your loss with other people, not your child. They need your support and your love. Go to a support group or find someone to confide in for yourself…. It's not easy letting go of the hopes and dreams you had for your child, but new hopes and dreams can emerge."

In order to be able to support your teen, it is incredibly important for you to get the help and support you need, and to be able to connect with other parents going through the same process. In doing so you will encounter parents ahead of you on this journey and be able to learn from their experiences. You may want to join an online parent support group, go to a local support group or PFLAG meeting, or possibly see a therapist. At Gender Spectrum, we not only hold conferences and other events for families, but we also have call-in support groups and online forums for parents to connect with others and gain support and knowledge. These are safe contexts in which to share your fears and concerns with others who truly get it and can offer advice that is meaningful. There are an increasing number of in-person support groups popping up in communities around the world. If there isn't a local group, you could consider starting your own group. You will feel so much stronger when you realize that you are not alone on this journey. Parents from all walks of life are going through the same things all around the world. Many are waiting to share their experiences with you. And it may seem impossible now, but you may someday do the same for someone else!

Choosing Your Next Steps

"Follow your child's lead. Take care of yourself so you can take care of your child. By accompanying your child on their journey, they will lead you to some amazing places and new discoveries of not only your child, but of yourself."

You cannot control your initial feelings or what others will think about you or your teen. It is not up to you or because of you that your child's gender is unfolding in a way you never imagined. But you have choices about how you will respond to this unexpected turn of events in your life. It is time to shift your line of questioning away from what caused this and turn instead to what you can do to support your child at this difficult time. How will you be their ally and help to fortify their inner resilience? How can you support and nourish your child's self-confidence and self-esteem? It is easier to meet a difficult circumstance with fear and blame, but if that is where you are, it is essential to shift your response to one that is more helpful, accepting, curious, and understanding.

Once you are able to shift from blame, your decisions and actions can be guided from a place of love. This is the best place from which to make important, life-impacting decisions. And love is certainly the best place from which to engage in discussions about gender with your teen. A sense of kindness, compassion, and deep caring can lead you and the rest of your family. It is important not only for your teen, but for everyone in your teen's life—family, extended family, your community, and beyond—to feel that love and care are guiding the process. Blame creates distance; compassion and caring create connection.

We have seen wonderful things happen for parents and their

children in this moment where you are right now. The future can be exciting, fulfilling, and filled with hope. It's time to move forward from here and create it.

---

1   HRC and Gender Spectrum, *Supporting and Caring for our Gender Expansive Youth*, 2013.

Chapter 2

Understanding Gender and the Gender Spectrum

"There's a learning curve for trans youth and their parents, and by the time young people tell their parents about their identity, they're already thoroughly informed and waiting for us to catch up."

DESPITE THE FACT THAT EVERYONE interacts with gender every day, most of us have never received any formal education about it. It's actually incredible to realize this! Unfortunately, this is precisely why there is so much confusion and misunderstanding about transgender and non-binary teens. We know that you may be overwhelmed and confused as a parent right now. We will help to guide you through these feelings and be better able to support your teen through their teenage years. But having worked with thousands of families raising transgender and non-binary kids, we know that what will actually help you the most, before exploring the issues you may be most concerned with in having a non-binary or transgender teen in your life, is to have a strong foundational understanding of gender. Expanding your perceptions of gender will allow you to meet your teen where they are, and help you be more prepared for the discussions and unique challenges to come.

We know that some of you have been supporting your child in their authentic gender for years. If this is the case for you, we strongly suggest that you read this chapter, even though you may be tempted to skip it. We have information for you here as well. Understandings of gender continue to evolve, and no matter how much you may have already explored gender, there is always more to think about. Whenever you open yourself up to learning about subjects you feel you know inside and out, you create the possibility of getting an invaluable morsel that can help to transform your understanding or that can lead to an unexpected "aha!" moment.

Understanding the Difference Between Sex and Gender

When someone has a baby, usually the first question everyone asks is, "Is it a boy or a girl?" This seemingly innocent question reinforces the ever-present notion of the binary gender system. What is the binary gender system? It is our culture's current framework of gender: that there are two genders, boy/man and girl/woman, and that we can know someone's gender from the moment they are born. However, this way of looking at gender is oversimplified. It is based on three deeply held, but nonetheless flawed assumptions, that:

1. Sex and gender are the same.
2. There are only two gender options.
3. This core aspect of self is determined solely by looking at a baby's genitals when they are born.

Sadly, this limited understanding of gender has a significant and costly consequence. People who don't meet this definition of gender are frequently marginalized because they are seen as being different. With over seven billion people on the planet today, isn't it funny that we would think that we could divide everyone into only two categories? When we are uncomfortable with those who don't fit into these two available options, we risk, as a society, losing access to the potential contributions of many of its members.

The idea that sex and gender are the same has become so common that it is rarely questioned. When a person is born, their genitals are used to determine their gender. Yet sex and gender are not interchangeable. A person's assigned sex and their gender are not always the same. While sex is about our biology, gender includes so much more than just our bodies.

Gender is the word used to describe what we consider to be "masculine" or "feminine." Yet, what is expected of a "man" or a "woman" can differ significantly in different cultures. Likewise, what is considered to be masculine and feminine varies based on a person's background, age, and culture(s). Many of the ideas we have about gender are characteristics and behaviors. We then associate those characteristics with "male bodies" and "female bodies," thus gendering the body.

However, these nonphysical qualities that we think of as gender are actually separate from a person's sex. A person's assigned sex reflects the physical characteristics of their anatomy (their genitals). It does not necessarily reflect their personal preferences, what they like to do, or how they feel about themselves. And so, while sex and gender appear to be interchangeable, they are not.

For many people, it is not a problem that it was assumed that because of the genitals they were born with, they were raised to be a girl or a boy. This has not caused much or any personal discomfort. But for people whose sex and gender are not aligned, the assumption that they should be aligned can be a source of struggle.

If Gender Is Not Based Only on Our Genitals, Then What Is Gender?

Gender is a bit more complex than we were raised to believe. Gender is part of our personal identity; it is also part of our social identity. As a culture, we use the word gender to refer to the interplay of a person's body, the way a person sees and presents themself, and the way they are perceived and recognized by others.

Stay with us here. Don't worry if you feel confused. This will all come together as you read through this chapter and the next one. It is completely normal to be confused when you begin to understand that something you always thought was a simple and straightforward part of life is not that simple after all.

Nature or Nurture?

There is ongoing debate as to whether the differences that exist between people result from biological differences or from the differences in the ways that children are raised. In other words, are gender differences innate (nature) or learned (nurture)? This debate of nature vs. nurture, although compelling, is another binary and oversimplified way of looking at things.

In reality, there are many factors that influence gender that cannot be easily separated. Each of us has innate characteristics *and* we are socialized from the moment we are born. This intertwining of nature and nurture is what makes us uniquely who we are. When people wonder if non-binary and transgender people are born that way or if it was somehow caused by the influence of their parents or from past traumas, they miss the diversity that is inherent in life.

Nature interacts in its environment and produces a beautiful, wide-ranging variability that is essential to survival. Nature (biology) and nurture (the environment) aren't one-dimensional either. Biology is complex. Humans are, on average, 99.9% genetically identical, but the small biological variation generates the tremendous diversity we see all around us. The environments we interact in help shape us, but it is not one specific thing that does so. It is the millions of inter-actions—and our perceptions and experiences of them—that shape what we call "nurture." So trying to figure out if anyone's gender—whether they conform to what society expects or not—is a matter of nature or nurture is fruitless. It also limits our ability to understand, appreciate, and value one another.

We are at a crossroads in time now, when simplistic thinking about gender is being replaced with models that explain the diversity we see every day around us. Instead of seeing gender as binary, with anything that doesn't conform deemed to be wrong and in need of correction, it is time to embrace a model of natural variability that enriches and includes all of us.

How Gender Is Taught, Learned, and Reinforced

"All I wanted for Chanukah when I was six years old was a pink princess castle. Instead my parents got me a boring gray castle, I think it had some knights and dragons, I'm not sure, because I never played with it. And you know, I wasn't a kid who cried a lot but all these years later I remember sobbing when I opened that present. It wasn't just that I didn't get what I wanted, it's that I somehow knew already that the things I wanted most were not okay with them."

Gender is all around us; gendered messages and gender expectations bombard us constantly. Upbringing, culture, peers, schools, commu-nity, media, and religion are some of the many influences that shape our understanding of this core aspect of self. Practically everything in society is assigned a gender—toys, colors, clothes, hairstyles, and behaviors are just some of the more obvious examples. Parents, care-givers, and others (influenced by their own gender and cultural values) communicate their expectations of what is appropriate for each gender through their interactions with the child (forms of eye contact, which toys are offered, how they are touched). These expectations are then integrated and internalized by the child. It is this gender socialization from the time we are born that often influences so many of the things we may later consider to be personal preference. For example, gender socialization determines for a child what to wear, what toys to play with, what kinds of play are allowed, what they should be interested in, and what skills they're encouraged to develop.

How you learned and interacted with gender as a young child directly influences how you view the world today. This explains why the youth of today view gender differently than you might. The cultural messages of gender communicated to them are different from the messages of gender that were conveyed to you as a young child. Roles that were once linked to gender are changing in families, society, education, employment, and the media.

> **Assigned sex:** We will be using this term to reference the sex a baby was determined to be, and legally classified as, by a visual observation of their genitals at birth. This determination often misses not-visible intersex configurations. In binary systems of sex determination, there is no room for anyone who has more complex genitalia (or more complex internal reproductive anatomy, or chromosomal variations) to be assigned a sex other than male or female.

> **Assumed gender:** We will be using this term to reference the gender identity a person is presumed to have based on their sex assigned at birth. For example, a person who was assigned male at birth has the assumed gender of a boy/

man. A person who was assigned female at birth has the assumed gender of a girl/woman. It is when either of these individuals articulates or asserts a gender identity that is different from their sex assigned at birth that we realize their gender was wrongly presumed from the start.

Through a combination of social conditioning and personal preference, by the time they are three years old, most children prefer activities and exhibit behaviors typically associated with their assumed gender. Parents, extended family, care providers, and society all encourage children to act within their assumed gender roles and provide positive reinforcement when they do. This understanding of what is expected and desirable for their gender is internalized by the child.

Because what is expected for each gender is communicated so frequently right from birth, it's understandable that most people accept this culturally enforced gendering as a given. In fact, most people cannot imagine life any other way.

When the gender expectations of your environment line up with your own internal sense of self, then there might not have been a reason to think about your gender before. As a result, people rarely question what gender really is, or stop to wonder how their gender might be or might have been different without this socialization and reinforcement. It's only when there is a situation where these expectations don't line up for you, or for someone you know, that you begin to question how gender came to be defined this way.

Dimensions of Gender

"I never learned any of this stuff when I was growing up... it was new to me. But now I feel more comfortable... OK not comfortable, but knowledgeable about my kid's gender and what it means to her. And I am learning a lot about myself in the process too."

You won't be surprised by now to hear that we won't be discussing gender in the traditional binary way. Instead, we utilize a model that incorporates a spectrum of characteristics, including a person's body, gender identity, and gender expression. When you understand these aspects of gender and recognize that they are separate but linked, a more nuanced understanding emerges that accounts for each person's unique experience of gender. Gender can be seen as a rich tapestry, recognizing the intersection of societal expectation with one's body, identity, and expression. There is a variety of possibilities for each of these aspects of gender; therefore, no two people experience gender in exactly the same way. It is personal and social, public and private. Your gender is uniquely yours.

A person's gender is the complex interrelationship between:

Body: our experience of our own body, combined with how others/society genders bodies and interacts with us based on our body. Our body is used to determine our sex.

Identity: our internal sense of gender, who we privately know ourselves to be. Our gender identity can be the same or different from the sex we were assigned at birth.

Expression: our public gender—how we present our gender in the world and how society, culture, community, and family perceive, interact with, and try to shape our gender. Expression is also related to gender roles and how society uses those roles to try to enforce conformity to current gender norms.

Each of these dimensions can vary greatly across a range of possibilities. A person's comfort in their gender is related to the degree to which these three dimensions feel in harmony. Let's look more closely at each of these dimensions.

Body

"I really believed he was a boy. I mean he has a penis! I had no idea that you could be born with a penis but be a girl. That blew my mind! But I did a lot of damage coming to understand this basic fact. If I could tell other parents one thing it would be—don't believe what you've been told about gender. It is all a lie. It will save you so much time if you just accept that you have been duped."

"I am a boy and have always known this. Some boys are born with vulvas rather than penises. If everyone understood this my life would be so much easier. Because they don't I am told I am transgender. But I am not transgender. I was never a girl. I have always been a boy."

At birth, a cursory examination of a baby's external genitals is used to assign their sex. In actuality, sex characteristics are much more than external genitalia; they also include physical attributes such as sex chromosomes, gonads, sex hormones, and internal reproductive structures. At birth, however, only the visible genitals are used to assign sex and thus to identify individuals as male or female. Once assigned, sex is used to assume gender.

Sex Is Not Binary

Contrary to common understanding, sex characteristics are not simply binary. There are more than two variations of humans. Normal human development is represented across a spectrum. Variation can occur in any of the sex characteristics including a person's chromosomes, gonads (ovaries and testicles), and genitals. When these bodily variations stray outside of culturally established standards of male and female, we use the term "intersex." Being intersex is a natural part of human biology; it is just less common. Some of these intersex variations are visible at birth, but many are not.

Sometimes a person is not aware that they are intersex until they reach puberty or even adulthood. Some people never know. Even though this variation is a natural part of being human, our simple binary (either/or) model of sex characteristics keeps us from educating children about this natural variance. As a result, there is often inbuilt shame and secrecy associated with being on a less common place of the anatomical spectrum. When there are only two available options, instead of a spectrum, anyone who does not fit into either of the available options is perceived as "other."

At least 1 percent of the population is born with some form of sex variance. Yet, in most parts of the world, there are only two possible categories to select from when determining the official sex of a baby for legal documentation and classification. Despite the medical awareness of the complexity of what actually makes up a person's sex characteristics, we continue to use only a cursory visual exam to determine a person's sex. Some countries, such as France, Nepal, Australia, New Zealand, and Germany are leading the way in providing more options for sex/gender on legal documents. Hopefully, soon there will be more widespread understanding of the true spectrum of human biology.

So what exactly is a person's sex? Is it the perception of your genitals at birth that goes onto your birth certificate? Does your sex change if you come to understand that your internal reproductive organs do not match your external ones? Does it change if you surgically modify your body? Is sex fixed, or can it change? Who gets to decide where the line is for that change? These are important questions to consider.

In most cultures children are told from the time they are young that what makes a boy a boy and a girl a girl is their genitals; what makes a man a man is his facial hair, his height and his body hair, and what make a woman a woman is her breasts, her curves, and her soft skin. These notions about bodies impact how each of us feels about our gender. These stereotypical assertions regarding how bodies are gendered leave many people's experience marginalized; this can be particularly true for someone who is transgender or non-binary. For those who have a body associated with a certain gender but do not feel that they are that gender, their body can become a source of discomfort and struggle. This discomfort and struggle can be internal—wishing that they were born with body parts or reproductive capacities that they do not have. This struggle can be connected to wishing that others would recognize that their body *is* reflective of their gender, just not in the ways we have been taught to assume. This struggle can revolve around the assumption that all transgender people want to surgically alter their body when they feel fine about their body and wish others would stop assuming that they don't. This struggle can revolve around parents refusing to acknowledge their child's gender because of their genitals. Or it can revolve around parents refusing to support body modification their transgender or non-binary teen needs in order to find congruence in their gender. Given that society generally combines sex and gender as though they are the same thing, the body can become an internal and external battleground for transgender and non-binary people.

Gender Identity

> *"I really understood that my child was a girl when she revealed how she thought of herself inside her head. It started when she was little. For example, she was playing with two friends who were boys and they were all three chasing the "bad guys" in our backyard. However, while the friends were being Batman and the Hulk, she was being a butterfly princess. Her actions looked exactly the same as theirs, but how she perceived herself was completely different."*

> *"People ask me how I know I am non-binary. I just have to laugh! I just ask them the same question: How do you know you are a girl?"*

> *"My dad asked me if I was sure I was a boy. I told him I had no doubt in my mind."*

Gender identity is a person's deeply held sense of their gender—as male, female, both, neither, or something entirely different. Gender identity is an internal experience. We do not choose our gender identity; rather, our gender identity emerges from within. It is believed to be an inherent aspect of a person's makeup and cannot be regulated or determined by others.

It can often be difficult to understand what gender identity is because it's such an intrinsic part of who we are. Because it's deeply personal and privately understood, it can be difficult to think of it as a distinct aspect of who we are, and equally challenging to articulate this sense of who we are to someone else. The tendency is to try to equate gender identity with other aspects of gender and self, such as body parts, personal expression, sexual orientation, or even personality. Our gender identity remains even if our sexual and romantic attractions or outward expression change. It is who each of us feels our self to be.

Gender identity is separate from anatomy, although for many people, their assigned sex, their gender expression and their assumed gender line up; this is where the assumption that they are one and the same stems from. Interestingly, what a culture typically perceives as gender has little to do with the gender identity of an individual.

Because many things influence how and when each person comes to identify their gender, people recognize their non-binary and transgender identities at various points throughout their lives, rather than all at the same point in life. The accelerated brain development of puberty, increase in hormones, and pubertal physical changes all converge in adolescence making it a common time for a new gender identity to emerge, resurface, or be declared. This can be especially true in puberty for those teens who begin to feel their body changing in a direction that does not feel "right."

Once a new or newly revealed gender identity emerges in adolescence, it is extremely unlikely that it will "revert." It may take a bit of time for the teen to know for certain whether what they are experiencing is truly an issue of gender identity or if it is a need for a more expansive gender expression, but if it is gender identity, it is probably here to stay. Understanding that there are many different gender identities allows us to recognize the unique configuration of each individual without placing value or judgment.

Because gender identity is an internal experience, it is not possible to know someone's gender identity without asking them. While a person's gender identity and gender expression are often related, they are distinct dimensions of gender. So using gender expression to determine a person's gender identity can be a risky (and potentially embarrassing) assumption to make!

Gender Expression

"Who I am on the inside stays the same, but sometimes I just like to wear different kinds of clothes. I generally dress in men's clothing, but every once in awhile I'll wear something more feminine. I'm not trying to make a statement; it's just that those clothes feel like me that day."

Gender expression can be thought of as a person's public gender. It is what other people see and is present in all of our interactions with others. Our gender expression is how we live our gender in the world (e.g., our clothing, hairstyle, grooming patterns, behaviors, and mannerisms). It is also how society, culture, community, and family perceive, interact with, and try to shape our gender. Gender expression is a social communication of gender and includes both intentional and involuntary gender cues. Gender expression has three parts: *gender presentation* (how we present our self to others—and what they see, whether we intend them to see us that way or not); *gender norms* (the rules and ideas about how a culture thinks males and females should look); and *gender roles* (the behaviors we expect and think are appropriate for each gender).

In many ways, gender expression seems pretty straightforward. We often think that we know someone's gender based on the type of clothes and accessories they wear. It turns out that, much like the other dimensions of gender, expression is a bit more complicated.

There are also aspects of gender expression that are subtler, such as a person's voice and communication patterns, their emotional expressiveness, demeanor, and the way they move. Gender expression refers to all the different things a person does that communicate gender, intentionally or not. What is considered to be typical gender expression for men and women varies from culture to culture, because how gender is expressed varies from culture to culture.

Because a person's gender expression is the first thing we see when we look at them, we use these cues to "read" someone's gender. Having been taught a binary system of gender, our brains take the visual gender cues a person presents and attempt to classify that person into the category of male or female. We subconsciously rely on combinations of countless cues to do this. We can become confused, uncomfortable, or even angry if making a simple binary classification of someone is difficult or not possible because of missing or conflicting gender cues. While each of us hopes to communicate our gender so that others see us as we would like to be seen, that is not always the case.

Gender Presentation

"As a freshman I started to grow my hair and wear makeup. I still identified as male because I didn't know anything else. Everyone told me I must be gay so I thought I was—even though that didn't feel right to me."

"As someone assigned female at birth who likes to be seen as masculine, I find my expression of my gender and other people's perception of my gender do not always align. For example, I may be intentionally expressing myself in a masculine manner, but others may still very much see my gender cues as female. This can feel very invalidating to me."

Gender-based discrimination often begins as a reaction to a person's gender presentation. When a person's presentation falls outside their society's expectations for their gender, their gender is considered to be nonconforming. As a result, people who express their gender in ways that go against the current social gender norms often have a very different experience of life than those whose gender expression conforms to what's expected. The more a person's gender presentation falls outside of current cultural expectations, the more gender-based discrimination they typically experience. To the degree that gender cues are perceived to be absent or conflicting in a person, the greater the discrimination they face on a daily basis.

Boys seen as feminine at any age, and girls thought to be too masculine (especially as they move into their teens) face a variety of challenges. Pressures to conform at home, mistreatment by peers in school, and condemnation by religious, cultural, or other institutions are just some of the difficulties facing a teen whose gender presentation does not fall in line with the binary gender system. In fact, although bullying of children and teens often takes the form of homophobia (with such slurs as "fag" and "dyke"), in reality, these kids are frequently being bullied and teased for not fitting into typical gender norms, rather than for their sexual orientation.

As children become teens, their parents or guardians may be less responsible for deciding their hairstyles or clothing purchases, potentially leading teens to more freely express themselves. With this increased ability to express themselves, it is a common time for presentation styles to change and for gender-nonconforming self-expression to emerge in a more pronounced way.

It is important to understand that having a nonconforming gender expression does not necessarily mean that a person is transgender or non-binary. Many people who have a nonconforming gender expression feel comfortable identifying as the gender assumed for them at birth. One's gender expression may or may not be consistent with one's assigned sex, socially prescribed gender roles, or internal gender identity.

Gender Norms

"I don't know when these things stopped bothering me so much. When I was young, the sexism of our culture drove me bananas. But now I have just found ways to live with it. I don't always know the most helpful way to talk about this with my child who goes back and forth between wanting to fit in by conforming to gender norms and wanting to be a caped revolutionary destroyer of gender norms!"

Societal expectations of gender regulate and create the gender norms for that society. Gender norms can be thought of as spoken and unspoken rules about gender expression. Norms around gender expression change across cultures and over time. It is worth noting that since cultural gender norms shift with time, what was once nonconforming often becomes accepted over time. In the U.S., for example, a quick examination of history related to men wearing earrings or women sporting tattoos shows how social expectations of gender expression change. Even the notion "pink is for girls, blue is for boys" is relatively new. Prior to the mid-twentieth century, pink was associated with boys and blue with girls. Likewise, women and girls have worn pants for some time of course, but only recently are we beginning to see men and boys wearing dresses and skirts.

Given the prevalence of the binary gender system, from the time we are young, we all face great pressure to conform to our culture's narrow definitions of "boy" or "girl." Those who don't conform can experience discomfort or even distress from the pressure they feel to be different from how they truly are. But if we were to take away the pressures to conform to social norms, the range of possible gender expressions could be limitless.

Gender Roles

"I realized I was 'different' when I was the only kid in my class who was best friends with both the boys and the girls. Everyone else was very polarized, but I moved back and forth with ease and comfort."

Gender roles are the culturally accepted standards of masculinity and femininity. Gender roles reflect societal expectations of what one should do and how one should act, think, carry their bodies, and even feel based on their gender. Gender roles are what dictate "appropriate" gender expression within a culture. These social constructs of gender are communicated through every aspect of our lives, including family, culture, peers, schools, community, the media, and religion. They are the context that sets the expectations for gender expression.

What is expected of a man or a woman can expand as time passes and societal needs and desires change. As Dr. Adrienne Harris says, "We have to keep putting words like feminine and masculine in irony-conveying quotation marks. With these rhetorical devices, we signal our understanding that these terms only have meaning in particular and unique contexts and that these contexts shift constantly."

However, expectations still remain for what is considered masculine and feminine, and even though there are countless tolerated exceptions and variations to every gender rule, there are also consequences for those who step outside of those exceptions. The further a person steps outside the social expectations of their gender, intentionally or unintentionally, the more pressure, ridicule, and discrimination they experience.

Youth Enforce Gender Roles for One Another

A 2014 study tracking the ways that fourteen-year-old students in a school in Lisbon, Portugal interacted with their ideas about masculinity and femininity found that being raised in a culture with strict gender roles led to a negative impact on the overall physical and mental health and well-being of the teens.

The researchers found that the students, regardless of gender, regulated their behaviors in order to adhere to gender norms. For example, all of the female students restricted their food intake despite being in healthy weight ranges. The girls restricted their food intake as a means of reaching the feminine physique considered sexy, despite the need for increased calories during adolescence. Girls also restricted their physical activity at school because they were teased by boys to act more feminine, or for fear of looking unattractive while being active. Girls also felt they must downplay their intelligence in order to not intimidate boys as there was the impression (held by both girls and boys) that boys are supposed to be smarter. Boys, on the other hand, felt compelled to prove their masculinity, if they were slighted in some way, through acts of violence like hitting and slapping one another. Boys also felt like they were supposed to suppress their emotions as a way of appearing manly and were pressured to drink alcohol as another way of proving their masculinity.

It became clear to the researchers that both boys and girls struggled with constant pressure to self-regulate their behaviors in order to adhere to gender norms. This stress appeared to undermine self-esteem and to increase gender-related anxiety. The impact of gender self-monitoring crossed all social groups. When interviewed in one-on-one interviews, the students universally expressed feeling compelled to regulate their behaviors according to gender expectations and did not like doing so. When the students learned that everyone in the study felt limited and restricted by these expectations, they were astonished.

They found in the study what we see every day in our work at Gender Spectrum: that once teens realize how much effort they are putting into acting their gender according to prescribed societal scripts, students stop policing each other so heavily. There is greater tolerance for gender-nonconforming behaviors. Violence decreases, and more girls start participating in physical activities. The culture of the students shifts after becoming aware of the impact of cultural gender messaging. Gender roles limit people in many more ways than they are aware of, and shedding light on this is all that is needed for youth to loosen the restrictions placed upon them.

Gender vs. Sexual Orientation

"Very early, we thought she'd turn out to be fabulously gay. We were totally OK with that. We were just wrong."

"Although my child is thirteen, she is neither exploring nor sure about sexual orientation—gender identity clarity came way before now."

One final distinction to make is the difference between gender and sexual orientation, which are often incorrectly conflated. When someone's gender expression or identity is perceived to be inconsistent with others' expectations, they are frequently assumed to be gay. But gender is about who we are, and sexual orientation is about who we are attracted to physically and/or romantically.

Why is it so critical to distinguish between these two notions? Although they are different and essential aspects of our self, people intertwine them when observing behavior in order to make assumptions about someone. It is not uncommon to "read" a young person's gender expression and assume that it tells us something about their sexual orientation. The teenage boy who is gentle, prefers theater to sports, and is soft-spoken is assumed to be gay, and the adolescent girl who buys clothes in the boys' section, likes to build things, and favors a short haircut must be a lesbian. These are faulty conclusions. What someone wears, how they speak, hold their body, etc. is about personal preference and gender expression, not their sexual orientation. These assumptions may keep you from accurately seeing your teen and understanding who they are. When we think about gender identity or gender expression as sexuality, we are attaching a meaning that may have nothing to with the young person's authentic self.

The Gender Spectrum

"Both my parents are first-generation Americans. I first came out as gay because my family perceived me as male and I was attracted to other men. But when it comes to my gender, I actually identify in the middle. It's taken a lot of time for my parents to accept my sexual orientation, but they don't know the extent of my gender identity. I don't think I'll talk to them about my gender anytime soon because of cultural and language barriers. I know that they think I'm a good person and that's enough for me."

Gender in All Its Beautiful Variations

Either/or gender expectations discourage us from expressing ourselves in ways that may conflict with how society dictates we should look and act. This societal pressure leaves most people with their genders unexplored. It also prevents a lot of people from expressing themselves in the ways that they would naturally prefer. Studies indicate that self-policing and external policing of gender are firmly in place by the time we are of preschool age. This process of gender regulation is so ingrained that we hardly even recognize its existence, except when we encounter elements of it that personally rub us or someone close to us the wrong way. Whether we recognize it anymore or not, our current system of gender limits *everyone* from true self-expression.

Alone, each dimension of gender (body, gender identity, and gender expression) challenges the binary model so common in many cultures. But when considered as a whole, the diversity of gender truly unfolds. Just as three dimensions of space provide a more detailed landscape for understanding physical objects, the dimensions of gender provide a much richer model for exploring this fundamental aspect of ourselves. Taken together (while understanding the infinite ways in which the dimensions can interact), we can begin to capture gender's complexity.

For many people, the elements of their gender are aligned. That is, their body, gender identity, and gender expression all line up. Their assigned sex and their assumed gender are aligned. An adjective sometimes used to capture this alignment is "cisgender." The prefix *cis*- comes from Latin and means "on the same side as" or "on this side of." While perhaps the most common pattern, even this arrangement has tremendous room for variation. Think of the people you know whose body (as far as you know) and gender identity (as far as you know) line up, but express themselves in a range of ways regarding appearance, interests, how they move their bodies, use their voice, etc. As long as gender expression doesn't fall outside the boundaries of what is considered the norm, they're still considered cisgender. Nonetheless, the term "cisgender" is an important one in that it names the dominant experience, rather than simply assuming it to be the default or "normal" way to be.

When a person's assigned sex does not line up with their gender identity, they may identify as transgender. Where "cisgender" refers to someone whose identity is aligned with their assigned sex, "transgender" refers to someone whose identity is "across from" their assigned sex. Gender expression for transgender individuals, as with cisgender people, can be anywhere along the spectrum. For example, some transgender teen girls and transgender women might not gravitate toward dresses, while some cisgender teen boys might in fact enjoy wearing dresses. This may be about preferences, but may also be indicative of the context in which they find themselves and how safe they feel in expressing themselves in the manner they feel is most congruent with their innermost self.

In addition to someone identifying as transgender, a person whose assigned sex does not align with their gender identity may have a non-binary gender identity, meaning they don't fit into any traditional gender box. Some non-binary people consider themselves to be under the transgender umbrella and some don't. We will explore this in depth in the following chapter.

Beyond the Binary

While some individuals fall within "traditional" gender identities, others identify outside of this binary altogether. They may not identify with being either a boy or a girl, experience themselves as a blend of both, or see their gender as fluid. Someone with a non-binary identity may express themselves consistent with a binary presentation, or outside of any particular gender norms.

Life outside the binary isn't just about gender identity: It can include the other two dimensions of gender as well. Intersex and other people who have a non-binary representation of sex characteristics fall outside the biological sex binary and its assumed binary of bodies; and those who present themselves outside expected gender norms and roles are non-binary in their gender expression. Someone can be binary in one dimension and non-binary in others. For example, someone assigned male at birth, who identifies as a boy, and likes to wear dresses is binary in body and identity, but non-binary in expression. His non-binary expression doesn't change his identity—he's still a boy, just a boy who likes to wear dresses.

Gender-Expansive

Gender-expansive is an umbrella term we sometimes use in our work to describe individuals who broaden their culture's gender norms for identity and expression. It acknowledges that there are many ways in which people stand outside the binary, each person having a personal experience of gender. The term gender-expansive helps to describe and affirm personal experiences and expressions of gender that cannot be positively categorized using existing language. It recognizes that it is society's narrow perceptions of gender and the consequent limitations that it imposes that must be questioned, rather than the individuals who don't conform to them.

Discrimination Is Often Based on Expression, Rather Than Identity

> "I was harassed much more when people weren't sure if I was a boy or a girl. After I transitioned, I only got harassed in places where people knew I was trans. Otherwise they just think I am a cisgender boy and treat me well."

In public discussions regarding gender, people tend to talk about discrimination in terms of gender identity. In other words, they say that transgender or non-binary people face a lot of discrimination. There's no question that is true—discrimination regarding gender identity is pervasive. However, in most cases of day-to-day discrimination, harassment, and violence, people don't know what someone's gender identity is; they only see how someone expresses their gender. The more gender-nonconforming someone is in their appearance and mannerisms (expression), whether or not they have a transgender or non-binary gender identity, the greater the likelihood of discrimination.

Gender-nonconforming people, whether they are transgender, non-binary, or cisgender, often experience discrimination on a day-to-day basis. When a person is visibly gender-nonconforming, the way that people interact with them in public is somewhat unpredictable. The degree to which people respond negatively or positively to a gender-nonconforming person is often linked to not only how their gender nonconformity is perceived, but also the ways that racism, sexism, and transphobia play into the picture.

If someone's gender is ambiguous, androgynous, or just unclear due to missing or mixed cues, strangers may consciously or unconsciously stare at them, trying to figure out if they are male or female. It's possible that someone whose gender presentation is ambiguous, or seems to give mixed messages, will be questioned if they use a public gender-segregated facility such as a bathroom or locker room. If a stranger engages in a conversation with someone, and they are confused about the person's gender, they might try to avoid using pronouns so that they don't make a mistake and misgender the person. Depending on the specific circumstance strangers react to gender-nonconforming people with a range of feelings including anger, fear, anxiety, or annoyance, making the situation potentially uncomfortable or unsafe for the transgender or non-binary person.

Other circumstances, however, can be far more frightening. The more a person's appearance is seen as gender transgressive, regardless of their gender identity, the more they are at risk for harassment and even violence. Because of fear, sexism, misogyny, and other types of prejudice, known transmen and transwomen, as well as people assigned male with a stereotypical feminine expression, are particularly targeted for harassment.

In terms of violence, the problem is worst of all for transwomen of color as the discrimination they face is a combination of racism, sexism and transphobia. According to the National Coalition of Anti-Violence Programs, in 2015, there were reports of twenty-two transgender people being murdered in US hate crimes. Among the victims of these crimes, nineteen were Latino and/or Black, nineteen were women, and two identified as non-binary.

Gender and Privilege

"I hate to admit this, but I had never really thought about my gender very much before. I mean, I just hadn't thought about it that deeply. I guess I didn't have to. That has definitely changed over the last couple of years as I've struggled to understand my child. I've learned a lot!"

Anyone whose body, gender identity, and gender expression align—anyone who is cisgender—benefits from gender privilege. Like many forms of social privilege, this is frequently an unexamined aspect of our lives. By default, most social environments and institutions are designed around the simplistic binary model of gender. If you can use a restroom without being questioned or feeling unsafe, that is a privilege. If you receive needed medical care, shop for clothing in stores without being harassed, or take a flight without worrying that TSA will stop you because you don't appear as they think you should based on your identity documents, that's gender privilege. For a transgender, non-binary, or visually gender-nonconforming person, each of these (and many more examples) is a constant reminder that they move about in a culture that really does not account for their experience. Social privilege comes from an assumption that one's own perspective is universal; whether related to race, class, faith, language, or gender, privilege comes from being part of the "norm."

The daily need to make judgments about what one does, wears, or says based on other people's perceptions of their gender is a burden that many people never encounter. These everyday reminders of being different are also constant reinforcement of being "other."

Lifting the Damaging Burden of Conformity

When the natural variability of gender is denied, we deny the authentic experiences of many people. As we become more attuned to the oppression faced by those who do not fit neatly into society's limited understanding of gender, we become sensitive to the personal and societal costs of the binary gender system. As one of the most fundamental aspects of a person's identity, gender deeply influences every part of one's life. In a society where this crucial aspect of self has been so narrowly defined and rigidly enforced, individuals who exist outside its norms face innumerable challenges. Even those who vary only slightly from the norm can become targets of disapproval. As Anne Fausto-Sterling so aptly says, "When we discourage free expression of self and identity of the individual, we impose the damaging burden of conformity."

Often, well meaning and supportive parents of transgender teens transfer their binary thinking about gender onto their children (simply switching from one box to another) and thus are not able to be the full allies that they could be in assisting their child to explore the gender they truly feel themselves to be.

Yet this does not have to be the case. By appreciating the uniqueness and validity of every person's experience of gender, we can develop greater acceptance for all. This will create not only greater inclusion for individuals who challenge the norms of gender; it will also create space for all individuals to more fully explore and celebrate who they are.

Chapter 3

Embracing the Complexity

"My son only wears his skirts at home now. He just got tired of people assuming he is a girl. But whenever we go out of town, his skirts are packed. Somehow he is invigorated again to see the world as he feels most comfortable and he does not mind explaining to people who assume he is a girl that no—he is a boy who likes to wear skirts... or likes to have his hair in a bun."

OUR SOCIETY IS ON THE cusp of a new frontier when it comes to gender as more people recognize that trying to constrain all people into two categories no longer works. We are grappling with issues related to gender in meaningful ways, trying to embrace rather than contain the richness and diversity of gender.

Gender trailblazers are making inroads for the rest of society to come along safely into new and unexplored territory. In their desire to be their authentic self, your child may be one of the first visible transgender or non-binary people in their school, place of worship, or community, putting them out front in ways they never desired. But let's be clear, being a gender trailblazer is not a chosen role. Your child did not choose their gender anymore than you chose yours, nor would anyone choose the stigma and discrimination that currently come with being transgender or non-binary. Nonetheless, over time, many gender-expansive people arrive at a deeper appreciation for the unique perspectives their less common gender allows them to have. We have spoken with many transgender youth who have come full circle to a place of realization that they are proud of who they are and would not want to be any other way. *You*, however, do get a choice. You do not get to choose the gender of your child, but you do have a choice about how to support them on their journey. The choices you make during this crucial time period of adolescence will have a tremendous and lasting impact. We encourage you to support your teen willingly, with a sense of adventure and a fierce desire to protect your child no matter what it takes. Neither of you chose this, but life has a way of taking us to wonderful and unexpected places.

We will help you get up to speed so you are ready to join your teen on the next part of their journey. No child should have to feel that they belong in the category of "other," be marginalized, or face discrimination just for being themselves. Transgender and non-binary teens, as well as all teens questioning their gender, desperately need and deserve all the support they can get in a world that has yet to fully understand them. In order to do this, you must continue to deepen your understanding of what gender is and how today's teens are expressing gender and leading our entire culture toward more expansive territory.

As parents, we want our children to be safe, valued, and respected. We want there to be a place for them in our society. In order for there to be room for everyone in society, we have to take a few critical steps. The first and most important step is to recognize and acknowledge that the system of gender that has been in place simply does not work for everyone. We all need to shift our thinking and understanding to a more inclusive model that values gender diversity. To do this, we need to be able to see and recognize that as a society, we require a deeper and broader understanding of gender, where restrictions that cause unnecessary pain and suffering are expanded to make room for everyone. This benefits not only transgender and non-binary people, but all of us. Expanding both our personal and our cultural understandings of gender has exciting and intriguing implications.

In this chapter, we first explore the ages at which a person realizes that they are transgender or non-binary; we then go on to examine the natural spectrum of gender identities and gender expressions. Even if you have a child that went through a social gender transition years ago, read on. It is crucial to acknowledge that your transgender or non-binary teen may undergo a gender maturation during adolescence, and you will need to be there to meet them with a more sophisticated understanding of gender if and when this happens. Working with a teen around issues of gender is very different from working with a young child.

Changing Expectations of Youth and Gender

"Having had a transgender brother all my life, I have a broader understanding of gender than other teens my age. I feel like I am always educating people!"

People have always had a personal sense of their gender. The shift that is taking place now is that people who do not fit reasonably within the binary expectations of gender are seeking to express themselves, and appealing to the human right to be free from oppression in doing so. This is especially true for the youth of today. In the past, a greater percentage of people subsumed their personal gender and allowed themselves to remain confined to one of the culturally available boxes.

Many youth of today are now neither willing nor able to tolerate the restrictions that requires. Their starting place is a much more inclusive understanding and acceptance of gender, not just for themselves but for everyone. What generates excited conversation about gender among parents is often met with a yawn by youth. There is a pervasive attitude of cultural insistence: "I will not deny myself to make you comfortable." As a society, we are on the verge of a paradigm shift surrounding gender.

The Myth of Gender as Stable and Unchanging

"I just stopped feeling like a girl. I had no idea what my gender was, I felt kind of like a boy and kind of like a girl but at the same time neither of them. When school started I joined Queer Straight Alliance (QSA) and I found out about more genders than just male and female. At first I found out about gender fluid, and that fit more than male or female, so I thought I was gender fluid. Sometime around October, I found out what gender neutral is and that fit the best at the time. Until March or April, I thought that I was gender neutral but then I learned what agender is, and that has fit the best. Starting around July or August, I started questioning my gender again, and I still am."

Most of us were raised with the false impression that everyone is born as one of two genders and that everyone's gender remains constant throughout life. It can be difficult to understand that a person's gender identity can form and reform at different points in life because one of Western culture's long-held beliefs about gender is that it is constant and unchanging. While it is certainly true that the majority of people do feel comfortable within the boundaries of the sex assigned to them at birth and their assumed gender, it is not true that a person's sense of gender remains exactly the same throughout life. For some, their sense of their gender changes more than for others.

Gender Is a Part of Self That Is Always Evolving

"Gender is fluid, gender can change, and that is OK and doesn't make it any less valid. And gender isn't just male to female and the stuff in between; it's much, much more than that. Also, you don't 'decide to become' the gender you identify as—YOU ARE THAT GENDER."

It can be valuable to think of a person's gender as something that grows and matures over time. For everyone (including you), gender is evolving. As you look back on your life, you may see times when your gender expression differed from what it is today. As society changes and expands the expectations and allowable manifestations of gender, people reflect these changes, each in their own way. The social progression of gender is experienced and expressed in all of our lives. Yet not everyone spends time reflecting on the evolution of their own gender, and most hardly realize how they have personally changed over time; it was a gradual and natural progression. It is precisely this societal evolution of gender that has allowed for a greater number of transgender and non-binary children and youth to express themselves authentically at a younger age and for our society to be willing to consider their experiences as valid and worthy of protection rather than something aberrant, worthy of punishment or conversion therapy.

Gender Stability

Gender stability is an understanding of your gender that remains consistent over time. People of any gender identity can have a stable gender identity; in fact, most people have an early sense of their gender identity and begin to voice it as early as two years old. We don't think anything of this when a child's gender identity matches their assigned sex at birth and assumed gender; as a matter of fact, we expect it. Only when they express something different does it get our attention.

Some transgender and non-binary kids are clear from the beginning. As soon as they have language, they state a clear gender identity. Others may just have an internal sense that something is different about their gender and not have the language or information to clearly communicate this feeling. The consistency of the feeling that something is different about their gender is a form of gender stability for some transgender and non-binary teens.

An increasing number of parents are listening to their children when they assert a gender identity that is different from their assumed gender and are allowing their child to evolve in ways that are appropriate for them, rather than trying to change them to fit cultural expectations. It is often with great relief that parents of transgender or non-binary teens relax in the knowledge that their teen has been persistent and consistent in their assertion of their gender since childhood. It is this persistence and consistency that have afforded a growing number of children and youth the ability to seek social congruence before puberty and to provide some of them the opportunity—through puberty suppressants and hormone therapy— to go through the puberty that matches their internal sense of themselves. (See *The Transgender Child* for more information on gender development in children.)

There are also transgender and non-binary children who are not clear enough in their communications for their parents to understand what they are trying to say, or who don't say anything to their parents because they are afraid. Some of these children feel stable in their gender identity regardless of when they are able to seek congruence or be accepted by others in their authentic self. Gender identity is an internal understanding of one's gender. It isn't dependent on other people recognizing, accepting, or supporting it. Thus even without external validation, a person can have been stable in their transgender or non-binary identity long before they receive external acknowledgment of it.

Please note that people with a fluid gender or those who feel themselves to be a blend of genders or multi-gendered can also feel stable in a fluid or more complex experience of gender.

If a teen is coming to terms with a sense of a new gender identity or is questioning their gender identity, it may not be stable. Stability will come once their identity is further explored.

Adolescent Gender Identity Consolidation

For many teens, there are new expectations for them in adolescence in regard to their gender that feel even more confining than those in childhood did. For example, girls who were allowed or even encouraged to have a more stereotypically masculine self-presentation and gender expression (often called tomboys) may now find themselves faced with expectations that they will grow out of these behaviors or feel pressured to express themselves in more stereotypically feminine ways in order to be accepted. Boys who always had a strong circle of friends who were girls may now find that people assume they are gay just because of who they hang out with. The pressure to conform to gender norms is closely tied to the pressure to appear straight, because teens who do not conform to gender norms are often assumed to be gay or lesbian.

While teenagers may feel at odds with their expected compliance with restrictive gender roles and expectations, most teens can find a way to deal with this discomfort within acceptable, or at least mostly acceptable, parameters. It may cause annoyance and frustration for them and may be perceived as rebelliousness by their parents, but it won't cause them serious distress. These are areas of tension in many families and have been so for time immemorial.

Navigating personal desires and preferences in order to avoid being ostracized or harassed distracts youth from manifesting their full potential in other areas of life. We strongly encourage our teens to resist social pressures regarding drugs, sexual activity, and other risky behaviors (placing emphasis on the ability to resist peer pressure as an indication of moral character), while simultaneously encouraging conformity to gendered social expectations.

Deepening of Gender Identity in Adolescence

"Now here I am at sixteen and realizing that I am struggling with my gender, and have been for a long, long time."

There is a natural process of individuation and identity development that occurs in adolescence. Although there is a deepening awareness of one's gender identity in adolescence for all teens, those for whom their assigned sex and gender identity align may not even realize that they have undergone a deepening of identity. It is more of a process of reinforcing an already known sense of self. This deepening can feel internally validating. It is often this increasing gender confidence and internal consolidation of self that allows a teen to feel comfortable moving into the world of dating. For some teens, the process of exploring who they are includes awareness of their gender identity, and they wonder how this part of themselves fits into their overall identity. They may confirm that they are cisgender through this exploration, or they may find that they are non-binary or transgender. Regardless of gender identity, adolescence can bring a richer understanding of their gender.

Some Teens Realize They Are Transgender or Non-Binary in Adolescence

"Until puberty, I didn't really think I had a gender."

Because of the misunderstanding that gender is constant and unwavering, a parent can often be confused and suspicious when their teen reveals that their gender identity is other than their assumed gender based on their sex assigned at birth. However, there are many people whose transgender or non-binary identity emerges after childhood. Some of the teens who express that they feel they are transgender or non-binary for the first time in adolescence have finally found the strength and courage to voice something they have always known about themselves, whereas others are truly coming to this realization for the first time. They may or may not have felt "different" in childhood. It is often easier to make it through childhood as one's assumed gender than through adolescence, which is filled with body changes and sexual emphasis. For this reason, a number of teens only come to recognize their feelings related to their gender, or only learn the language to describe their feelings, when they are in puberty.

It is often the transition from essentially gender-neutral bodies to the development of secondary sex characteristics (breasts, body hair, voice changes, etc.) that leads to this recognition. For some teens, puberty causes their body to look less and less like the gender with which they have always identified. They may not even have consciously recognized their gender identity until their body began to change. This results in a mind-body disconnection prompted by unwanted physical changes during puberty. It is that disconnection that may begin to ring some internal alarm bells.

**When Transgender Teens Realize They Are Non-Binary and
Non-Binary Teens Realize They Are Transgender**

With the developmentally appropriate deepening of gender identity in adolescence, some transgender teens will come to recognize a more non-binary gender identity, or may begin to express themselves in a more expansive manner. Transgender teens who transitioned before puberty may find that their transgender identity is actually more fluid than they had previously thought. Likewise, some teens who have previously identified as non-binary realize they now have a binary identity and are transgender. We will explain more about non-binary identities throughout this chapter.

Evolving Language of Gender

The more that language evolves to describe various gender experiences, the more people you will encounter who fit into categories you may not have known existed before. It is also true that once people hear new vocabulary to describe various experiences, the more they may realize that they too have a more complex gender than they had realized or named before. There is a tremendous expansion in language about gender—it's hard to keep up with all the terms and what they mean. As Dr. Adrienne Harris says, gender's language has been breaking down, breaking open, and breaking free. The multiplicity of terms can initially feel bewildering, but stay with us and it will become more intuitive as you read on. Keep in mind that in addition to terms being defined within the chapters, there is a glossary in the back of the book as well.

What Is Transgender?

The term transgender is used in various ways, so it is always good when you hear it to check which meaning the person is using. It can be used as an umbrella term to encompass many identities and describe anyone whose gender identity does not match their sex assigned at birth, or whose identity or behavior falls outside of stereotypical gender norms. Used this way, "transgender" or the related use of "trans" can potentially refer to all people who fall outside the limits of their society's rules and concepts of gender. These terms can also include everyone with a non-binary gender identity or gender expression. When the word transgender is used to encompass such a broad group of people, including agender people and non-binary people, it often has an asterisk, as in trans*.

For the purpose of this book, rather than as an umbrella term, we use transgender to refer to people who experience deep feelings of incongruence with their assigned sex and associated sex characteristics, and feel alignment with what many often think of as the "opposite sex." For example, this would include someone who was assigned a male sex at birth and had an assumed male gender but knows her gender to be female. We use it as a cross-gender identification. As mentioned, some people with non-binary gender identities also identify as transgender; however, for simplicity in communication, we will use transgender to reflect people who identify explicitly as a boy/man or girl/woman."

When we use the term transgender, we are referring to those people who want to align aspects of their gender to reflect their inner experience. It is common for transgender people to switch their pronouns and change their names; they may or may not pursue medical congruence measures. For some transgender people, there is a desire to synchronize their sex characteristics (hormones, secondary sex characteristics, and/or anatomy) with their identity, although this is not true for all transgender people. When we use the term transgender by itself, we are referring to people who feel most comfortable in the gender binary, yet the incorrect gender was assumed due to their assigned sex at birth. While the primary motivation for transgender people is to align dimensions of their gender for their own sense of self, it is also important for many transgender people to be perceived by others the way they see themselves.

Some Common Misconceptions About Transgender People

There are many misconceptions about transgender people that are sometimes reinforced by media, public figures, and maybe your own family, friends, or coworkers. Much misinformation comes from people who don't know transgender people and who may be repeating what they have heard or read. Inaccurate information can be harmful and create misguided fear of and backlash toward transgender people. That's why it is so important to address these misconceptions.

Myth: There Is One Common Transgender Experience

There is a common misconception that transgender people all have the same internal and external experiences. With more than one million people in the U.S. alone identifying as transgender, they are as diverse as any other group of people. They are from all socioeconomic backgrounds, ethnicities, races, religions, and family structures. What unites them is the experience of incongruence with their assigned sex, and the daily oppression of societal discrimination and social pressures to conform.

Myth: True Transgender People Know They Are Transgender From a Young Age

> *"Just because I didn't always feel this way does not mean I don't feel it now!"*

As we've stated earlier, some transgender people do know that their gender identity is different from what has been assumed for them from an early age. However, people can learn or confirm that they are transgender at any age. It is very common for youth to understand or confirm this about themselves as they enter puberty or any time during puberty. This can happen as their sense of self and their gender evolves, or when they learn terms that for the first time describe their lived experience.

Myth: All Transgender People Feel Like They Are Trapped in the Wrong Body

Although this is a common concept often cited in the media to reflect transgender people's experiences, it is not a universal experience. Some transgender people do feel that they are trapped in the wrong body. Others, however, do not feel that there was a mistake made with their body, but rather that there was a mistake made with their gender assignment. And many other transgender people love their bodies, but do not like the gendered assumptions that others place on their body. Feeling trapped in the wrong body is not required to be transgender.

Myth: All Transgender People Hate Their Bodies

Although it is true that many transgender people experience a disconnect with certain body parts and features, and some would go so far as to say that they hate these body parts, there are many others who accept, love, and are comfortable in their bodies. We work with a lot of transgender children who were afforded the opportunity (through the use of puberty suppressants) to undergo only the puberty corresponding to their authentic gender. These youth develop the secondary sex characteristics of the sex they feel more aligned with. There are also teens who do not desire to remove or change their genitals. They feel comfortable in their bodies. There are plenty of transgender men who went through their natal puberty and bind their breasts to achieve the appearance of a flat chest when clothed, but still feel connected to their breasts and do not want them removed. Hating your body is not a requirement for being transgender. Likewise, needing or wanting to surgically alter your body is not a requirement. It is important to note that altering one's body so it matches one's sense of self does not mean that a person hates their body; body modification can be an act of self-love.

Myth: Transgender People Aren't "Real" Men/Boys or Women/Girls

Of all the myths about transgender people, this is perhaps the most divisive and hurtful. Transgender people are no less real in their experience of gender than anyone else, including cisgender people. Claiming that someone is not real undermines their very existence. It is this myth that perpetuates violence and widespread discrimination. There are many ways to be a man or a woman, and assigned sex and biology are not the only determinants.

Myth: Transgender People Are Mentally Ill

Being transgender is not a mental disorder. The distress associated with experiences of discrimination, lack of acceptance by family and society, and acts of violence committed against transgender people may understandably lead to anxiety, depression, or related conditions, but these are effects of oppression, not of being transgender.

Many transgender people experience gender dysphoria, which can be described as a feeling of disconnection with one's assigned sex and assumed gender. People who experience "intense, persistent gender incongruence" may be given a DSM diagnosis of gender dysphoria. This diagnosis is fairly controversial. Some believe that the diagnosis should be eliminated because it pathologizes gender incongruence in much the same way that homosexuality was historically pathologized. Others argue that the diagnosis is needed in order to provide care and to obtain insurance coverage. DSM diagnosis or no diagnosis, transgender people are not mentally ill.

Myth: Transgender Teens Are Just Confused

Just like cisgender people, transgender people know who they are. They may go through a period of confusion before finding the right label or identifier to reflect how they experience themselves, but that does not mean that what they feel is invalid. It can take a while to know how to express oneself simply because the gender socialization of mainstream culture does not include transgender as an option. Likewise, there are a lot of cultural stereotypes around transgender people to sift through when coming to claim one's identity, and not a lot of transgender role models to look up to. As our society changes, the confusion that some transgender people experience in their self-expression and identification will be significantly lessened. Because transgender people fall outside traditional understandings of gender, they typically think about their genders more than those who are cisgender. This level of self-exploration may show up as confusion, when what is more likely happening is an evolving understanding of who they are.

Myth: You Can Tell Someone Is Transgender Just by Looking at Them

"When people meet my kids for the first time and have known that I have a kid who is transgender, they always think it is my other child. It always gives us all a good laugh."

This has never been true and is less so now than ever before. Because there are countless children who are allowed to live in alignment with their true gender from a young age, and many of those youth are allowed to go through the puberty that they feel aligned with, there are a growing number of transgender youth whom you would never assume are transgender. Some transgender people do not want to or are not able to look as if they are cisgender and that, coupled with

cultural stereotypes, has people believing that they can visually identify all transgender people. However, you can never tell who someone
is by looking at them. It is very likely that you have met and known
transgender youth (and adults) and simply did not know. It is up to
all of us to stop categorizing people and their genders so that we can
make room for people to just be themselves.

Myth: All Transgender People Are 100 percent Sure and Feel 100 percent Male or Female

Asking anyone to be 100 percent sure about anything is a tall order. Give
some thought to your own life. If you are cisgender, can you say you are
100 percent feminine-identified, or 100 percent masculine-identified?
Most people cannot do this even if they do not identify as transgender.
It is unrealistic to expect anyone to be 100 percent sure of their gender
identity or 100 percent sure that it will not evolve—the goal is to be as
sure as you possibly can be. And remember, given the current levels of
discrimination in our culture toward transgender people, there is a lot
riding on the decision to walk this path. If your teen is telling you that
they are transgender, a good starting place is to honor that self-percep-
tion. From there, you can decide how to move forward.

Myth: All Transgender Men Are Highly Masculine and All Transgender Women Are Highly Feminine

As we look around our lives, we see a wide variety of gender expressions, preferences, and ways people relate to expected gender roles.
Think about it—how many different kinds of men are there in your
community or workplace? Then do the same for women. The variation is pretty staggering. When one identifies as transgender, it simply
means that their internal resonance is cross-gender from their assigned
sex. It does not mean that they will want to conform to one common
stereotype or another. As with cisgender teens, there is a lot of variation in gender expression among transgender youth.

Myth: Transgender People Are Actually a Third Gender

Although some transgender people may also have a non-binary identity or sense of self, as we have said, we use "transgender" to reflect people who identify explicitly as male or female. There are people who identify as another gender, or as not having a gender at all. These people fall under the "non-binary" umbrella. Most transgender people do not identify as a third gender and do not wish to be perceived that way. They feel comfortable with the existing categories of male and female, they just feel they belong in the other category than the one they were assumed to belong in. Some transgender teens do not identify with being transgender at all. They experience themselves to be a boy/man or girl/woman despite the genitals they were born with. They believe there are many ways to be a man or a woman. Given the negative societal messaging regarding what it means to be transgender, they may not relate that term to themselves. This doesn't mean they deny their assigned sex, simply that they will not be told what identity to assume.

Myth: Transitioning Is Cosmetic, and Not Medically Necessary

"After surgery, I finally felt my body looked like the gender I had always known myself to be."

Perhaps because an increasing number of people have aesthetic surgeries (such as breast or pectoral muscle implants, face lifts, liposuction, etc.), it is difficult to understand that for some transgender people, medical transition is a necessity and not just a cosmetic preference. Medical congruence measures can be critical in relieving gender dysphoria and in achieving a sense of personal alignment, and they can be a life-saving treatment for some. With an attempted suicide rate upward of 40 percent and research clearly indicating that medical congruence measures commonly alleviate gender dysphoria and related mental stressors, why shouldn't this be an available option for all transgender people who desire it?

Myth: All Transgender People Have Surgeries and Go on Hormones

The flip side of this is that there are transgender people who choose not to, cannot afford to, or cannot safely have hormone therapy and/or gender-affirming surgeries. This does not make them any less transgender than those who do.

Myth: Reaching Congruence Is Simple

> *"Figuring out the steps it would take for me to feel secure in my gender was challenging. At first, I thought a simple doctor's appointment would change things, but soon I realized it was much more than doctors."*

Many people are under the misconception that reaching a sense of congruence as a transgender person simply requires one surgery. However, the process of reaching congruence is an extended and often complicated process that is about much more than whether or not to seek hormonal or surgical measures. In fact, a large percentage of transgender people do not end up having genital reconstructive surgery at all, even if they do elect to have other gender-affirming surgeries. There are many arenas of life that must become aligned in order to feel congruent, potentially involving pronoun and name changes, sharing information with family and friends at school and work, and negotiating environments that may be, to different degrees, hostile or supportive.

Then there are potential legal congruence measures that require changing legal documents, including formal name change, birth certificate, passport, driver's license, health insurance, and school registration to name but a few.

For those who choose to pursue medical congruence measures like hormone therapy or surgeries, there are many doctor appointments, medications, and/or other treatments that may be required. The process takes both time and resources.

If you find that you are using the desire for or degree of congruence measures to assess the validity of your child's experience, or if they are holding themselves up to this standard, it is crucial to stop and reconsider. Recognize that the experience of transgender people is complex and takes place over time. There is no one right way to be transgender—only what is right for each individual.

Myth: All Transgender People Are Gay

It is important to remember that gender and sexual orientation are different aspects of self. Being transgender does not imply any specific sexual orientation. Sexual orientation is not linked to anatomy or to gender identity. Therefore, as with cisgender people, transgender people may identify their sexual orientation as straight, gay, lesbian, bisexual, pansexual, etc.

Adding to this confusion around sexual orientation and gender identity is the fact that some transgender teens first come out as gay before recognizing that they are actually transgender. Being gay is often more acceptable than being transgender in this day and age. Once a person comes to understand their gender identity, they may realize that they had previously confused it as a sexual orientation. Adolescence brings all these identity issues to the forefront at the same time—it is no wonder that it can be confusing. However, transgender men want to be seen as men sexually, and transgender women want to be seen as women sexually. With whom they choose to be sexual depends on their sexual orientation.

Proper Usage of the Word Transgender

Transgender is an adjective describing a state of being. As in, "Our transgender daughter is going to a great school." People commonly misuse the term by saying "transgendered." However, it is not a verb, so this is not proper usage. It is also not a noun, so it is not appropriate to say, "My son's best friend was just kicked out of his home for being a transgender."

Non-Binary Gender Identities

"I looked at the term gender fluid but it never felt right to me. It's only when I got the curiosity to look up the word non-binary did it really click with me and it was a stunning revelation. I cried a lot that night because it explained so much and felt so right."

Having a binary identity is currently the most common form of gender identity, in part because it is the predominant option available in Western societies. However, more and more people express that they do not have a static gender identity, or feel that they are both or neither of the available binary gender options.

What Is a Non-Binary Gender Identity?

Non-binary is a term covering any gender identity that doesn't fit within the two gender categories of male and female. Although it is an imperfect umbrella term, for the purposes of this book, we like non-binary to communicate the experience of people whose gender identities cannot be defined purely in terms of the binary system of exclusively a boy/man or girl/woman.

People who have a non-binary identity may, in fact, identify with one or both of the binary genders, at least in part; others may experience their gender to be completely non-binary. Non-binary allows a person to not have to attach a name to their gender.

Some people do not experience themselves to have a gender. For the purpose of this book we have also included them in non-binary gender identification, although they may not use this term for themselves since it is a term that still relates gender to the binary system, and they may feel no resonance with the entire construct of gender.

Some people who have a non-binary identity have two or more genders, a gender that shifts, or a singular, fixed gender. Some people who identify as non-binary find gender to be multidimensional and thus believe that no one can actually fit their gender into the current binary system. Just like transgender people, some non-binary people desire physical modification or hormone therapy to allow their physical attributes to reflect their gender, and others do not. Likewise, some non-binary people undergo name and pronoun changes and legal identification changes while others do not.

Non-Binary Does Not Equal Intersex
It is common for people to assume that those with a non-binary identity feel this way because they are intersex. Intersex describes a person with a less common combination of hormones, chromosomes, and anatomy. However, as previously discussed, the spectrum of biology is separate from gender; intersex people represent the same spectrum of gender identities as everyone else. Although a person's experience of their biology may influence to a greater or lesser degree the way they experience their gender, their biology alone does not determine their gender identity.

Some Common Misconceptions About People Who Identify as Non-Binary
There is tremendous cultural resistance to recognizing people with

non-binary genders. For the most part, non-binary people are invisible. Perhaps because of an unwillingness to accept the possibility of more than two genders, the common misconception is that there is no such thing as non-binary genders. The foundations of sexism are based not only on male/masculinity being privileged over female/femininity, but also on forced conformity to binary gender expectations. When we are able to recognize that there are genders outside of the binary, we free everyone from the pressures of conformity.

Awareness of people with non-binary genders is so limited that their existence is marginalized. In order to move forward toward greater understanding, it is important to recognize the stereotypes and myths surrounding non-binary people.

Myth: People Who Say They Are Non-Binary Just Can't Decide Or Are Confused About Their Gender

"I've never been more sure about my gender than I have since coming out as non-binary. I always felt both male and female, but thought there was something wrong with me. Now that I know there are others who feel this way, I know it's not me that's confused... It's everyone else."

The presumption here is that the gender binary is absolute, and that any person expressing a non-binary gender will eventually settle on one of the two choices once their confusion subsides. Although many non-binary people do choose one of the binary gender designations for the sake of legal documents, bathroom use, ease of day-to-day life, etc., this does not necessarily reflect their inner experience of themselves. There is often no confusion on the part of people who have a non-binary gender or no gender. Rather, the challenge comes in trying to be oneself in a society that requires conforming to only one of two designated genders. Of course, for many non-binary, or agender people, there are times of confusion. Navigating a path so few have publicly discussed leaves many on their own with little to no guidance and support. This does not negate or invalidate their experience of themself.

Myth: This Is Just a Fad

> "Sometimes people ask me whether or not having more media attention on transgender issues allowed me to come out as non-binary. I am who I am regardless of what's happening in our culture and society. I just feel fortunate there are now role models who can help me name my experience."

There have been and still are cultures that recognize people who are neither male nor female or who are considered to be a blend of both genders.

This myth assumes that a person's non-binary identity will wear off, and they will come to their senses. It further assumes that non-binary identities are new and that it is popular to claim a non-binary identity. Perhaps this comes from the increased visibility of a few non-binary people in celebrity culture. In reality, even though some youth do respect peers who are willing to be themselves, being non-binary has not suddenly become a ticket for teens to become popular and accepted in schools. There is a cost to youth who assert a non-binary gender identity, and our experience clearly indicates that youth do not do so unless they have spent enormous time considering the identity they wish to assert.

Myth: You Can Wear Whatever You Want, Or Do Whatever You Want, but It Doesn't Mean You Are Not a Girl Or a Boy

> "My mother is really open and she always tells me she loves me just as I am. I can wear what I want and do the things I

like around her...but she still calls me her daughter. This hurts because I've told her like a million times that I am non-binary. I wish she would understand. I wish she could see me like I see myself. I am her child, but not her daughter."

Gender expression (clothes and preferences) is different from gender identity. The problem, in addition to the joining of gender expression and gender identity in this myth, is the dismissive way it insists on assigning a binary gender to everyone. A person with a non-binary gender identity does not experience themselves comfortably within the categories of male or female. This is not just about how they look or what they like to do, it is about who they know themselves to be. Confining non-binary people into a social construct that does not account for them effectively requires them to pose as someone other than who they are. While it may take some time to fully understand, if your teen has told you that they are non-binary, respect their sense of self.

Myth: Everyone Is a Blend of Feminine and Masculine; You Don't Need a New Word Just for You

Agender people and some non-binary people do not experience gender to be a spectrum within, between, and/or beyond male and female. Rather, they experience gender to be a reflection of endless personal possibility that is not confined to two genders. The purpose of language is to communicate. If existing terms and identifiers do not adequately communicate a person's gender, then they absolutely should use language (including a new word) to help others understand their identity and experience.

Myth: You Are Just Trying to Make a Political Point

One's gender or non-gender identity is simply a part of oneself, not a political statement. When a cisgender person identifies as a man or a woman, we don't say they are just identifying that way to be political. The same is true for non-binary (and transgender) people as well.

Common Non-Binary Identities

Below are some commonly used non-binary identities. As with all gender terminology, these terms take on different meanings in different geographic regions, communities, and age groups (and are changing all the time). However, this list will give you an understanding of many of the most common terms people are using at this point in time in the United States.

You will notice that some terms have similar definitions. With language this complex and evolving, it is important to respect the labels or identifiers that people choose for themselves. For example: One person may call themselves bi-gender while another with a relatively similar experience may refer to themselves as gender-flux, gender-fluid, genderqueer, or demi-gender. There are non-binary identified people who use the pronouns assigned to them, while others prefer to use gender-neutral pronouns. Some of the following terms are used by people who identify as non-binary; however, keep in mind that the same term can be used by a person who feels separate from the gender system altogether. Most importantly, if your child is using one of these terms to identify their gender, ask them what it means to them!

Neutrois, Gender-Neutral, Gender-Free, Agender

> *"My identity rests in an ambiguous place. To me this is what being gender-neutral means. My place is definitely somewhere in between the spaces of man and woman."*

These are all commonly used identity terms that people who do not feel they have a gender use. Some of the people who use these terms feel a connection to the concept of gender, but feel they do not have one. Others cannot even understand what gender is because they do not experience it within themselves. Still others feel like they are a person with preferences and personal expressions, but that those things are not gender, and to call it a gender is to support sexist notions.

Androgyne/Androgynous

Androgynes feel themselves to be simultaneously masculine and feminine—although not necessarily in equal parts. They frequently have both female and male gender characteristics. Some feel they are a blended gender, neither masculine nor feminine. This inner androgyny may or may not be reflected in their appearance.

Bi-Gender, Multi-Gender

A bi-gender person identifies as two genders. It does not necessarily mean they identify as a man and a woman, just that there are two distinct genders with which they identify. They may identify as both at the same time, flow between genders, or feel they are a blend.

People who have more than two gender identities, either at the same time or sometimes shifting between them, may identify as multi-gender.

Gender-Fluid and Agender-Fluid

People that are gender-fluid have a gender, or genders, that change. Gender-fluid people move between genders—not necessarily masculine and feminine. Gender-fluid people tend to not experience their gender as something static, but rather as a dynamic experience. They might have multiple distinct sides of their gender, and often their gender presentation shifts accordingly. Gender-fluid people may have a fluid sense of gender or experience themselves as having lots of different genders.

Gender fluidity conveys a wide, flexible range of gender expressions or gender identities, with interests and behaviors and/or an internal sense of self that may change, even from day to day. Gender-fluid people may feel they are a girl/woman some days and a boy/man on others, or a combination, or possibly feel that neither term describes them accurately. Gender-fluid people may fall under a multi-gender, non-binary, and/or transgender gender identity. Some people identify as agender-fluid, which describes a primary gender identity as agender, but can fluctuate or move fluidly through other genders.

Gender Flux

Gender flux can be an identity similar to gender-fluid, but it usually indicates a movement between specific genders rather than fluidity. Often, but not always, one of the genders is non-binary or agender, or possibly one gender identity is fixed, and the other part or parts are in flux. It also can describe the experience of gender-fluid people as in "I experience the most gender flux when I move from school to work."

Demi-Gender, Demi-Fluid, Demi-Flux

Someone who identifies as demi-gender identifies partially with one (or more) gender(s). For example, a demi-guy or demi-boy identifies partially as a boy/man/masculine, but not entirely. Demi-gender can be a subset of bi-gender or multi-gender, but does not have to be. A demi-gender person may identify as demi-fluid or demi-flux. This indicates a part of one's identity remains stable while the other part or parts are fluid. Often a demi-flux person feels that the stable part of their identity is gender-neutral or non-binary.

Intergender

Intergender is an identity for those who experience their gender to be a combination or blend of genders, or an identity that is between genders.

Non-Binary
Some people simply claim non-binary as their gender identity.

Pangender
This is an identity that reflects multiple gender identities and gender expressions. Some people use it to indicate that they are all genders.

Gender Identifiers That Signify a LGBQ Orientation
People of all sexual orientations use the previous gender identities. The following are a few gender identities usually claimed only by people who identify as part of the LGBQ or pansexual communities.

Butch
This can be a lesbian or queer masculine gender identity, gender expression, or gender role. The word butch has different meanings for different people. It is generally associated with queer-identified individuals whose gender expression is perceived as masculine. For some, it is related to more traditionally masculine gender roles, while others may use it as a gender identity.

Genderqueer
Genderqueer is an umbrella term to describe non-normative gender experiences. Genderqueer is often a combined gender identity, gender expression, and sexual orientation. Genderqueer individuals typically reject static categories of gender and sexual orientation. For some, genderqueer is a non-binary identification, and for others, it is not. Genderqueer can often include an element of challenging the construction of gender.

Femme
Femme is a lesbian or queer feminine gender expression, gender

identity, or gender role. For example, one can be a genderqueer femme or a gender-fluid femme. The word femme has different meanings for different people. It is generally associated with a lesbian or queer person whose gender expression is perceived as feminine. For some, it is also related to more traditionally feminine gender roles or identities.

Stud

Someone assigned female at birth who identifies as masculine physi cally, mentally, and/or emotionally. This word is most frequently used within black and Latina lesbian communities. A stud may be cisgender, non-binary, or consider themselves transgender. Some live full-time as men.

Transmasculine

This is someone who was assigned female at birth, but who identifies as more masculine than feminine. This is often a subset of a gender-queer identity. Some people will describe themselves as "masculine of center" as a way of describing where they see themselves on the masculine and feminine continuum.

Transfeminine

This is someone who was assigned male at birth, but identifies as more feminine than masculine. This is often a subset of a genderqueer iden-tity. Some people will describe themselves as "feminine of center" as a way of describing where they see themselves on the masculine and feminine continuum.

Intersections of Gender Identities

People often have multiple gender signifiers. For example, a person could be a bi-gender genderqueer who slides between male and gender-neutral identities. Or they could be a transgender genderqueer man, or a gender-fluid stud, or an agender-flux woman. The possibilities are endless (and sometimes a bit confusing).

Why So Many Options?

Why do we need all this terminology? For someone who has always been comfortable with the sex they were assigned and the associated gender, it can seem like this plethora of new words is confusing and unnecessarily complicated. However, for the people for whom gender does not fit into an either/or category, these terms are both necessary and liberating; they tell their specific gender story.

Non-Binary Gender Presentation and Expression

There is no standard way that a non-binary person looks. The similar thread among them all is that they are trying to be comfortable within themselves and hopefully understood by those who matter to them most. Some people who experience their gender as non-binary feel gender dysphoria with parts of their body while others don't. Some undergo some form of medical alignment measures while others don't. It is highly personal and individualized. There are non-binary people who are gender nonconforming in their appearance; they may look androgynous or give mixed gender cues. Others present their gender in a traditional and conforming way. Some people present mixed or somewhat confusing gender cues while simply naturally expressing themselves without any statement involved, while others intentionally present in a way that is meant to confuse people.

Our brains like organization and so try to categorize and classify our experiences in order to make sense of them. Harvard University researchers have found that when first seeing someone, our brains try to classify their race and gender before anything else. These are some of the most primary classifications we have. Interestingly, they are also some of the hottest social topics. People who present themselves in ways that cannot easily be classified into established categories or those who fit into marginalized categories confuse our brains, and their place in society is called into question.

As we personally and culturally expand our notions of both race and gender to include the complexities of lived experience, we establish new language and new ways of conceptualizing gender. What was once thought of as a limited binary system is expanding in order to integrate much broader understandings of gender.

Diversity is key to evolution.

"Nature loves diversity, society hates it."

—MILTON DIAMOND

Non-Binary Genders Across the Globe

Documented by historians and anthropologists, the diversity of gender is a normal part of the human experience, across cultures and throughout history. Examples of individuals living comfortably outside of typical male/female expectations and/or identities are found in every region of the globe. The abilities of various societies to incorporate non-binary understandings of gender are clear indications of the capacity for cultures to normalize these experiences.

What are some of the terms and societies that include these nuanced notions of gender? One example is the idea of the "two-spirit" person observed in many first nation cultures of the Western hemisphere. These are individuals who possess a sense of self that transcends the male/female binary. Like everything else associated with gender, there is no single two-spirit experience; rather, more than one hundred fifty tribes have various traditions, terms, and/or social roles for these individuals.

Another non-binary understanding of gender is seen among the Bugis culture of Indonesia. Located in Sulawesi, the Bugis recognize five distinct genders: men, women, *Bissu* (a version of two-spirit), *Calalai* (someone assigned female, with many male roles and attributes), and *Calabai* (someone assigned male, with many female roles and attributes).

In India, the *Hijra* represent another non-binary understanding of gender. Since ancient times, these "male-born" individuals live as a distinct gender, with many feminine characteristics, roles, and traditions. In late 2014, the Indian Supreme Court issued a ruling formally recognizing the *Hijra* as a third gender, with formal documentation, and government hiring and college acceptance quotas throughout the country. The court's pronouncement followed similar rulings in Pakistan, Bangladesh, Nepal, Germany, and Australia.

Muxe is a term derived from the ancient Zapotec language of the Yucatan region of Mexico. Some *Muxes* choose to live full-time as women, while others have a more nuanced and fluctuating gender identity. In some parts of Mexico they're marginalized, but in Juchitán, they tend to play a more integral role in society as teachers, nurses, caregivers, seamstresses, and event planners, among other professions. In the Dominican Republic, there is a small rural village of individuals known as *Guevedoces*. These are intersex people who at birth appear to be biologically female, but at puberty begin developing in a more typically male manner, including the emergence of a penis and testicles. These are young people around whom a set of various role expectations and traditions have emerged. In the Arabian Peninsula, the country of

Oman has a third gender category of *Xanith*. In Ethiopia, the *Ashtime* are sometimes described as "wobo," or crooked. In fact, the cultures of ancient and modern Africa have an array of gender traditions and designations. These examples and many more all represent more complex understandings of gender than allowed for by a simplistic binary model.

With the reemergence and awareness of non-binary notions of identity, many of the non-binary and third-gender communities are reclaiming their designations and traditions. As with terms like queer and others with negative connotations in larger society, these identities are becoming emboldened to claim their places at the gender table, creating more space for each of us to assert our own authentic sense of self.

Chapter 4

Achieving Gender Identity Consolidation

"I learned about transgender people when I was eleven. I never considered I might be trans because everything I knew about trans was weird. I am not weird. I feel normal so I never considered that I might actually be trans. Once I finally saw someone who I really liked and respected and learned he was trans, I realized that there was room for me in that term too."

THE CENTRAL TASK OF ADOLESCENCE is identity consolidation. Identity consolidation is the creation of a strong, stable sense of self with which to move into adulthood. It is vital for the adults in a teen's life to understand that transgender and non-binary youth require a tremendous amount of support during adolescence while they are coming to terms with their gender identity and integrating it into their adult identity. The years when your child's gender is consolidating are some of the most vulnerable in their life. Our goal in this chapter is to let you know what is happening developmentally during this time for your child so that, in turn, you can help your teen to understand it, reassure them that what they are going through is a normal process, and together strategize ways to help them through it.

Most parents are not prepared to have a transgender or non-binary child. Parenting is incredibly demanding regardless of the child and their specific needs; however, when you find yourself in unfamiliar territory without sufficient knowledge or support, even well-meaning parents can back away from their child, thinking they aren't able to help them as needed, or believing their child needs space and that they are doing okay. Yet we know from experience that all is not as it appears on the outside with teens. Your teen needs you, especially throughout their gender consolidation process, which can continue into their mid-twenties. Once they reach identity consolidation you will begin to breathe a little easier. Of course, even once your child has come to terms with who they are and has reached a certain level of congruence, it doesn't mean that their struggles with gender are over. Your role and involvement in their day-to-day gender journey may shift, but your love and support will remain a stabilizing force in their lives.

> *"We no longer discuss gender on a daily or even weekly basis. He is very secure in who he is. But sometimes, something will trigger his body dysphoria, and he goes back to being very tender and vulnerable again. It is so great that he knows he can come to me and discuss these things."*

Gender Identity Formation

*"I started doing my own research and then I talked to a couple of
my friends...and they helped introduce me to all of the culture
and terms and things to help me figure out the big question mark
that is me."*

Adolescence is a time when changes in the body and the brain result
in a deepening of both gender and sexual identities. When a teen is
coming to the realization that they are or might be transgender or non-
binary, it can be a difficult time in their lives. While some teens realize
it "overnight" and find relief in finding language for their experience,
many have a drawn-out process of recognizing and coming to terms
with a gender identity that does not correspond to their assigned sex.

Although all teens go through identity development and it can be a
confusing process for them, for transgender and non-binary youth, it
can be even more complicated.

They must deal with internal and external gender expectations
while attempting to uncover and articulate (even if only to themselves)
their own inner gender identity. Due to pervasive social stigma, this
identity is not usually one they want, or would choose, and it is often
associated with shame, guilt, and fear of rejection from family, peers,
and greater society. If and when they come to accept their identity, they
often struggle with how to express it, how to tell their parents, and how
to fit in. This process usually results in a struggle between the desire to
authentically be who they are and the desire to be like everyone else.
Many teens keep this struggle quiet until a time when hiding their identity creates so much inner conflict that taking the risk of being more
open is considered the only decision possible. This is a very tricky path.
For the many teens who have to navigate this path without support
from family and friends, the journey can be more than they can handle.
Even with your love and support, it can be a monumental task.

It is a deep human need to feel whole and coherent. We all want to feel that we know who we are, and that who we are is recognized and accepted by others. For younger teens, there is a strong desire to blend in, a goal that can seem impossible and therefore stressful for transgender, non-binary, and questioning youth. As teens mature, in addition to wanting to be recognized and accepted by others, they often yearn to be unique. In this process the drive to be whole—authentically who they are—can outweigh the desire to conform and fit in. Nonetheless, the desire to be understood and accepted remains throughout life.

Achieving Gender Consolidation

At some point in our lives, we all undertake a process to feel whole in who we are—we need to integrate the different aspects of our identities, including gender, race, physical abilities, sexual orientation, appearance, and religion. This is called identity consolidation. When this journey is centered around an identity that falls outside of social norms, as with your child's gender journey, the process is more challenging.

As you recognize and acknowledge that your child's gender journey can be an isolating one, you can find strategies to counter that isolation and help your child develop a sense of self-coherence. Self-coherence is not so much about what is visible on the outside—such as personal appearance or even names or pronouns—but it's the inner sense a person has that they know who they are, that they like who they are, and are comfortable in their own skin.

While this journey toward wholeness can in many ways span a lifetime, we have come to recognize through our work with youth and families that there are some common benchmarks along this path during the teen years.

There is a common developmental pathway from gender identity formation to gender identity consolidation, although the journey is different for each person. Everyone goes through this process around their gender, not just transgender and non-binary people; however, to the degree that someone falls outside society's gender norms, the process is likely to be a more conscious and possibly more complicated one.

> *"For my first child, the teenage question of 'Who am I?" played out in a number of different ways. She changed her name in eleventh grade, changed it back in twelfth. She had many different hairstyles and tried out multiple piercings. Some of the piercings stayed, but most did not. She experimented with different social groups and kinds of music. She took our whole family on a wild ride. She is 'cisgender' as they say. My transgender teen did not explore clothing or hairstyles or piercings—he is very gender normative. His process was more internal than external. He struggled with self-worth and his right to be himself. Once he found a resting place with these deeper questions, he developed more meaningful friendships."*

Unique Issues for Transgender and Non-Binary Teens Who Have Lived in Alignment with Their Gender Identity Since Childhood

> *"Our teenage daughter has been living in her affirmed gender for over ten years now and I kind of wish that I had seen her actually wrestle more with her gender identity through those years. On the one hand, I realize that is a silly thought. I have not once questioned my other (cisgender) daughter's understanding of who she is. But at the same time, as we're considering these major medical procedures, it would be reassuring to know my transgender daughter has wrestled with this as much as I have! I am left wanting something carved in stone that says, 'Yes, this is her gender identity*

and you are doing the right thing.' So far, no engraved tablets have
fallen from the sky and I don't expect them anytime soon."

If a transgender or non-binary teen has lived in alignment with their
gender identity since childhood, some aspects of gender consolidation
in adolescence may be easier than for those teens who either came to
this awareness later in life or who were not allowed to express their
authentic gender identity. However, even for teens who have been living
in their affirmed gender since childhood, adolescence is not always an
easy time. Childhood may have felt like a bubble as the gender-related
concerns revolved around names, pronouns, clothing, and making
sure they had access to the correct bathroom. Once adolescence hits, it
becomes much more complex. What may have once felt like a steady,
manageable path suddenly becomes more challenging and uncertain.
It is so for you as a parent as well; having "gotten on board" when
your child was young, it can be quite disconcerting to be once again
challenged by your teen's reexamination of their gender as a teenager.

Teens who have been supported in their transgender or non-binary
identity since childhood go through the same stages of gender identity
consolidation that all other teens do and are as likely to refine their
gender identity in adolescence. Perhaps their identity is shifting toward
a more complex or less binary identity. Others may come to recognize that childhood assumptions about what forms of body modification they would want for themselves no longer hold. A realization of a
gender identity shift (e.g., from transgender to non-binary, or from non-
binary to transgender) brings with it the same fears and concerns as
others have who are encountering their gender incongruity for the first
time. It also brings an additional fear that the outside world (including
parents and other family members) will not see their gender as valid if
it continues to evolve. Thus, the struggle to acknowledge a changing
identity may be very difficult and fraught with deep anxiety that may
trigger a new identity crisis around their gender.

It is important to note that in our work, we have yet to see even one transgender or non-binary teen who was affirmed in their gender in childhood realize in adolescence that they are cisgender. Mostly their gender identity remains constant and simply deepens in adolescence. However, we have seen transgender teens realize that they are non-binary and non-binary teens move to a transgender identity.

The Pathway to Congruence

"Now that I have been on hormones for six months and more changes are starting to happen, I'm completely comfortable in my identity. So, I don't really even consider myself a trans girl anymore; it's more just like I'm a girl who just happens to be transgender. I feel like I'm just myself."

"Watching my kid look in the mirror for the first time wearing the clothes of their choice was an amazing moment—they were just beaming."

"My teen started wearing a binder and his confidence went way up, his anxiety way down. It's been great to see."

A key element of gender consolidation and positive identity formation is the process of reaching a feeling of congruence. Gender congruence is reached when a person has accepted their gender identity and feels satisfied with how they are physically and socially expressing their gender. For some, whether or not they are cisgender, transgender, non-binary, or agender, congruence involves a certain level of compromise or reconciliation between their internal feelings and the currently desired or available options for external expression. For your non-binary or transgender teen, congruence should not be considered an endpoint. Rather, congruence should bring an internal sense of peace in relation to their gender. Typical congruence measures for a transgender or non-binary person may include appearance changes (hairstyles, clothing, accessories); name and/or pronoun change(s); body modification procedures; and legal document changes (gender markers, birth certificates, etc.).

> *"Breasts became a big topic in my house! As a teen, my daughter was unhappy with her breasts being as small as they are. Her body did not look like what popular culture was telling her that a woman was supposed to look like. She didn't think she looked feminine enough. At the same time, my transgender son was worried that he would look too feminine and wanted a flatter chest than he has. Who knew parenting would be so complicated?! Over the last year or so, I'm happy to say that my daughter is getting more comfortable with her body, and my son has found that testosterone has given him more of the flat chest he is looking for. They both deserve to be happy in their bodies."*

Teens Have Fears Too

Keep in mind that teens have their own fears, whether they are spoken or not. Those we hear most often are:

- "Will I have access to blockers (puberty-suppressing medication)? And if so, will it be soon enough?"
- "Will my body betray me somehow, letting everyone know things about me that I only tell those who I trust completely?"
- "Will I be able to get cross-hormones, or be stuck waiting to begin puberty while everyone else's bodies are changing?"
- "Will I find someone who loves me as I am?"

Ultimate Goal: Identity Consolidation

All of the tasks of adolescence work together toward the ultimate task of creating a positive self-image, positive identity, and a clear sense of self. As mentioned, the central task of adolescence is creating a strong, stable sense of self with which to move into adulthood (identity consolidation). Identity consolidation occurs when a person has acknowledged important parts of themselves and arrives at an integrated, positive sense of self.

We will review the developmental tasks that support identity formation in the following chapter. We will now specifically examine the process for identity consolidation for all youth, with special focus on transgender and non-binary youth. Much of what we cover here regarding the stages of identity consolidation can be used across the board when considering other marginalized identities your teen might have and how they too are integrated. In the chapter on fostering resilience in your teen, we will explore multiple ways that you can assist your teen in forming a positive self-image.

The point in late adolescence or young adulthood at which gender identity consolidation happens for your child will directly impact how many of their years at home will be marked by increased gender-related anxiety, angst, and (most seriously) depression. Identity consolidation is not a linear process and, as such, there is not a magical moment where gender issues are over and everything becomes easy. However, with parental vigilance toward warning signs of depression and self-harm, transgender and non-binary teens can navigate the heightened emotions of adolescence and emerge successfully into adulthood similarly to other teens. For most transgender and non-binary youth who experience family support, adolescence will be in line with the social, cognitive, and emotional development that all teens experience—simply with additional gender-related challenges. However, if you notice your teen's identity consolidation process is extended, don't worry—this is not unusual. Every person is on their own developmental path.

The Six Stages of Positive Gender Identity Consolidation

A stage model can provide a useful framework for a parent, caregiver, or other adult to understand the process of positively integrating a transgender or non-binary identity. This framework can be helpful for all people seeking to support a transgender or non-binary teen.

Keep in mind that gender identity consolidation is an organic process that is not always linear, and it occurs for all teenagers, not just transgender and non-binary teens. Youth can be in more than one stage simultaneously, or return for a deeper dive into an earlier stage. It is useful to conceptualize the process by which people identify their gender, come to accept it, and when necessary (as with transgender and non-binary gender people), transform it from a stigma-based, negative identity, into a positive one. Of course, the impact of intersecting identities contributes to the timeline of the identity consolidation process as well.

The model we set forth is based on research in adolescent identity formation and influenced by our experience with transgender and non-binary youth. It represents a journey marked by the progression from confusion to tolerance, acceptance, and pride.

Unique Manifestations, but Common Stages

The stages of identity consolidation can look and feel different for each individual. A number of factors influence a child's experience, including individual brain development, pubertal state, abstract thinking skills development, desire to conform, as well as external factors like family, school, and community support (or lack thereof). It is a flexible model, so don't worry if your child's path zigs and zags a bit throughout their development. This is natural. Also, some people have more of an endpoint in their identity and expression, and once they reach it, they find their resting point. For others, both identity and expression continue to evolve, and consolidation is reached once congruence with their then-current sense of self occurs. As you read through the stages, please remember that your teen may be anywhere along this path of identity integration.

Stage 1: Dissonance

> *"Even when I was little, I didn't feel like a girl boy—only when I was told that 'girls and boys are very different,' is when I realized I thought differently than everyone around me."*

The initial stage of identity consolidation, Dissonance, is marked by tension. Teens in this stage feel confused, limited, and to some extent, controlled by social and cultural expectations about gender expression, gender identity, and gender roles. In the case of emerging transgender and non-binary identities, this confusion sometimes leads to denial regarding their gender.

Awareness of discomfort or distress is usually conscious, but some emerging transgender and non-binary teens may or may not associate the discomfort with their gender. They know something is "wrong," but they may not understand why or how to describe it. At this point, it is not usually clear for the teen (or those around them) if the struggle is with their gender role, gender identity, or gender expression. Sometimes, assumptions may be made that a teen is struggling with sexual orientation, not gender. Many teens experience a crisis at this stage, and you may see significant changes in their behavior. Risky behaviors may emerge as a way to manage the feelings of shame, low self-worth, and anxiety that commonly arise as they become aware of their gender confusion.

We all seek inner coherence, a sense that we are a whole and integrated person. There are times when we might lose contact with ourselves, but come back to it again in a new way. However, it feels awful and chaotic while drifting in a place of internal incoherence. Undergoing a personal overhaul makes for a messy time, and can be difficult for those around them to understand what exactly is going on. These periods of incoherence can lead to depression, withdrawal, self-harm, drug use, promiscuity, and anxiety. If you see these in your child, talk with them to see if they can pinpoint what is happening. They may not have language for it yet, but they may be able to communicate pieces of what's happening for them in a way that allows you to help them reduce confusion and reassure them that they will be able to work through it to a place of greater comfort.

Stage 2: Comparison

> "I just kept looking at everyone around me—am I like that person? Or maybe like that person? I was a teenage girl comparing myself to the young men I saw on the bus, on billboards, and on TV. Eventually I realized that everyone I was comparing myself to were guys, and a sense of never girls or women."

In the next stage, Comparison, teenagers find themselves looking at other youth and adults, trying to see where they do and do not match up in relation to their gender. They may try especially hard to fit the expectations of their assumed gender in their appearance and behavior. They may or may not be aware that the urge to fit in is trumping their urge to be themselves. For many transgender, non-binary, and questioning teens, there is often a tremendous amount of distress, emotional pain, and struggle in this phase, which leaves these teens extremely vulnerable. For the average transgender or non-binary teen, the internal conflict around gender becomes more conscious in this stage.

In this stage, transgender and non-binary youth who are just coming to realize their gender identity for the first time, or are realizing that their feelings about their gender are not going away and they have to finally deal with them, may compare themselves to others as a part of coming to terms with this awareness. Teens who are on the verge of acknowledging that they are transgender or non-binary often have difficulty recognizing themselves in the gender identities they see expressed around them. These youth may try other "alternative" identities on for size that are traditionally more accepting of variation in gender presentation, such as lesbian, gay, bisexual, or queer identities, and only later realize that they are actually transgender or non-binary. Because denial of one's emerging awareness of being transgender or non-binary is more difficult at this stage, anxiety can be extremely heightened. This stage is sometimes characterized by risky behaviors with particular tendencies toward disordered eating, depression, self-harm (including attempted suicide), and sexual confusion.

The swift pubertal body changes of adolescence can lead to new levels of body dysphoria. Before puberty, body dysphoria is typically more easily relieved with clothing and hairstyles. It is no longer quite that simple once puberty begins. The body changes of puberty may be met with extreme self-loathing, directed acts of self-harm toward the secondary sex characteristics of the body, disordered eating and/ or dissociation, a sense of detachment from physical and emotional experiences. In the Comparison stage, as well as part of the first stage (Dissonance), if youth are connected with mental health providers who do not have significant experience working with gender and teens, they may be diagnosed with depression, anxiety, or an eating disorder, while leaving the gender issue unacknowledged and unaddressed.

Stage 3: Tolerance

> "My daughter has been struggling to find the language that feels right for her, but I can see her shifting to a more comfortable place within herself. She worries less what others think of her, but she's still more isolated from other kids at school than I wish she was."

Stage three, Tolerance, marks the beginning of the steps toward self-acceptance. For all teens, this is the beginning of the shift away from needing a conventionally defined gender expression and toward initial acceptance of their individuality. All teens are striving to define and assert a clear sense of self in this phase and are exploring how they want to be seen and express themselves.

By the time a teen is able to say to themself, "I am probably transgender" or "I don't know what my gender is, but it is not what I have always been told," they have moved into the Tolerance stage and have a greater level of commitment to defining this new sense of identity. Locating and identifying what that identity may be can take many forms. Teens often explore a series of different identities, labels, and presentations until they find the best fit during this stage. This can exacerbate the preexisting awkwardness of adolescence. If you observe your teen moving from one label to another, it is understandable that you might wonder if they are going through a phase of experimentation, causing you to discount the validity of their gender exploration. In reality, your teen is simply going through a process of elimination as they figure out who they are (and who they are not).

The increasing visibility of transgender, non-binary, and gender-expansive role models may provide a sort of roadmap for your child to define their own gender. However, it is quite likely that none of these people will represent the exact gender your child experiences themselves to be, making it even more difficult to see a reflection of their self out in the world. Sexuality can be another arena for some teens to explore their gender. It can be through sexual expression that some teens come to find their truest sense of themselves in relation to their gender.

At some point during this stage, teens try to connect with others who also do not feel congruent with their assumed gender. They are highly likely to turn to the Internet as a means of trying to locate and interact with others who may be undergoing a similar process of self-exploration. Such connections can provide tremendous relief for your teen, offering both support and confirmation.

A hallmark of the Tolerance stage is increased feelings of isolation and alienation. Your teen may be struggling with shame, secrecy, guilt, and pressure to conform to what is expected of them socially, culturally, or within your family. The greater the perceived pressure to conform and the risk of rejection associated with it, the more likely the teen will isolate themselves and explore their gender internally more than externally. Dysphoria, depression, eating disorders, self-harm, and suicide risk continue to be potential consequences of this dynamic.

Perhaps the most important way to interrupt these self-destructive patterns is through the presence of an accepting adult. If transgender and non-binary teens have adults in their lives who are supportive, it is easier for them to stay open during this stage, creating space for them to begin claiming their identity ("I am transgender" or "I am gender-fluid," etc.). Once they are able to state affirmatively who they are, or at least start trying different labels on for size with a sense of hope, they enter the next stage of self-acceptance.

Stage 4: Acceptance

> "See, when you first look at me, 'Oh yeah, are you a boy?' I'm like, 'Um, no.' And then they give me a look, but it's all a natural thing. [I'm] in the middle. What middle means is a rare person."[1]

All teens in stage four, Acceptance, begin to claim their personal preferences—whether for grooming, clothes, or activities. They are generally more comfortable with their personal gender expression. Secure that their gender identity is not threatened by their preferences, teens in this stage become more confident in asserting who they are. Identity is more settled, and they claim their personal gender identity as well as their gender expression. In short, there is a growing sense of coherence that is coming into focus.

It is important in this stage for non-binary and transgender teens to begin to seek out experiences that normalize their gender identity. This usually coincides with increased contact with other transgender or non-binary people. As they reach greater self-acceptance, often as reflected by others' acceptance of them, they begin to get more comfortable out in the world.

The gender identity labels a teen uses may change over time, but if the inner sense of self remains coherent, then identity formation has stabilized (even if the stability is within the malleability of a gender-fluid identity). Most people will come to an awareness of a single gender identity; others find that they have a mixed gender or multiple genders. Rather than a source of distress because of feeling different, however, this hard-earned sense of self is quite liberating and empowering for many teens.

Once gender identity coherence is established, the task at hand is to see what is required for your teen to reach a state of congruence, which is an alignment between their inner and outer selves. If you recall the discussion regarding the three dimensions of gender, identity is just one aspect. Congruence is when each of us gets all three dimensions to line up, in the ways that are right for us, to the best of our ability. For some, finding an identity label that fits is enough. For others, congruence comes with changing one's personal presentation or style. Yet others may need a pronoun and/or name change, or medical options such as hormone therapy or surgery. The process of coming to a sense of congruence is highly individualized. But for everyone, regardless of gender, it is the ability to have the internal sense of their gender in harmony with their body and gender expressions at a level where they experience a sense of "this feels right" or at least "right enough."

This stage can last for quite a while; it's not uncommon for it to take place over many years and to overlap with the next two phases. It not only includes accepting one's identity and inner feelings, but also searching for a way to show the world who we are. This will be reflected in your teen's appearance, presentation (mannerisms, etc.), and in their interactions with others. Choosing to seek congruence despite possible cultural stigma, discrimination and harassment can be an agonizing but life-saving and affirming choice for transgender and non-binary people.

Although your teen can look more assured in their new gender expression, more confident in their walk and the way that they carry themselves, this stage is still an exceptionally vulnerable time. Their coherence can be very fragile, often more fragile than they appear, and it can be very disconcerting for them to cope with those who do not affirm their gender. The negative reactions of others can crumble their newly emerging self-confidence. Likewise, when someone is new to their identity, they have not yet clarified their lines of privacy and they may find themselves in emotionally or physically dangerous situations. This risk is compounded if a young person experiences rejection from family, religious, ethnic, or cultural communities.

An individual knows they have reached congruence when they experience a sense of peace and wholeness that they never had before. Other changes that come with congruence can include a lifting or lessening of chronic mental health issues, greater comfort in one's body, and greater confidence. Congruence is essential in terms of positive identity formation and satisfaction with life. But without the next two stages, positive identity consolidation has not yet occurred. We want to emphasize that reaching coherence and congruence does not imply resilience. The foundation is still shaky despite outward indications that could suggest otherwise.

Stage 5: Pride

> *"I've accepted myself and that's just as important as others*
> *accepting me. But I'm not always brave enough to be my whole*
> *self in the 'real world.' I don't think that makes me any less*
> *proud—the world still has a lot of growing to do before people*
> *like me can feel safe to be open about who we are."*

This fifth stage, Pride, marks the turning point toward positive identity consolidation. For all teens, this is the point where they take pride
in themselves and appreciate their uniqueness. They are able to see
that gender is expansive, with room for everyone to be themselves.
This is often accompanied with a shift out of shame or hiding aspects
of themselves that are not consistent with social gender norms and
into claiming who they are (e.g., "I am a boy who knits," "I am a female
jock," "I don't wear makeup," etc.). Teens in this stage take pride in
proclaiming who they are. For transgender and non-binary teens, this
is the stage when gender identity is consolidated.

The Pride stage marks the shift from the inner work of understanding one's gender to the external process of creating connection
and community. As in the previous stage, Acceptance, the Pride stage
is a time when positive links with transgender and non-binary teens
with whom they can relate, either online or through local groups, is
critical. Finding these communities provides spaces where their life
experience is normalized rather than marginalized.

With the emergence of gender pride, transgender and non-binary
youth can feel at odds with the inequities of society at large. For some,
this naturally leads to activism or greater advocacy on behalf of themselves and others who face gender discrimination. This can take many
forms, such as being a role model for others, working for social justice,
or taking part in protests. Often there is an increased desire to tell their
story, and many avenues and formats exist for them to do so. Some-

times, this initial experience of pride can be accompanied with a sort of aggressive tone or an "in your face" attitude. Having found their voice, there is a natural and understandable desire to use it to be heard.

Whether someone openly engages in activism or quietly makes their way, this phase marks the shift internally to a place of acceptance and pride. In this stage, transgender and non-binary youth continue learning to live and relate to others with a new or newly articulated gender. With increased openness, there may be some new encounters with stigma and discrimination. But unlike earlier stages where these negative experiences threaten emotional stability, gender pride is a key component of developing resilience to these social ills.

With this pride comes recognition of positive aspects that go along with their individual identity, as well as the larger communities they may be part of. This provides new meaning in life and serves to greatly reduce risks for the negative coping mechanisms described in earlier stages.

Stage 6: Consolidation

> *"When I was in high school, I had a very rough time. I was teased and tormented for being too girlish. But I found refuge in being Hawaiian, being Kanaka Maoli. My purpose in this lifetime is to pass on the true meaning of aloha—love, honor, and respect. It's a responsibility that I take very seriously."*
>
> *—KUMU HINA*

In the final stage, Consolidation, a person's gender identity becomes integrated with other aspects of their identity such as race, ethnicity, family, class, and religion. How many other aspects of identity there are to integrate, and how tolerant their particular communities are, will affect the time it takes for all identities to consolidate and integrate into one multidimensional identity.

Whether or not your child is still living at home at this point, you will see a greater peace in your transgender or non-binary child in this stage. Both you and they will be able to see a worthwhile future for them with multiple opportunities. In this stage of consolidation, relationships are stronger and usually marked by greater levels of acceptance. Relationships with family and friends are enriched and strengthened through mutual respect and authenticity (if they are accepting and supportive). Likewise, the impact of non-accepting people in your teen/young adult's life is greatly reduced.

Perhaps the greatest hallmark of the Consolidation stage is the confidence and strength that radiates from your teen/young adult. Having been through such a transformative and often difficult experience creates an inner strength of identity that is powerful and results in deep inner resilience.

Self-Esteem and Identity

One of the primary responsibilities of parents and caregivers of adolescents is to assist their teen in acquiring a healthy sense of self. The road to adulthood is not expected to be neat and tidy. Adolescent growth and development are expected to be awkward. When a teen is transgender or non-binary, their adolescence involves not only the expected awkwardness of the teenage years, but also an additional and often much more difficult element of self-discovery. This gender-related discovery process takes many different individualized trajectories and, as with all adolescent growth, some teens (and families) have it easier than others. Allow your teen the time they need to explore themselves and their gender—but do everything you can to monitor their progress and to help keep them safe throughout their consolidation journey.

Low Self-Worth Can Delay Self-Acceptance

"Because true belonging only happens when we present our authentic, imperfect selves to the world, our sense of belonging can never be greater than our level of self-acceptance."

—BRENÉ BROWN, DARING GREATLY: HOW THE COURAGE TO BE VULNERABLE TRANSFORMS THE WAY WE LIVE, LOVE, PARENT, AND LEAD

Non-binary, transgender, and other gender-expansive youth often feel that there is something inherently wrong with them. They can feel that they are not "normal". Cultural expectations of gender roles and what it means to be a "real" man or a "real" woman are found throughout society. It is difficult not to internalize that there is something wrong with you when genders like yours are not positively mirrored around you. This can lead to a lack of self-worth and low self-esteem, which can lead to difficulty claiming your gender identity.

Self-Loathing

One thing that is very difficult for parents to accept (and often to realize at all) is that it is highly likely that before identity consolidation, your transgender or non-binary teen may actually hate themselves. They may brutally judge and attack themselves and question their reason for living. This can lead to shame—and the deep-seated fear that they are unlovable and have no inherent value as a person. Self-hatred of this level can lead your teen to substance use, self-harm, eating disorders, suicide, or other self-destructive behaviors. Self-loathing is very common for transgender and non-binary teens due to internalized stigmatization—believing negative gender-related messages that they get from media, peers, religion, and maybe even family. It is quite a dilemma because in order to successfully manage their marginalized identity, your child needs a fairly high level of self-esteem, and yet it is that same stigmatized identity that negatively impacts self-esteem.

Empathy and Understanding Reduce Shame

> "When [our teen] was really struggling with the thought that he might be a girl, we listened. We tried to show him through our actions and words that we understood his struggle and that whatever was true for him was OK with us. We told him that if he was a girl or a boy, or some combination of the two, we were good with that. We just wanted him to know that we thought he was unique, special, and loved."

Coming to a place of self-love and acceptance will not happen overnight. This is a lengthy process that requires truly coming to terms with who one is. This is what positive identity integration is all about. In the meantime, there is a lot that you as a parent can do to cultivate your teen's self-acceptance. The next chapters of the book go into specific supportive parenting things you can do, as well as ways to help your teen build resilience. Reinforce actions that move your teen toward self-compassion. Research has shown that self-loathing recedes when we help others. If you can, engage in meaningful volunteer work together or other activities focused on others. Let your teen know in no uncertain terms how much they mean to you. Create regular time to be together. Actively listen to your teen. Empathize and remind them that you see their beauty.

Actively Reinforce Encouraging Messages of Value and Self-Worth

"We live in a world where most people still subscribe to the belief that shame is a good tool for keeping people in line. Not only is this wrong, but it's dangerous. Shame is highly correlated with addiction, violence, aggression, depression, eating disorders, and bullying."

—BRENÉ BROWN, DARING GREATLY: HOW THE COURAGE TO BE VULNERABLE TRANSFORMS THE WAY WE LIVE, LOVE, PARENT, AND LEAD

Through your words and actions, regularly express to your child how loved they are by you. It may not always seem like it, but your child needs to hear:

I love you.

I trust you.

I believe in you.

I value your experience of yourself.

I know you can handle this.

You are very, very important to me.

You are creating the life you want to live.

You are not alone.

You have value.

Your warmth and support can be a constant during these challenging times while they are acquiring a solid and positive sense of self. As a parent, when you demonstrate warmth and love you provide a safe base. In doing so you will be supporting their emotional and mental health and the benefits will be widespread and lifelong.

---

1   This is from the film: http://aplaceinthemiddle.org/film

Chapter 5

Goals of Adolescent Development

"We had thought the teen years were going to be very difficult for our child. It turned out so much better than we could have imagined. As his body grew into the body he had always imagined having (through the help of puberty blockers and testosterone), he gained such confidence in himself. He is kind, compassionate, well-rounded varsity athlete and an overall great person! Don't let people scare you about these years. Just stay connected to your child."

"As I read widely about the teen years, I was able to put my gender-fluid daughter's adolescence into better perspective. Some of the things that I had been so focused on turned out to be normal parts of adolescence and had nothing to do with her gender! I really think all parents who have transgender or gender-fluid teens need to know that not everything is about gender. I think if she had been my second child instead of my first, it would have been easier."

THERE AREN'T MANY OF US who, if given the chance, would willingly trade adulthood for a return to adolescence. While there are blessings in those teen years, they are also tumultuous.

Every teen, regardless of gender identity or gender expression, grapples with the significant developmental challenges that they are faced with throughout adolescence. The emotional and physical rollercoaster known as puberty is just one factor. Changes in their brain and the impact those changes have on their ability to read and respond to increasingly complex social dynamics add another layer. Is it any wonder that, when you add the typical disrupted sleep patterns that teens experience on top of all of this, your teen is often stressed, moody, and overwrought? Our goal in this chapter is to help provide information about what is happening for your teen at various stages of adolescence so that what you're seeing in their behavior and in your interactions makes a bit more sense. We will highlight what is universal for all teens and what has a different twist to it for transgender, non-binary, and questioning teens. We want to emphasize the importance of staying engaged with your teen during this time, even when you don't feel like it. With transgender and non-binary teens, there are additional serious health and well-being implications (depression, self-harm, and suicidal tendencies) in the teenage years that you need to be aware of.

The overview of adolescent development that follows will introduce you to the changes that are occurring; while this knowledge may not make your journey with your teen less aggravating, scary, and/or frustrating, hopefully it will allow you to understand just how much they are grappling with.

Adolescents experience enormous changes in every facet of their lives as they transition from childhood to adulthood. As parents, our goal is to assist our children in accomplishing the many developmental tasks of adolescence in order to help them successfully launch into adulthood. With transgender and non-binary teens, this also involves supporting their process of personal development and sense of self so that they are secure in their gender and feel congruent with themselves (meaning they have accepted their gender identity and feel satisfaction with their appearance and expression of gender). Identity consolidation, the process of integrating different parts of one's identity, is a universal task of adolescence; once it occurs, youth are ready to emerge from adolescence into adulthood. For transgender and non-binary youth, achieving this developmental milestone of identity consolidation is a more nuanced and often much more difficult process. Having a solid understanding of the developmental processes of adolescence will assist you in parenting your teen during these years.

Puberty is difficult; struggling with gender identity issues makes it even more challenging. Combine this with any additional struggles your teen or family may have and parenting effectively throughout puberty can feel overwhelming. Take heart. You're not alone. We are here with you, as are thousands of families raising their transgender and non-binary teens at this very moment. Together we are forging new territory and helping to create a safer, more inclusive world for everyone.

Although the goals of adolescent development are specific to emergent adulthood, the areas of the brain that are undergoing the most change are the same as those that saw rapid growth during infancy and toddlerhood. So again, although gender identity forms initially in the toddler years, it is no surprise that it is revisited in adolescence. For all teens, adolescence marks a period of rapid biological, psychological, and social development rivaling only the rate of change of infancy and early childhood. During this time teens not only grow in size, but in thinking capacity, sexual development, and emotional maturity.

Adolescence as a Time of Opportunity

Although there can be a tendency to focus on the challenges that teens face and what we can do to help them (and ourselves) survive adolescence, for most young people, adolescence is a period of normal, healthy development. The majority of teens, including non-binary and transgender teens, who have supportive adults in their lives succeed in school and move into adulthood without experiencing serious health and safety issues. Despite all of the stories we hear otherwise, many families successfully navigate this period of time together.

Take the time to truly appreciate the wonders of adolescence. It is an incredible time in the human lifecycle with astonishing growth in virtually all aspects of self. When you take the time to understand the capabilities and vulnerabilities particular to adolescent human development, you can better utilize the research and resources to support your teen in lifelong mental health and wellness.

The Teenage Brain

The changes in the brain during adolescence are dramatic. The flexibility of the brain is one of the hallmarks of adolescence, and it is both a strength and a vulnerability. What can seem too much to bear for a teen one day can be manageable (and sometimes exhilarating) the next. This fluctuation can be challenging for teen and parent alike.

It is especially important during this time to be on the lookout for warning signs that your teen is suffering. We tend to dismiss a teen's behavior as a product of raging hormones or attitude as they assert their independence. Of course, those aspects may indeed play a role, but the many ups and downs of adolescence are evidence that there is a lot of change happening inside their brains. Brain imaging studies show that teenage brains actually function differently from adult brains, requiring us to frame adolescent behavior in a whole new light. In some very important ways, the brains of teenagers do not look like adult brains until they reach their mid-twenties.

The intense development of a teen's brain is complicated by the fact that two essential components of this process occur at different rates.

In early adolescence, the part of your teen's brain that enjoys risk-taking (the limbic brain) accelerates its rate of growth. This part of the brain is dominant throughout the first part of adolescence. Later in adolescence, the parts of your teen's brain that are responsible for impulse control and the awareness of cause and long-term effect (the frontal lobes) start to mature. The frontal lobes regulate the functions associated with adult behavior. Thus, impulse control and the ability to plan ahead, anticipate, and support goal-oriented behavior mature later.

In fact, the development of our prefrontal cortex (the front part of the frontal lobes) is a lengthy process. It goes through its own growth spurt shortly after puberty and does not finish maturation until a person is twenty-three to twenty-five years old. Once the prefrontal cortex has developed, more mature decision-making and improved communication skills can solidify. In other words, during adolescence, the critical thinking functions of judgment and insight do not keep pace with the increase in the gut response/emotional regions of the brain.

This explains, at least in part, why younger teens engage in riskier behavior, have more heightened emotions, and are not always able to have the levels of foresight and insight that parents and other adults in their life expect and desire. Asking a younger teen, "Didn't you think about what would happen?" may be an unanswerable question; in many ways, some younger teens are developmentally unable to do so.

Teenage Development Is Uneven
Teens enter adolescence with the body and mind of a child and leave adolescence ten or so years later with the body and mind of an adult. It is a remarkable process! During these years, there is not only naturally staggered development, but there is also a great deal of individual variation within the developmental process. Healthy development in teens is uneven. This is why teens can seem so young some days and older than their years on others. It is also why it remains critical to stay involved and continue to provide healthy limits and boundaries

for your teen until they are developed enough to be able to make wise decisions on their own. Talk with your teen about your own process of setting boundaries (when appropriate) so that you model for them the steps involved in making healthy decisions.

Brain-Related Emotional Response

Teenagers experience emotions very intensely; it is a normal part of adolescent brain development. Brain imaging reveals that teenagers cannot read the emotions of others as accurately as adults can, often incorrectly or inconsistently recognizing emotions on someone's face. Add to that evidence suggesting that the teenage brain reacts in a more intensified manner to emotionally loaded imagery (as compared to children and adults) and what you have is a teenager with a heightened emotional reaction, often incorrectly interpreting what they are reacting (or overreacting) to!

Thus it is completely normal for a teen, especially a younger teen, to have impulsive, emotionally reactionary responses rather than thoughtful responses to the events in their lives. Many teens, due to a combination of brain and hormonal changes, experience a newly intense level of emotions such as rage, fear, sexual stimulation, aggression toward self and others, and overall excitement. It takes a number of years for more areas of the brain to become involved in the processing of emotions, in order to gain a greater sense of equilibrium and control when it comes to managing emotions and accurately interpreting the emotions of others. Until that time, teens have a tendency to misread the emotions of those around them and to respond in an amplified manner.

While difficult for any young person, this creates even more challenges for non-binary and transgender teens. Perhaps already hypervigilant and on guard for slights from their peers, they may (accurately or inaccurately) believe that other teens feel disdain or dislike for them based on their gender. In response, they may have a heightened reaction or even take self-harming, impulsive actions.

During adolescence, there is also a dramatic increase in social self-consciousness and the desire to fit in. Research demonstrates that the teenage brain finds peer approval to be highly rewarding and satisfying, much more so than the brains of children or adults. Another relevant area of development that creates emotional conflict in the teenage brain has to do with abstract thinking. Abstract reasoning helps us assemble and hold multiple ideas at one time. In adolescence, it facilitates a teen in being able to make inferences about other people's thoughts and feelings. This commonly results in a teen being able to hypothesize about what they suppose others think or feel about them.

This potent combination of increased self-consciousness, the desire to fit in, and the perception that they know what someone else is thinking about them can significantly increase vulnerabilities in teens who are confronted with teasing, harassment, or social isolation. The fear of being targeted for their gender and the desire to fit in can be a volatile combination for teens and especially difficult to negotiate.

Hormonal Influences on Adolescent Behavior

"Since our daughter started taking estrogen, it has been very interesting to see her response to it. I think she feels really great about the changes she's seen (and of course what has not happened). She's very proud of her breasts! But she is definitely more up and down emotionally. Especially as the doses have increased, we see her getting weepier, more moody. But she can also joke about it—when we get on her about her attitude, she will sometimes say, 'Well what do you want? I'm a hormonal teenager!'"

There is an enormous hormonal cascade during adolescence. The adolescent brain secretes adrenal stress hormones, sex hormones, and growth hormones, all of which influence brain development. Hormones impact social and sexual behavior in addition to regulating growth patterns and supporting bone health. In addition to the sex and growth hormones, stress hormones also impact the brain and behavior. Add to this the variability of the timing and length of a teen's puberty, and it is easy to see why these hormonal influences can throw anyone into a state of emotional turmoil. Keep in mind that as challenging as it can be to be the parent of a teen, it is much more challenging for the teen.

When it comes to non-binary and transgender teens, conceptualizing the impact of adolescent hormones is more complex than for cisgender teens. There are multiple versions of puberty that transgender and non-binary youth can potentially experience:

- Their body's natal puberty (if they don't begin blockers at puberty's onset)
- A partial natal puberty that was suppressed with hormone suppressants, pushing a pause button at the point of hormonal development they had reached when suppressants were started
- Puberty consistent with their affirmed gender through hormone therapy at the age when their body was entering puberty naturally (this usually includes suppressants of their natal hormones at the same time they are taking hormone therapy for alignment with their affirmed gender)
- Puberty consistent with their affirmed gender through hormone therapy after being delayed, perhaps for two or more years, by the use of suppressants
- Natal puberty followed by a second puberty consistent with their affirmed gender by means of hormone therapy

Each of these variations of puberty brings a different experience of hormonal elements to consider: from a temporary suppression of sex hormones to the possibility of undergoing puberty twice—each time with a different set of dominant hormones. These options create a less common hormonal experience for adolescence and should be taken into consideration as you make decisions about medical interventions.

Sleep Loss, Hormones, and Depression

> *"My transgender daughter has a lot of anxiety at bedtime. She is not open about being transgender, she transitioned a long time ago, and almost everyone has no idea that she was assumed to be male at birth. I think her sleep struggles are because she has so much constantly on her mind about keeping her gender under wraps that she has a hard time quieting her mind when it's time to go to sleep. She is definitely sleep-deprived and I worry about her."*

Some of the brain and hormonal changes of adolescence affect sleep regulation and can be a factor in the teenage predisposition to stay up late. However, adequate sleep plays a central role in physical, mental, and emotional health. Sleep studies in teens reveal that lack of adequate sleep increases impulsivity and directly increases rates of depression. Sleep supports the brain to regulate emotions. Teens with chronic sleep deprivation experience greater levels of emotional distress. According to a 2015 study of almost twenty-eight thousand high school students in the United States in the *Journal of Youth and Adolescence*, for each hour of sleep loss, there is a 38 percent increased risk of feeling hopeless or sad and a 58 percent increase in suicide attempts. Sleep loss and depression go hand in hand.

As a parent of a transgender or non-binary teen, one of the most important roles you have is to help them regulate their emotions through healthy sleep patterns. It is only during sleep that many essential brain, hormonal, and body functions occur. The average teenager needs more sleep than both adults and younger children, yet frequently they get less. It is recommended that teens get 9.5 hours of sleep per night, but only 15 percent of teens get the required sleep during the school week. The American Academy of Pediatrics says that insufficient sleep in teens is a public health issue. Chronic sleep loss damages mental and physical health, education, and driving performance.

Sleep issues can be especially complicated for transgender and non-binary teens. According to a study of nearly one thousand transgender teens in Canada, 73 percent of teens say they always or often have trouble falling or staying asleep. This may sometimes be linked to stress related to gender identity. In a U.S. research study, many teens shared experiences of worry just at the moment when they were trying to sleep—a moment often infused with a quiet vulnerability.

Make Sleep a Priority

Parents play a vital role in helping teens get the sleep they need. Encourage your teen (and set expectations accordingly) to get proper sleep, rather than trying to make up for it on the weekends. Research on more than fifteen thousand students found that teens with set bedtimes that allow for sufficient sleep are less likely to suffer from depression or contemplate suicide. Helping your teen establish a consistent sleep schedule will make a tremendous difference. Be aware of these signs of sleep deprivation:

Irritability in the afternoon

Depression

Poor school performance

Trouble concentrating

Mood swings

Hyperactivity

Nervousness

Aggressive behavior

Stages of Adolescence

The developmental milestones of adolescence occur gradually, simultaneously, and in a layered fashion. Each milestone is dependent on others in order to be fully accomplished. Therefore, it is valuable to understand the general themes of early, middle, and late adolescence. Again, remember that if your teen suppresses puberty at any point, or initiates hormone therapy after previously going through natal pubertal development, some of these tasks of adolescence may be acquired on a less traditional timeline. However, regardless of the timeline, healthy development of the core areas identified in the following sections will facilitate preparedness for adulthood.

Early Adolescence

Rapid physical growth and sexual maturation are the hallmarks of early adolescence. Most young teens have mixed feelings about their changing bodies. Thus, it is natural that body image and concerns regarding physical acceptability are often at the forefront in the minds of young teens. Early adolescents are trying to establish their individuality as separate from their parents. There is usually an increased desire for privacy during these years. Younger teens are also often moody. As they pull away from their parents, they often turn to their peers for guidance and support, leaning on each other before they are able to fully stand on their own. The influence of their peers, rather than their parents, becomes primary; conformity becomes a governing theme. At this stage in adolescence, teens want to fit in—both in terms of physical appearance and social behavior. A thematic question for teens of this age is "Am I normal?" which can lead to constant comparison to others.

During early to mid-adolescence, a teen's expression of gender is typically quite rigid and stereotyped. Gender role socialization becomes very strong, and both adults and peers police gender role conformity. As a result, younger teens will typically participate in increased gender-stereotyped behaviors. This is due to a combination of emerging body changes, hormones, efforts to be romantically attractive, peer and adult pressures, and the powerful need to fit in.

Coming to realize that their body is changing in the wrong direction (or is not changing at all because of the use of puberty suppressants) can cause tremendous anxiety for transgender and non-binary youth at this stage of adolescence. The increasing pressure to conform to gender roles often causes new and heightened levels of anxiety, internal turmoil, and conflict for these teens.

Middle Adolescence

Middle adolescence is marked by a rapid increase in cognitive abilities resulting in new thinking skills and an interest in experimentation. Abstract thinking is beginning to develop. Physical development and sex drive may be more advanced for this age group. They often make risky and rebellious choices without an ability to understand the impact of their decisions. They are working toward behavioral maturity and independence from their parents, but they are also very self-absorbed. They may be hostile toward adults and authority figures.

Coping skills increase and impulse control capacity begins to be more developed as they become more self-directed. Although peer allegiance and social group identity remain strong, as they move through this phase, peer influence begins to decrease. The increased inclination to engage in gender-stereotyped behaviors peaks during these years and then begins to subside. Social skills increase and with them the desire to learn more sophisticated conflict resolution skills arises. During this time teens commonly try to organize the world into categories of just and unjust, right and wrong; and this period of binary thinking is often a time of increased family conflict. Personal identities, such as race or ethnicity, are also beginning to strengthen. Many teens in this phase of adolescence gain greater clarity (if they did not have it before) about what their gender and sexual orientation are, rather than just what they are not. Teens in middle adolescence are usually more at home with their new bodies, which leads to greater confidence. With this confidence, they may turn their attentions toward dating.

Middle adolescence is a period of especially high levels of vulnerability for transgender and non-binary teens. With these emerging thinking skills, greater levels of depression and anxiety can arise for transgender and non-binary youth. As they begin to see outside of their personal bubble, they may not be able to see a positive future for themselves. Isolation can loom large for those desiring social interactions but facing rejection or harassment. For these reasons, middle adolescence is a time of increased risk for self-harming behaviors, suicide attempts, and gender-related disordered eating.

Late Adolescence

Late adolescence is a period of frequent change and exploration throughout all areas of life: school, family, home, work, and social roles. Developing the skills necessary for functioning as a member of society may extend until their mid-twenties. Older teens become more self-aware; with this comes an awareness of identity and individuality separate from both family and friends. Older teens relate to individuals more than groups, establish their personal ethics and values, and tend to be idealistic and philosophical. As they identify their personal values, they are capable of respecting differing values and viewpoints and appreciating diversity. Achieving psychological independence from their parents during this period, older teens increasingly learn to relate to their family as adults. Conflicts with parents naturally decrease as they learn to balance their independence with connection to their parents. In addition, they:

- increase their ability to compromise;
- become more capable of complex and intimate relationships

and more concerned with serious relationships including what
kind of person would best suit them as a partner;

• use self-reflection to ask themselves what kind of a person they
  are and who they want to become;

• are more likely to engage in sexual activity;

• become more comfortable with body image and reach greater
  acceptance of their physical appearance; and

• are future-oriented and become more focused on college and/or
  career goals.

As they consolidate their personal identity, they are less driven by
peer approval. It is still a time of identity exploration, but the scaf-
folding is in place and feels more secure. Teens in later adolescence
tend to be aware of individuality and even celebrate it, participating in
fewer gender-stereotyped behaviors as gender identity becomes more
stable and expectations about appropriate forms of gender roles and
gender expression become more flexible. Older teens are more prone
to examine themselves and to discover that who they are as an individual is made up of many different characteristics that are separate
from their internal gender identity. At this point, youth are more likely
to feel confident and secure enough to enjoy activities that interest
them, and to present and express themselves in ways that feel natural
to them, whether or not they fit into societal gender stereotypes or peer
and parental expectations. Their understanding of gender becomes
more broadly defined.

As with their cisgender peers, gender identity stability happens
for older non-binary and transgender teens as well, although positive identity consolidation may not be achieved until into their mid-
twenties. For some non-binary and transgender teens, positive identity consolidation may require leaving home and finding others like
themselves and a community that values them. Those with supportive
families and community are often able to reach a greater level of

identity consolidation before leaving home. However, keep in mind that this period of late adolescence is one of increased risk for substance abuse and demeaning sexual behavior for transgender and non-binary youth if their self-esteem is not supported effectively. Suicide attempts are more likely to be successful in late adolescence.

> *"All my college-essay letters, like, have something to do with being transgender, because I feel like it's just like a really big part of me. Since then, I auditioned for [college name]. I met a lot of cool people. I was one of two black people there. That was awkward."*[1]

The Tasks of Adolescence

With this background on the changing teenage brain and the stages of adolescence, we now turn our attention to the primary developmental tasks of this important period in your child's life. As you know from your own life, human development isn't linear. We circle back through things time and time again; it's natural for all of us (including your teen). Personal experience, individual characteristics, and temperament all come into play with regard to how a teen travels through adolescence. So don't worry when you see tasks you thought were complete for your teen coming back for another round. It is all part of the process.

Let's start with the various markers of your teen's path toward adulthood. Based heavily on the work of Rae Simpson of the Harvard School of Public Health, the following areas are widely recognized adolescent development tasks required to support the healthy launching of teens.

Character Development and New Thinking Skills Integration

This task requires teens to take their newly heightened critical thinking skills and apply them to the development and understanding of the values that will guide their character as adults.

Teens Must Learn to:

* *Acquire and integrate new intellectual abilities*
  In early adolescence, the tendency to think concretely begins to give
  way to the ability to think abstractly. Teens are moving from egocen-
  tric thinking to the ability to conceptualize outside of themselves,
  thus developing empathy. However, the skill is still limited, leaving
  them feeling vulnerable and challenged to truly see another's point
  of view. Although this is a slow process that deepens throughout
  adolescence and into adulthood, the intellectual growth process
  really begins to accelerate in middle adolescence.

* *Adjust to increased cognitive expectations at school*
  Teachers challenge students to hone their newly developing abstract
  thinking skills, requiring them to apply their skills throughout the
  curriculum. The material is usually more demanding and since the
  rate and speed of cognitive growth are individualized, the material
  can feel alternatively thrilling, exhausting, or frustrating depending
  on a teen's personal cognitive abilities at any point in time.

* *Develop new communication skills*
  Intellectual maturation demands increased verbal skills to
  adequately communicate about more complex concepts. As prep-
  aration for adulthood, teens must acquire an expanded vocabulary in order to express themselves competently. They must also
  develop their social skills to include nonverbal communication,
  inferences, and sarcasm.

* *Develop a personal value system*
  It is developmentally appropriate for teens to actively question
  the beliefs and moral standards of their family, community, and
  culture. They identify a value system that resonates with their

personal concepts of what is right, just, important, and meaningful. Rather than accepting at face value what they're told, they
want to explore for themselves what makes sense. Combined with
their growing cognitive abilities, this process of exploration can
take many forms, from philosophical questioning, to experimentation with new and different beliefs, all the way to rejection of
commonly held values. Many teens find a greater sense of heritage,
cultural, and/or ethnic identity during adolescence. By late adolescence, teens have usually identified the guiding principles for their
own life, and many develop a greater moral and ethical inclusivity
than they were raised with.

- *Enhance problem-solving, decision-making, and conflict-resolu-
  tion skills*
  During adolescence, teens move from emotionally based, either/
  or solutions to a more sophisticated ability to weigh a variety of
  options as they seek to solve problems and resolve conflict. They
  begin to develop the ability to be more rational, find constructive
  solutions, and move toward compromise and collaboration. Teens
  learn to work with ambiguity, impulse control, planning, organizing
  thoughts, weighing consequences, and respecting other people's
  opinions and needs. As teens mature, they are able to recognize
  their own biases and to see the impact of their decisions on others.

- *Cultivate a sense of character*
  With their own moral code in place and the ability to solve problems, teens become able to take responsibility for their choices.
  Character is the intersection of a teen's values with their actions.
  Character development means becoming a person of integrity and
  becoming trustworthy. It involves doing what your heart knows is
  the right thing to do. Requiring self-reflection, self-knowledge, and
  a fair amount of self-control, developing strong character leads to

self-respect and often earns respect from others. Adults in a teen's life can provide opportunities and support for this level of development, encouraging them to be the best person they can be and providing them with opportunities where they can explore and practice treating others with kindness, compassion, and fairness.

Independence, Competence, and Coming Into Their Own

Teens Must Learn to:

- *Develop emotional maturity*
  Adolescence brings with it a depth and range of emotions that most teens have not experienced in the same way before. Over time, their ability to successfully manage intense, fluctuating emotions becomes more practiced. Teens learn how to manage stressful situations that elicit strong emotional reactions in healthy ways that don't involve self-harm or hurting others, utilizing coping skills to manage emotions and stress without acting out. As teens become more self-aware, they are able to identify and understand not only their own emotions, but also those of others. Emotional sophistication, which deepens throughout adolescence, allows a teen to communicate their own complex emotions, to have empathy for others, and to take responsibility for their own emotions. Adults can facilitate this emotional maturation process through healthy modeling of emotional expression, empathy, and healthy communication. Emotional maturity is linked to self-awareness and one's values, both evolving throughout adolescence.

- *Develop increased behavioral maturity*
  Gradually throughout adolescence, teens learn greater self-control. However, before that occurs, especially in early and middle adolescence, they tend to engage in risky behaviors as they are more

focused on immediate gratification. As their brains develop the ability to think through the potential consequences of their actions, teens frequently act in ways that can jeopardize their social, physical, sexual, and emotional safety. As they mature, they are more able to synchronize their behaviors with the increased recognition of potential negative impacts of impulsive decisions, as well as to align their actions with the emerging awareness of their long-term goals.

- *Effectively take on greater responsibilities*
  Throughout adolescence, teens learn to take on more mature roles and responsibilities. They may have greater responsibilities at home and in the running of the family, or have jobs and obligations outside of the home—in addition to managing their academic load. As they mature, they begin to learn accountability and to fulfill expectations independently, preparing them for the roles they will assume as adults. In early adolescence, teens tend to do a sloppy or incomplete job with new roles; they tend not to be able to track effectively or to truly care about all that is required to complete a task or responsibility. As they mature, they begin to take pride in their ability to be reliable and to take on more adult-like responsibilities.

- *Transform family relationships*
  Adolescence marks the transition from dependence on parents for virtually all of their needs to independence and autonomy. Teens sway back and forth in these years between their need for the continued safe, secure, and dependent relationship with their parents and the strong drive to become their own person. Teens are shifting from identifying as an extension of their parents to establishing separate identities. As they strive to discover who they are as independent people, they often push their parents away in order to create the space for self-discovery. During this

often-trying period for all involved, it is best to strive to maintain closeness and connection while supporting your teen in their independence.

By late adolescence, teens will begin to renegotiate their relationships with their parents. They will often reestablish relationships with their parents on new terms that respect their autonomy as an emerging adult and reflect their desire for closeness and connection. Likewise, if your relationship with your teen was not close to begin with, or they experienced rejection from you, it may be up to you as a parent to try to rebuild the bridge of connection honoring their new maturity.

- *Establish professional goals*
  Teens prepare for adulthood in part by planning for their futures. Whether they intend to pursue ongoing education or go straight into the workforce, teens begin to shape their ideas for the future and develop goals and plans to reach those goals. This is a natural part of identity development as they begin to envision what kind of life they want for themselves and what they want to do in the world.

- *Engender competence*
  In order to successfully launch into independent living, teens need to believe that they have both the abilities and skills to do so. Adolescents need opportunities to identify their passions and practice the skills needed to develop them. Likewise, they need contexts in which to try new things, receive training, and utilize their growing skill sets.

Develop Positive Body Image and Healthy Sexuality

"At first we thought he wouldn't date in high school. Not many people know he was assigned female at birth; he has chosen to keep that private. Dating could complicate that. But he met someone who does not live in his town and they have been together for a few years now. She is completely fine with our son. She has no problem seeing him as a boy. They care deeply for each other. She was mad at him when he initially disclosed about his gender history—but her anger came from him not telling her sooner. She felt like he didn't trust her and her feelings got hurt. What was incredible to us is that she had never known of transgender people, but had no problem with it."

Teens Must Learn to:

- *Adjust to new physical changes*
  Teens must adjust to a completely new physical sense of self. At no other time since infancy does the human body undergo such rapid and significant physical changes. There is a large gain in weight and height, as well as development of secondary sex characteristics. As a result, it is perfectly normal for teens to become somewhat obsessed with their bodies and physical appearance. Having a positive body image means feeling comfortable in your body and feeling good about the way you look. Many teens struggle with a positive body image as they sift through the messages from the media that they are inundated with regarding what a perfect body looks like. They must go through the process of coming to terms with their own body if they feel it does not measure up. People who have a positive body image are able to separate the way they look from their sense of self-worth. People with a negative body image often feel overly self-conscious and ashamed of how they

look. Negative body image can lead to depression, low self-esteem, and disordered eating. Teens may need active support in learning how to develop a positive body image.

- *Manage their sexuality*
  During adolescence teens identify their sexual orientation and face any feelings they have around this awareness. They also begin to integrate their gender identity, gender roles, and what gender means in relation to sexual relationships. During adolescence teens begin the process of discovering their own sexual values, whether or not they are engaged yet in sexual activity with others.

Relationships, Social Development, and Connection

Teens Must Learn to:

- *Deepen relationships with peers*

  "I have grown closer to many of my peers due to the fact that I can be more true to myself since I am out to them."

  Because teens develop increased empathy in adolescence, their relationships naturally deepen as they are able to take another's perspective into consideration. They are able to apply their developing communication skills and empathy to conflict resolution in all of their relationships. Peer friendships play a significant role in teenage life. In adolescence, friendships become based less on shared interests and move to being based more on shared ideas, perspectives, and values. Peer groups have a major role in teenage life. There is a correlation between the degree to which a teen can make friends and have a peer group to associate with and their ability to move successfully through other areas of development.

All that is needed for this is to have one or two good friends. It doesn't have to be a large social group. Peer relationships can play a significant role in a teen's self-concept. Friendships deepen and become more stable in later adolescence as they are able to use their increasing social and emotional skills. This lays the ground-work for meaningful adult relationships.

• *Develop romantic relationships*

> *"My child's strategy toward romantic relationships is to put them on hold until she is older—possibly post-surgery. In some ways, it makes me sad that she's not fully participating in this part of adolescence but, I have to admit, I'm also relieved!"*

Romantic relationships begin to flourish during adolescence. In addition to having a forum in which to practice their developing interpersonal skills, romantic relationships give teens the opportunity to explore their values regarding intimate relationships. Teens can learn and practice cooperation skills, interdependence, compromise, and empathy through dating. In early adolescence, dating is more for fun and exploration, often occurring in groups. As teens get older, dating can turn into true romantic relationships, where they can experience intimacy, affection, support, and friendship. There is usually physical as well as emotional intimacy. Romantic and sexual relationships during adolescence pose both promise and problems. They can be a way for teens to learn more about who they are and what they want from relationships. In this way, they can affect a teen's self-esteem. On the other hand, teens may not know themselves well enough to create a healthy intimacy with another person, or know the difference between enhancing and nurturing relationships versus those that are damaging or exploitative.

- *Forge new relationships with mentors, role models, and parents*
  Teenagers often develop meaningful relationships with adults
  outside of their immediate family. These may form with teachers,
  coaches, mentors, bosses, or parents of their friends. They begin to
  learn to turn to others for support, guidance, and connection. As
  teens form positive bonds with other adults, they learn to navigate
  more mature ways of interacting that can then carry over into their
  interactions with their parents.

Adolescent Identity Development

The question of "Who am I?" is a recurring theme throughout adolescence, leading teens through a process of gaining a sense of themselves as unique individuals.

Identity is complex and dynamic, with multiple dimensions that
form each person's unique sense of self. Identity is influenced by how
we see ourselves, how others see us, and how we see others; it has both
personal and societal factors that intertwine. While identity formation
is a lifelong process, foundational pieces of identity are formed during
adolescence.

All identities are not valued equally by society at large. Some identities are highly valued; others are marginalized or stigmatized and
devalued in mainstream social contexts. The greater the stigmatized
identity—and the more stigmatized identities a teen has—the greater
the social marginalization they will likely experience. Given that
society continues to stigmatize non-binary and transgender people,
your teen needs as much support and help as they can get to construct
a positive sense of self.

Two fundamental aspects of identity are self-concept and self-
esteem. Self-concept is the picture one has of oneself and is determined by one's own perception of their qualities, talents, experiences,
and goals. It can also include one's beliefs. For example, your teen's

self-concept may be based on being Latino, non-binary, attracted to boys, musically inclined, athletic, spiritually focused, and planning to become an architect. Self-esteem is how a person places value on their self-concept. It is the emotional evaluation and regard they have of their own worth. Self-esteem can be influenced by others and by social perceptions of various aspects of one's self-concept. Positive self-esteem and self-confidence are linked to a positive self-identity. We will address numerous ways that you as a parent can help your non-binary or transgender teen with positive identity formation, self-esteem, and self-confidence in the upcoming chapters.

---

1   E. Brodsky, 2015, *The Year We Thought About Love* (documentary) http://www.theyearwethoughtaboutlove.com.

Chapter 6

What Keeps You Up at Night

"Sometimes I just can't sleep at night knowing that my sweet child is at such great risk just by being herself in a world that is not ready for her yet. I want to keep her tucked in my arms for the rest of my life. But she is a teen, so the next best thing is for me to get out there and try to make the world a safer place for her."

WE'RE GOING TO BE UPFRONT with you: This chapter isn't easy to read (it wasn't easy to write either). In our work, we hear again and again from parents the reverberating fear that harm will come to their child because of their gender—either by their own hand or as a victim of violence perpetrated by others. We ask you to hang in there with us and read this chapter because everyone raising a transgender or non-binary child needs to look at this issue with their eyes wide open. What we promise though is that we will not just leave you with disturbing statistics. Much of the rest of the book will provide you with specific information about what you can do to help reduce the odds of harm to your child, identifying the specific parenting approaches you can provide to help them.

To date, transgender and non-binary people have mostly been misunderstood and marginalized. Little research has been conducted to understand their experiences or what can be done to minimize the risk factors that affect them; however, that is beginning to change—and the research is sobering. Despite some signs of greater cultural acceptance and recognition, studies indicate that gender minorities continue to face significant challenges. Discrimination against transgender and gender-nonconforming people is pervasive and institutionalized, resulting in devastating effects on both short- and long-term physical safety, mental health, and overall well-being.

The research statistics may frighten you, but these are the very reasons why you do not have the luxury of time to slowly get on board with your child or to debate with family members, schools, and other communities as to whether or not they will choose to support your teen. The time to support your child is now. You are in a fight to keep your child from becoming one of these statistics—and research indicates what our hearts already know—your love and support make a tremendous difference.

The Research

> "[After learning my child was transgender], I just told my child—OK... I went away and started to research and came out with the conclusion that I needed to support 100 percent to avoid self-harm, suicide, drug addiction. And create in my child strong self-resilience, self-esteem, and self-confidence. And create a community for them to flourish in."

Transgender and non-binary people face discrimination in every aspect of life. Injustice ranging from verbal harassment and denial of services to physical and/or sexual assault is all too commonplace. It occurs in the family, at school, in public spaces, on public transportation, at the store, in the workplace, in the legal system, at the emergency room, in doctor's offices, when trying to secure appropriate ID, and when using the bathroom. For many people who are openly transgender and those who are visibly gender nonconforming, bias-related events occur on a regular basis, sometimes multiple times a day. The stress of others' judgment, prejudice, and rejection becomes compounded over time and can lead to tremendous, often intolerable levels of suffering.

Suicide

In 2014, the Williams Institute (UCLA School of Law) and the American Foundation for Suicide Prevention published a landmark study, "Suicide Attempts among Transgender and Gender Non-Conforming Adults." Survey data from over six thousand respondents (the largest survey of transgender and gender-nonconforming adults age eighteen and older to date), revealed the following:

- 41 percent attempted suicide, vastly exceeding the 4.6% of the overall U.S. population who report a suicide attempt during their lifetime.
- Other demographic variables found suicide attempts were highest among those who were younger (eighteen to twenty-four, 45 percent); multiracial (54 percent) and American Indian or Alaskan Native (56 percent); have lower levels of educational attainment (high school or less, 48 –49 percent); and have lower annual household income (less than ten thousand dollars, 54 percent).
- Respondents who experienced rejection by family and friends,

discrimination, victimization, or violence are at an even higher risk for suicide attempts. Of those who attempted suicide:

- 57 percent indicated that family chose not to speak/ spend time with them.
- 50–54 percent reported being harassed or bullied at school.
- 63–78 percent suffered physical or sexual violence at school.

While the Williams report is the most comprehensive study to date, others also reveal what we have known for a long time: Transgender, non-binary, and other gender-expansive people are at great risk for considering, attempting, or dying by suicide.

Adolescence Is a Dangerous Time

"If virtually one in two trans teens try to, or god forbid, succeed at killing themselves, we have a major social issue on our hands. I know that I can make a difference. I have to make a difference. My kid, your kid, all of our kids need to know they are loved and valued and that their existence has value."

Feelings of helplessness and loneliness coupled with family/social rejection and other kinds of discrimination can leave teens feeling that the challenges of day-to-day living are too great.

In 2015, results from an online survey of 923 Canadian trans[1] youth aged fourteen to twenty-five entitled *Being Safe, Being Me: Results of the Canadian Trans Youth Health Survey* were released. They revealed

---

1   "Transgender" in this survey were those who identified as "trans or genderqueer, or felt their gender didn't match their body."

that within the previous twelve months, 75 percent of fourteen- to eighteen-year-olds had hurt themselves on purpose without wanting to die; 65 percent of fourteen- to eighteen-year-olds had seriously considered suicide and more than a third had attempted suicide at least one time; almost one in ten had tried to kill themselves four or more times.

As in perhaps no other population, your transgender or non-binary teen is at great risk for attempting or dying by suicide. Regardless of which studies you review, which statistics you read, this reality is something about which you as a parent must be aware. As frightening as it is, ignoring your teen's vulnerability to suicide will not make it go away. But you cannot allow it to paralyze you either. As you seek to understand and come to terms with your teen's gender, recognition of the dangers facing your teen can spur you to take action to confront and change the conditions that lead to these grim numbers.

"My daughter, who had done so well, for so long, was suddenly falling apart. We had not even talked much about her gender for years and then a number of things happened that brought it all up for her. It's painful to admit, but it took me some time to realize that she needed me to be available to her in a very different way than she had before. I needed to shift what I was doing, including how I prioritized my time. I needed to touch base more frequently, to check in and explicitly ask how she was doing, and to just sit together and talk about things she felt like talking about. She was at risk, and the reality of that terrified me."

Acquired Capability for Self-Harm/Pain Tolerance

What causes teens to move from suicidal ideation to actual suicide attempts is complex. Nevertheless, one thing that is valuable to acknowledge is that repeated exposure to physical pain, whether self-caused or caused by others, can lead to a level of pain tolerance commonly noted in those willing to take their own lives. This can be the result of self-harming behaviors, sexual or physical assaults, or even previous suicide attempts.

Mental Health Risks for Transgender and Non-Binary Teens

"Our child suffered many years of anxiety and depression. We now know that fears around his gender identity were a huge part of his struggle. I'm not even sure he could have had the language to express this until he was well into adolescence. Counseling helped him find the words he needed for himself and to tell us he was transgender. I am so grateful that we were able to find someone to help him come out of what was a very scary place. I shudder to think what could have happened."

A retrospective study published in 2015 from the Sidney Borum Jr. Health Center in Boston clearly indicated that transgender teens are a vulnerable population that is at significantly increased risk for negative mental health outcomes compared to cisgender teens. Compared with the non-transgender matched control group, transgender youth have a significantly elevated probability of suffering from depression and anxiety and were at much greater risk for self-harming behaviors. Across these areas there was a two to threefold increase in risk compared to their cisgender counterparts.

The Canadian study found that the presence of depressive symptoms in these teens is clearly related to whether or not they have family support for their gender identity and gender expression. Only 23 percent of teens who felt they had supportive parents experienced depression, whereas 75 percent of teens who felt their parents were not strongly supportive experienced depression.

Feeling Unsafe at School

"Peers calling her names like 'it,' 'a he/she,' 'freak.' Some teachers also would get her name and pronouns wrong even after the legal name change."

Transgender and non-binary students report having little confidence in their school administrators. Two-thirds of the students who report incidents of discrimination and violence said nothing was done to address the related issues; in fact, coming forward often resulted in an increase in the negative behaviors directed toward them.

At Gender Spectrum, we have had success in facilitating positive and gender-inclusive school climates in all kinds of schools. Educators often remark that all students, not just those who are transgender or non-binary, receive greater comfort and safety to understand and express themselves as a result of their school's work in this area. Unfortunately, without comprehensive training, school is not always a safe haven for non-binary and transgender youth. For now, we will briefly summarize the research that reflects what transgender and gender-nonconforming youth of today commonly experience at school in the absence of gender awareness training.

In a 2013 study of 7,898 youth (aged thirteen to twenty-one), the Gay, Lesbian, and Straight Education Network (GLSEN) found the following:

- 60.5–75 percent of transgender students reported feeling unsafe at school because of their gender.
- 59 percent to 64 percent of transgender and genderqueer students avoid bathrooms and locker rooms due to feeling unsafe or uncomfortable.
- 75 percent of transgender students felt unsafe at school because of their gender expression.

- 59–60 percent of transgender and genderqueer students reported verbal harassment.
- 22–29 percent of transgender and genderqueer students reported physical harassment.
- 9–16 percent of transgender and genderqueer students reported physical assault.
- 31.6 percent of transgender students had been prevented from wearing clothes considered inappropriate based on their assigned sex.
- 42.2 percent of transgender students had been prevented from using their preferred name.
- 59.2 percent of transgender students had been required to use a bathroom or locker room of their legal sex.

A 2012 study about the relationship between gender-based victimization (GBV) and suicide in transgender people found the following:

- Of the individuals who had experienced in-school GBV, 14.8 percent (6.6 percent of the total sample of 290) reported that the GBV they faced was severe enough that it was the main reason or a contributing factor to them not completing high school.
- Both transgender women and transgender men who had experienced in-school GBV reported significantly more suicide attempts than those who did not.

Being able to learn in a safe and supportive environment is every child's right. But for transgender and other gender-expansive students, it is clear from the data that unsafe school climates and the resulting violence, bullying, and harassment interfere with this basic right—and can lead to higher incidence of suicidality.

Gender-Based Discrimination, Bullying, Violence, and Sexual Violence

Transgender and visually nonconforming people are far more likely to become victims of violence, including murder, simply because of their gender identity or gender expression. Sexual assault and sexual abuse statistics are also much higher for this population. The 2012 study also found that half of transgender respondents reported a history of forced sexual activity and 60 percent indicated that they had been physically abused during their lifetime.

All studies of transgender youth indicate significant exposure to gender-based discrimination and violence. In the 2015 Canadian study, 70 percent reported sexual harassment; more than one-third reported being physically threatened or injured; and 36 percent reported cyber bullying. In this same study, two-thirds experienced discrimination because of their gender identity and almost half experienced discrimination due to their appearance.

Because of the compounding discrimination of race and gender, transgender and non-binary teens of color experience higher levels of gender-based harassment and violence in their day-to-day lives than white students. Transgender women of color face disproportionately high rates of hate-related violence, with the highest rates of hate-driven murder.

As of their 2016 update, the Trans Murder Monitoring (TMM) Project has documented 2,115 cases of murdered transgender and gender diverse people in sixty-five countries around the world over the past seven years, including 146 in North America, 117 in Europe, and 1,654 in South and Central America. Of these 2,115 cases, 131 transgender, non-binary and visually gender non-conforming people under twenty years old have been reported murdered. More than one-third of these victims were under eighteen—at least five kids were under age fourteen.

Transgender Europe's Senior Researcher, Carsten Balzer/Carla LaGata, stated, "*The TMM figures show only the tip of the iceberg of homi-*

cides of trans and gender diverse people on a worldwide scale, as these cases are those found through Internet search[es] and cooperation with trans organisations and activists. In most countries, data on murdered trans and gender diverse people are not systematically produced, and it is impossible to estimate the numbers of unreported cases."

Homelessness

"When I was in a group home, I lost points because I didn't have long hair or wear dresses. Even my mannerisms got me into trouble. The staff would tell me I wasn't 'talking like a lady' or that I was being 'too gentlemanly' when I opened doors for girls. They wouldn't let me be me because, to them, I was outside of the gender boundaries they were comfortable with."

Homelessness is a serious concern for transgender and non-binary youth. Many leave home due to conflict, harassment, and abuse from family members. Others are kicked out of their homes because of their family's rejection of their gender.

The Canadian study, Being Safe, Being Me, found that more than one in four had run away from home in the past year. This was much more likely for those youth who had experienced physical or sexual abuse. Some studies indicate that LGBT youth comprise between 20–40 percent of all homeless youth.

Many of the programs in place to help keep teens off the streets, such as foster care, emergency shelters, transitional housing, community centers, and other youth-specific agencies, are not able to safely and effectively address the needs of transgender and non-binary youth. There are many reasons for this including lack of training for providers and foster parents, prejudice and harassment by the adults and/or the other youth in these settings, and institutionalized discrimination.

Many programs force transgender teens to be housed according to their assigned sex rather than according to their affirmed gender identity, and many are not allowed to express themselves consistent with their identity. Access to proper gender-related healthcare is frequently limited or withheld. For these reasons, along with the abuse or hostility encountered in temporary placements or shelters, many of these teens run away or avoid these places altogether—which causes them to end up homeless or in the juvenile justice system.

It is difficult to know how many transgender and non-binary kids are on the streets. Once they are there, many prefer to remain rather than go to shelters where they are likely to face high levels of transphobia ranging from confusion about where to house them to violence.

Juvenile Justice

The juvenile justice system is another arena where transgender and non-binary youth are overly represented. The first contact that these youth have with the juvenile justice system is usually a result of clashes with family over gender identity or gender expression. Transgender and non-binary youth are twice as likely to have been homeless, experienced sexual abuse, and suffered high levels of family conflict as other youth in the system. Charges of being out of control or incorrigible are commonplace when a teen is unwilling to change their gender presentation on the basis of parent or guardian objections. Thus, these youth frequently enter the juvenile justice system for just being themselves, instead of as a result of harmful behavior. Homeless transgender and non-binary youth commonly resort to criminal behaviors and sex work as survival mechanisms; this increases their risk of arrest and detainment.

Some homeless transgender youth may feel that sex work is their only option for income and the money needed to access hormones and other forms of medical care. Even when transgender and gender-nonconforming homeless youth are not engaging in activities that are criminalized, they face risk of arrest. According to a 2005 Amnesty International report, police regularly profile transgender and gender-nonconforming youth as criminals, and selectively enforce laws relating to minor "quality-of-life" offenses, such as loitering, public drunkenness, public urination, and littering. Transgender and non-binary youth may also be arrested for simply sleeping on the streets, in itself a crime in many places.

Addiction, Unsafe Sex, and HIV

The extra burden of managing a stigmatized gender identity or expression can increase an adolescent's risk of substance abuse, unprotected sex, and HIV contraction. According to one study, 10 percent of transgender youth reported trading sex; older youth were twice as likely to report trading sex than younger participants (12 percent vs. 6 percent). In addition to the burden of stigma, there is a direct correlation between teens who are mistreated at school due to their gender identity or expression and substance use and abuse; the greater the harassment, the greater the chances of substance abuse, unprotected sex, and HIV contraction. The risk increases substantially again for transgender and non-binary teens who do not feel love, acceptance, and support from their family. When teens feel safe and welcomed in their homes and schools, the likelihood of drug use, alcohol use, and unsafe sex decreases, as they are less likely to need such coping mechanisms to manage their pain.

Hormones and Decreased Depression

"Once he started testosterone, he would run into the room to show us new pubertal developments, hair on his lip, beginnings

of an Adam's apple, thicker hair. He was so excited to go through puberty! Such a contrast to the constant fear that he would not start blockers soon enough and would grow breasts before they had a chance to work."

Research studies continue to demonstrate that transgender and non-binary youth who find congruence through medical measures experience decreased psychological stress and increased overall well-being. Most specifically, it appears that initiating hormone therapy leads to a marked decrease in levels of depression, anxiety, and stress, as well as increased self-esteem and quality of life. Some studies reveal that, after initiating hormone therapy, psychological distress markers of transgender people were comparable with those of the general population. It is equally important to note that many of the transgender and non-binary teens who desire hormone therapy but are forced to try other alignment measures first do not get this same relief of mental health symptoms. Until hormone therapy is initiated, they remain at greater risk for depression and other mental health issues despite the other steps taken towards congruence.

Transgender Teens of Color Face Highest Levels of Institutionalized Discrimination

For gender-nonconforming, non-binary, and transgender youth of color, the combination of gender-based discrimination with pervasive cultural and institutionalized racism compounds the negative impact significantly, more frequently leading to devastating outcomes.

One report from New York City showed that 82 percent of homeless transgender youth were black and Hispanic multiracial individuals; they reported the highest rates of gender-based violence (GBV) at 71.4 percent. Transgender and non-binary teens of color are at greater risk of being targeted by the police, more likely to end up in the juvenile justice system, face greater levels of physical assault and verbal harassment in public spaces, and have higher levels of HIV contraction. Youth of color are less able to access transgender-related healthcare, leaving them more likely to use street hormones without the proper medical oversight necessary to ensure their safety.

Transgender and non-binary youth come from all walks of life. While all face enormous obstacles, inequities related to gender and race compound both challenges and risks for transgender and non-binary youth of color. While all gender-expansive youth need to see themselves reflected in culture and society, research with transgender youth of color indicates that seeing positive role models from their own communities has a very strong influence on self acceptance, self-esteem, and identity consolidation.

Visually Gender-Nonconforming Individuals at Great Risk

Whether someone is transgender, non-binary, or simply gender-nonconforming in their gender expression, people who are visually nonconforming in their gender are often at the greatest risk for physical attack, sexual assault, and police brutality than their transgender visually conforming counterparts. Visually gender-nonconforming individuals might include someone who has a beard and wears a skirt or a person whose appearance makes people assume they are male, but in fact they identify as female or non-binary and use women's restrooms. Visually nonconforming individuals are less likely to seek or receive medical treatment due to discrimination and are often refused transition-related care altogether. The Canadian *Being Safe, Being Me* youth study revealed that two-thirds of participants reported discrimination because of their gender identity and about half reported discrimination due to their physical appearance.

In Chapter 10, "What You Can Do to Improve the Odds," we examine the effect of various parenting practices on the long-term health of transgender and non-binary teens. While there are no guarantees or magic pills to ensure a child's well-being, there is some good news. There is strong evidence that family support is the key to greater health and well-being for these teens. Your love and support have a significant impact. By implementing evidence-based supportive parenting practices, encouraging resilience-enhancing activities, educating yourself on the subject, advocating for your child, and finding the necessary medical and mental healthcare, you can significantly improve the chances of your child living a long and meaningful life.

Are You Worried Your Child Is Considering Suicide?

Suicidal Warning Signs

Four out of five teens who attempt suicide give clear warning signs. It is important to take the following warning signals seriously and to seek help if you are at all concerned that your teen might be suicidal. These behaviors are not always indications of suicidal thoughts and feelings. You might be less concerned if you see one or two of these signs infrequently; however, when they happen at the same time consistently for more than two weeks, it can indicate a serious situation. Heeding the warning signs, seeking professional help, and reaching out and providing support to a struggling teen can literally save their life. Warning signs include, but are not limited, to the following:

- Talking about suicide
- A previous suicide attempt

- Making statements about feeling hopeless, helpless, or worthless
- A deepening depression, moodiness, or withdrawal
- Withdrawing from family, friends, and activities
- Preoccupation with death or a strong wish to die
- Dramatic weight fluctuations in any direction
- Taking unnecessary risks or exhibiting self-destructive behaviors
- Increased alcohol or drug use
- Neglecting personal hygiene and other matters of personal appearance
- Difficulty concentrating and paying attention
- Declining grades in school
- Showing signs of extreme cheerfulness following periods of depression
- Loss of interest in schoolwork
- Crying more often
- Sleep changes
- Changes in eating habits
- Out-of-character behaviors
- Disinterest in favorite extracurricular activities
- Visiting or calling people they care about
- Saying goodbye, hinting at not being around in the future
- Giving or throwing away prized possessions
- Increased physical symptoms: stomachaches, headaches, muscle pains, exhaustion
- Chronic anxiety or nervousness
- Expressing loneliness

Take special notice of these warning signs if there has been:

- A recent death or suicide of a friend or family member
- A recent romantic breakup
- A recent gender-related negative incident
- Increased conflict with parents
- Reports of other suicides by transgender or non-binary teens in the recent media

Don't Be Afraid to Ask

Always take it seriously if your teen says that they want to kill themselves. Get help immediately. The American Academy of Child and Adolescent Psychiatry recommends that if you are concerned, it is best to ask a teen directly if they are depressed and if they are considering taking their life. Contrary to the common fear that this will put ideas into their heads, it actually communicates your care and support to your teen and provides them with an opportunity to talk about their struggles.

Getting Help

The Trevor Project provides lifeline support via phone, chat and text for Lesbian/Gay/Bisexual/Transgender/Queer (LGBTQ) youth considering suicide. They will also provide support for parents and other caregivers who are concerned their child might be at risk. For more information, go to http://www.thetrevorproject.org/.

Chapter 7

Supporting Your Teen in Their Gender Journey

"The more we've dealt with the gender stuff in a positive way, the better her mood has gotten; it's like a cloud has lifted, she doesn't have headaches anymore. Probably three times a week, she'd go to sleep crying. She doesn't do that anymore."

Personal Gender

OUR SOCIETY'S TENDENCY TO THINK of gender in binary terms misses the richness and complexity of gender. As we have discussed there are multiple dimensions of gender: body, gender identity, and gender expression (including gender roles). Each of these dimensions is also informed by the unique intersection of identities that each of us contains. We are all more than our body, gender identity, and gender expression: We are also our race, ethnicity, class, sense of geographic place, family history, community's gender roles and expectations, etc. The truth is, there are countless ways that people express, feel, and identify gender.

Our personal gender represents how all of these identities and influences uniquely come together and are embodied within each one of us.

Personal Gender within a Family Culture

At times, it may seem like your teen's gender is in conflict with your family, culture, faith, or greater community; this can raise a complex set of loyalties that can pull you in different directions. This may be a theme you are familiar with as you may have had your own difficulty with gender expectations in your family and/or community, but the level of dissonance between the expectations placed on you and your personal gender may not have been as great as that of your child's. For your teen, this dissonance may be tremendous. The thought that being true to yourself might mean the loss of family and cultural support is too difficult for many to bear.

Gender isn't the only place where this potential cultural conflict is raised, but because it is an area that creates strong feelings from all that are involved, it may be particularly complicated to navigate. Your child very likely feels this tension as well. In our experience, teens struggle greatly to figure out how to meet family expectations without disappointing those they love, and they are keenly aware of the difficult place their parent may be in trying to address the needs of their child while simultaneously affirming their family beliefs, values, relationships, and expectations. Let your child know that you love and support them and want to work together to find a way forward that honors everyone.

Making a Place for Your Child's Gender

> *"My son is non-binary in his presentation. People often mistake him for a girl. He identifies as a boy but his long hair, sensitivity, beauty, and mannerisms cause him a lot of hassle. He does not want to change how he looks, but he can feel invalidated by those who think his appearance makes him feminine."*

How can you as a parent maintain your own identities while supporting your child to do the same? If we take as our starting point that each person is unique, then we must find a way for people who do not exist within the gender binary, or do not express themselves consistent with cultural norms and expectations, to still have a place within their family and their family's cultures and religion.

Many parents struggle with this. There are no simple approaches or easy answers. You will need to find ways to support your teen in their cultures. Whenever possible, ask your teen, "How can I help you make sense of and navigate these parts of your identity that seem to create a sense of conflict?" While exploring this personal question, you can ask yourself, "How can I support my child and get my family/community to do the same?" We have seen people of many different cultures navigate the reconciliation of child and community beautifully; while it isn't easy, it is possible. We are confident that you can find a way.

The choices made in this process can have long-term consequences on the health and well-being of your child. If your family or community is not willing to respect and accept your child, you may face the choice between supporting your teen and being accepted and validated by your family/community. Your child will internalize the choices you make in this situation. If you choose the validation of others over your support of your teen, your child will feel that they are alone in this process. This type of disconnection from parents/family can have devastating consequences.

How Far Along Is Your Teen When You Join Them on Their Journey?

Many teens come to the realization of their gender identity on their own. They may have struggled with their feelings for years before talking to you about it, keeping the conflict around their gender private until the risks of self-expression no longer outweighed the benefits. Other teens may let you know early on in their process of self-realization.

What your teen requires is specific for them—the timelines and next steps to take have to do with their particular needs and circumstances. Some teens take years to explore what is going on for them and to find a full sense of congruence; it is a slow unfolding. Others are very clear about the road ahead and are already moving at a fast pace toward congruence. If this is the case for your teen it may necessitate your getting onboard quickly or risking having your teen act independently to seek the changes they feel that they need, such as securing hormones via the Internet, rather than with your support while under the care of a doctor.

Your Teen May Not Be as Brave as They Look

Be aware that there is a common misconception held by many of the parents we encounter who feel that their teen seems to be on top of all this gender stuff, and believe that it is simply they, as parents, who need to catch up. Whereas this may be the case initially, the journey to full self-acceptance of a less common gender identity that is still so marginalized is long and multifaceted. Your teen may initially feel that they are required to act as if they are completely OK with themselves in order to win your support, but once they are more certain of your unwavering love, they may reveal to you (and possibly to themselves for the first time) just how scared or uncertain they are.

Become Your Teen's Ally

"After speaking to my therapist, I sat with my child and told her that if she wanted to live her life as who she really felt she was, that I would be with her every step of the way. It was as if I had given her the keys to a kingdom she didn't know existed. She said, 'You mean, I can do that?' I said, 'Of course!' And the process of transitioning began."

Whether your teen has just told you they are transgender or non-binary or whether your teen socially transitioned years ago, there are many areas of change and decisions that need to be made surrounding their gender during the years of adolescence. This is a critical time in your relationship. Teens and their parents do not always see eye to eye; when you add the nuances of gender expression and body modification decisions into the mix, adolescence can get downright complex. Combine that complexity with a strong dose of urgency from your teen and you can understand why this time feels so stressful. If your child perceives you as an ally, you are likely to experience less stress in your relationship. Being an ally doesn't mean that you have to agree with everything they want; it does mean, though, that they know you are on their side, actively working with them to figure out how to best meet their needs.

Be Available

Transgender and non-binary teens need additional support throughout the teenage years. You can truly make a significant difference in the long-term outcomes for your child if you remain available and stay connected with your teen during this time. Adolescence is rough in the best of times. Developmentally it is a time for individuation that naturally involves pulling away from parents and developing stronger peer relationships. Therefore, if you are to maintain a close relationship with your teenager, no matter how difficult, you must also afford your child the respect and autonomy they need during adolescence in order to grow.

Engage in Conversation

> *"She had been deeply depressed and isolated, so I asked if there was something specific going on. I could tell from her response that there was. I told her I wasn't leaving her room until she told me what was going on. She reluctantly said, 'I'm a boy.'"*

"My daughter seems so self-sufficient that I forget that she needs and wants contact with me. Sometimes it's just cuddling and watching a favorite show, but increasingly it's also about the ways in which she sees the world, matters of justice at school and in the larger world. It is often in these discussions that I hear her thoughts on topics she doesn't generally talk about, like gender. Without these 'big idea' discussions, I wouldn't know nearly as much about her everyday world and how she experiences it."

It is important to keep the lines of communication open between you and your teen around gender issues. Talk about your own experiences with gender and any limitations you have experienced because of gender norms so that your child understands that everyone has a gender story, not just gender-expansive people. If it's not already part of your pattern, try to raise the issue of gender with your teen regularly so that your teen doesn't think it's only something they want to discuss. One way to do this is to talk to your teen about gender as it shows up in media and pop culture. Teens are typically more open to talking about gender when the focus of the conversation isn't on them!

These conversations about gender serve a few purposes. They will help your teen with their own places of personal confusion and allow them to not feel so alone in their explorations. Conversations will help you to understand more fully what your teen is struggling with and who they experience themself to be. And finally, healthy conversations will allow the two of you to increase your connectedness, which will increase your teen's resilience.

Set the tone for these explorations so your teen feels your approval and support. Whenever you discuss gender with your teen, remember to maintain neutral or welcoming body language. Be aware of your facial expressions. Your words, your tone, and your body language ideally should all communicate approachability and openness. Your acceptance of who your child is can go a long way, so do what you can to let them know that you love them for being true to themself and that you want to know who they really are. Allow your teen the room to explore and to not have it all figured out yet. Let your teen know that home is place where they can be themself and not have to worry about rejection or judgment, particularly yours. Encourage your teen to open up to you so that together, as a team, you can explore what is right for them.

Celebrate Your Teen's Strength

When your teen sees that you understand what they are going through, you increase their feeling of connectedness and decrease their isolation. This fosters their resilience. Take the time to regularly acknowledge your child's strength. Let them know that you admire them. Be clear with your teen about your commitment to them and to their well-being.

Ask Questions (but Don't Interrogate)

Parents sometimes unwittingly question their children in a manner that can signal anger, fear, or mistrust. The same feelings can come through when asking questions about your child's gender. Nobody likes to feel as though they're being interrogated; ensure that your questions are truly questions.

Share with your teen which things you would like to know more about. Be curious and interested. One way to build connection during these kinds of conversations is to answer the same questions about yourself that you are asking your teen. When appropriate this can be a great way for everyone in your family to share about themselves and to get to know each other more deeply. If you have other children it is a way for them to feel involved and valued. It is important when discussing gender with your transgender or non-binary teen to understand as much as you can about their personal gender. Don't just ask what their gender identity is; find out what that identity means to them, and how they see their gender as part of the larger tapestry of who they are.

Be Open to Admitting Mistakes

> *"My partner came down pretty hard on our son, expressing that she did not think that hormones were appropriate for transgender teens. She closed down the conversation before it ever began. It definitely damaged their relationship. After speaking with other families in similar situations at length, she realized that she was wrong. She apologized and they worked through it, but it took some time."*

If you have previously approached conversations about your child's gender in a negative/opposing manner, know that it is possible to change the established dynamic, but it may take a little time for your child to trust your new openness and shift in approach. Your teen may become combative whenever you bring up gender now. This is likely because they feel defensive, misunderstood, hurt, or afraid of being judged. They may not be ready to talk to you about so personal a subject yet. The first thing you can do to regain their trust is to apologize and try again. Ask for a "do-over" and then share with them the response you wish you had made. Even if they are not talking, they will probably be listening. It may be helpful to write it in a letter and give it to your teen. If you do, know that this letter will mean a lot. Try to keep your concerns, doubts, or fears out of this letter. This context is neither the time nor the place for them. When asking for forgiveness for your past approach to their gender, communicate your love, support, and willingness to listen to your child's experience and help them in any way you can.

When Your Teen Is Silent

"More than a year since coming out to me via text, my kid still does not speak openly with me about their gender. We have many overarching talks at home about gender, but it never gets personal."

Some teens share with their parents their feelings about their gender and then shut down further communication on the subject. This may be a self-protective response to your original reaction. Or they may just feel the need to disclose to you, but are uncertain and questioning many aspects of their gender. Give your teen the space to share a little bit at a time. They may feel hurt or rejected if you responded in a way that was less than ideal, pressed them for more information than they were ready to share, or questioned the validity of their assertions about their gender. They also may be fearful of rejection or so confused that they do not know how to talk about it. Perhaps your teen was courageous enough on the day they told you, but that courage is now gone. If they shared it with you in an email or a text, talking face to face may feel too vulnerable. This can be frustrating as a parent, especially if you can see that your teen is suffering.

If your teen is having difficulty talking with you, encourage them to share with you in ways that make them more comfortable. Some feel best emailing or texting what they are feeling or going through. Others feel best talking to their parent on the phone, even if it is from their bedroom. Your teen may prefer to talk first to their sibling or a friend and have that person share with you on their behalf (or have both of them share with you together). Basically, do whatever you can to create a bridge of safety between the two of you so that you can reassure your child that no matter what they are feeling, you will be there for them and help them through it.

If silence is only one part of a set of behaviors that leave you and your child disconnected, you may have a larger problem. For example, if your teen withdraws after you tell them you think they should wait a year before starting hormones or that they need to continue going to their school despite being bullied, then the silence (and withdrawal) may be about the limit you set. If you suspect this is the case, check it out with your child. If the condition you set is causing them to disconnect from you, it will be difficult to know what is going on for your child. They may slip into depression, make plans to secure hormones on their own, plan to run away, or contemplate self-harm in reaction to this limit. Talk to them. Try to reopen the lines of communication. Anytime your teen withdraws can be a good time for family therapy.

When Your Teen Is Actively Questioning Their Gender

It's OK Not to Know

> "My daughter told us she is pansexual and changed her name to a gender-neutral name. At first, she thought she might also have a non-binary gender identity, but over time, she has come to realize that she feels female. It is her sexual orientation that is gender-neutral and gender-inclusive, not her gender identity."

It takes time to be able to fully get in touch with your gender. Because we are all socialized as our assumed gender (based on our sex assigned at birth), it can be a long process to disentangle from what we've been told about how to behave and be able to recognize who we authentically are.

Resist the urge to rush your teen to "decide" on a gender. It can be difficult to be in a place of not knowing—it's more comfortable when things are definitive. Yet when it comes to gender, sometimes the only way to find the right fit is to try something on and live with it for a while. This is a process that cannot and should not be rushed.

Demonstrate to your teen your commitment to learning with them. Let your teen know that it is OK to be confused or overwhelmed, that they are not alone because you are a partner with them in this process. It is completely normal for them to be afraid and uncertain as they explore what their gender is and what this may mean for their future.

Whether they act like it or not, your child wants your approval. One of your goals is to help your teen disentangle their self-discovery process from their desire for your approval and fear of your rejection. One of the most beautiful gifts that you can give your teen is your encouragement. It can help your teen come to a place of personal awareness and self-acceptance that they wouldn't otherwise have been able to achieve on their own.

Let Your Teen Know That They Are Normal

Being transgender or non-binary is completely normal—but your teen may not know this or feel that way about themselves. Throughout history, many people have felt they were transgender, belonged to another gender, or were a blend of genders. Some cultures still acknowledge multiple genders. Non-binary and transgender people are everywhere, although they are not always visible. You can share with your teen that we all interact with transgender and non-binary people on a regular basis but may not know it. They are dentists, parents, teachers, flight attendants, models, architects, etc. They are part of society and always have been. If your teen feels isolated, you can share books, videos, blogs, and films that feature the diversity of transgender and non-binary people throughout time.

Help Your Teen Explore the Complexity of Gender

Your teen may not know very much about the complexity of gender. Many teens have heard about transgender people but may have some misconceptions about them. Teens frequently tell us they thought they weren't transgender because they were told that if they didn't know they were transgender as a young child, they couldn't be transgender. Although it is great that people are becoming familiar with transgender children, it is unfortunate that some people don't realize that it is perfectly natural to recognize one's transgender or non-binary gender identity at any point in life.

Teens are often not even aware of the existence of non-binary identities. They may feel like the gender assumed of them is wrong, but they also don't feel like they are the "other" gender. They don't see people with non-binary gender identities in the world around them, certainly not positively represented in mainstream culture, so sometimes it is up to us as parents to let them know that non-binary gender identities exist. Once non-binary teens get exposed to the idea that there is more than just male, female, and transgender, the world can open up and they can see room for themselves and claim their identity.

The Gender Spectrum

It is good to reassure your teen right from the beginning of your discussions about gender that gender is a spectrum and that each of us has our own, personal gender. Share with your teen that a person can be anywhere on that spectrum, or even feel like they are off the spectrum altogether. It may be that the only thing your teen knows for sure is that they don't identify with their assumed gender. This can be as true for a transgender teen who socially transitioned prior to puberty as it is for a teen newly expressing gender discomfort. When a teen is aware that they are not feeling comfortable in their gender, it is a natural response to want to know exactly where they will feel comfortable, to know exactly where they lie on the spectrum. We all want answers when it comes to the unknown. Unfortunately, it is not always what will allow a person to feel most comfortable. Sometimes, the only way to determine this is by trial and error. This process can be vulnerable and awkward. The adolescent journey of gender self-discovery is complicated by the fact that your child is figuring this all out while under the scrutiny of others. It is also compounded by the other developmental aspects of being a teenager. Your support during this period of questioning and confusion is invaluable.

Help Your Teen Understand That They Do Not Have to Be Gay to Be Transgender or Non-Binary

Some teens struggle with claiming their gender because they think that all transgender and non-binary people are gay or lesbian, and they do not feel that they are gay or lesbian. Explain to your teen that gender and sexual orientation are separate aspects of self. Being transgender or non-binary is about a person's gender. Sexual orientation is about whom a person is sexually attracted to. There are plenty of transgender and non-binary people of every sexual orientation.

Help Your Teen Understand That They Can Be Private About Their Gender and Still Be Transgender or Non-Binary

Some teens feel that the transgender people they have been exposed to on TV and elsewhere are not representative of who they experience themselves to be and so they think they must not be transgender themselves. The people they have seen may have a gender presentation different from their own, or perhaps your teen feels private about their gender and believes that in order to be transgender or non-binary, they would need to be vocal and political about gender. Your teen needs to understand that there are many ways to be transgender or non-binary. Remind them that they may never be aware of others who are private about their genders as they just blend in, so no one could point them out. Also reassure your teen that their gender and sexual orientation are separate. Being transgender or non-binary is about a person's gender. Sexual orientation is about whom a person is sexually attracted to. There are plenty of transgender and non-binary people of every sexual orientation.

Let Go of Preconceptions

"We were facing each other at the kitchen counter, and he hesitantly told me that he felt more comfortable in the boys' section at the store, like he belonged there and felt uncomfortable in the girls' section. He wanted to wear boys' clothing. I explained that he never had been a 'foo-foo' girl and that he was apparently just a tomboy. I didn't care what kind of clothes he wore. We went out and bought some new jeans and shirts. I basically dismissed what he was really trying to tell me, even though I let him express himself in whatever way he wanted. I didn't actually understand what he was really trying to express."

Being open to what is and trying to let go of preconceived ideas, notions, and preferences in regard to the gender identity and/or gender expression of your teen will allow for your teen to explore who they are without feeling like there is a script for them to follow.

Identities and self-awareness of one's identity can shift, deepen, and develop over time. Sometimes, these shifts are related to exposure to identities and expressions your teen never knew existed before, sometimes, these shifts are a result of personal maturation, and sometimes, they are from a release of internalized stigmatization. What your child chooses to call their identity might change over time, and it might not. Try to let go of how you think it's going to be and let it unfold naturally.

Living with the Unknown

"We had to start our child on medicine to suppress puberty hormones. He had always felt like a boy and a girl and we all needed time to figure out which puberty would be the right one for him."

Self-discovery is rarely linear. When it comes to gender exploration in adolescence, the path may involve a lot of trial and error before clarity is reached.

Do your best to give your teen the space to explore their gender and the ways they want to express it. By supporting and encouraging your teen, they will find places of personal expression and self-identification that feel right and make them feel good. In the beginning, it may be easiest for your teen to find the places that simply help them feel better. Over time and with your support your teen will organically move from confusion toward self-awareness, they will make decisions about self-expression, and settle finally in a place of stability and integration. It can be uncomfortable to go through this process that has no roadmap. Try to make peace with who your child is and the process of discovery—there can be a gift in the unfolding of a journey to an unknown destination.

Figuring It Out—One Step at a Time

Coming to terms with and expressing one's authentic gender is a journey where each step illuminates the next and the only way to learn if a step is right for your teen or not is to test it out. Even if your child has been clear about their transgender or non-binary gender for years, adolescence may bring with it many new and often unanticipated crossroads in regards to their gender. You will be able to see a little more of the path in front of you with each step that your teen takes toward identity and expression. You may not be able to see all the twists, turns, and side trails ahead, but you can reliably trust that each step will clarify the next. At each new stage, you and your teen will gain clarity, find the resources needed, and explore appropriate options. This process happens over and over again.

For example, if your teen knows they want to change their name to something that feels right for them, they might try a few names, decide on a name they really like, and begin using their new name. You'll both then figure out the best way to tell others in your social and family circles, how to address this change at school, formalize a legal name change (if desired), and update identity documents (if desired and where it's possible). That is an example of a fairly clear trajectory. Others are not so linear in progression. For example, you and your teen might have determined that hormone therapy was the next step toward body congruence only to learn after initiating cross hormones that it didn't feel like a good fit. Or your teen may have discovered that they are ready to express their gender a certain way in some settings, such as at their youth group, but maybe not at school. Encourage your teen to really tune in to how it feels as they try new things on for size and explore different parts of the gender spectrum. Each step reveals the next. Trying something only to discover it does not feel "right" does not indicate a reversal, confusion, or a matter of having made a wrong step; it's only that they can't always know what feels right until they try it out. Once they do, the best next step becomes clear. It is a process of refinement, moving from what feels wrong, to what feels better, and finally to what feels right.

Resist any urge to discourage ongoing experimentation or invalidate your teen's experience of their gender just because they are still a work in progress. Once your child has reached congruence (again, this may not happen until they are in their mid-twenties), you may want to breathe a sigh of relief. You should. It will likely get easier from here on out. But keep in mind that self-discovery and personal growth are lifelong processes.

How Do I Help My Child If They Are Struggling with Their Gender?

If your teen expresses that they do not feel "right" in their assumed gender, it is important to see if you can identify together what it is that is uncomfortable for them. Helping your teen to find what feels uncomfortable will help them to see where they might not feel like their authentic self. Once you find the source(s) of discomfort, then you can help them work one step at a time to find what feels congruent.

If your teen is sure about what they need to feel congruent but you are not onboard yet, consider allowing them to take steps that are reversible. This will buy you some time to increase your understanding of what is going on for your teen while letting them move forward on their journey. The same approach is worthwhile if you suspect that your teen may be rushing into things. Consider allowing them access to puberty suppressants and support reversible self-expression. But also know that this is a very fine line. As we have previously discussed, transgender and non-binary teens are highly sensitive to rejection and vulnerable to a number of increased risk factors. Also know that your teen does not need your permission to seek many of the changes they may wish to see in themselves. However, without your permission and support, they may look to get what they need outside safe medical sources and that puts them at significant risk.

Everyone Figures It Out Differently

"I started questioning around this time last year because I had a piano recital where I was wearing pretty gender-neutral dress clothes and my mom told me I looked androgynous. I didn't know why at the time, but I was thrilled the rest of the day. I didn't really believe in non-binary identities at the time, so I left it at I just wasn't traditionally feminine. I questioned a little

throughout that time, saying to a couple friends that I was pretty
sure I was a girl but who knows?"

People recognize their gender in different ways. For some people, it is a long process of one foot in front of the other, trying different things on for size before finding the right fit. Other people have more of an epiphany—a moment, or series of moments that they can pinpoint when they realized what their gender was.

It does not matter how your teen figures out their gender. There is no best way or right way. Figuring it out requires patience on the part of everyone involved. Your teen may already have a sense of what is the right direction for them. They may be clear about their gender identity and preferred expression and want to begin, or continue down, the path toward congruence. Other teens just know that something about their assumed gender is definitely not right, but they do not know what is right, yet.

Gender is a fusion of body, identity, expression, culture, and life experience that, when woven together, becomes the fabric of our identity—our gender. Of course it is complicated! Nontraditional behaviors, styles, and preferences do not necessarily mean that someone is transgender. These are components of self-expression that may or may not be tied to gender identity. Many teens need a broader range of self-expression in order to feel congruent, but also feel that the sex assigned to them at birth is a good match (at least as good a match as any). They may or may not feel that they are non-binary. These teens may or may not require medical interventions to feel aligned.

For example, your child who was assigned female at birth may identify as male, may not want to alter his body, but does want to change his name and pronoun, and wear the hair, clothes, and accessories that feel right to him…so his body looks "female" but his appearance is "masculine." Or your son may have a fluid gender expression, wearing pants one day and a skirt or dress with makeup the next, while remaining identified as a boy. Or perhaps your child who was assigned male at birth may identify as female and want to present herself as female in the world, pursue hormone therapy and legal changes in order to feel congruent, but isn't interested in surgical changes to her body. Your daughter may use a gender-neutral pronoun and bind their breasts, but still firmly identify as a girl and as your daughter. These are only a few of the infinite ways in which gender is lived in the world.

When you realize that gender inclusivity is about more than just accepting that some people feel like they were born in the wrong body and that actually there are countless gender identities and gender expressions possible, it can be hard to fathom. A complete paradigm shift is required of you. The generational gap may seem pretty wide at times like these.

Helping Your Teen Identify Areas of Discomfort

"I was crying over my first period when I was eleven, and my mother kept telling me that it was 'part of becoming a woman' but when I thought about it, I didn't want to become a woman; I didn't want to have that possibility or implication at all. I kept it to myself, because I thought I was a freak, but I just knew it was wrong, wrong, wrong."

Your teen may know the source(s) of their gender discomfort. However, some teens have a more global sense of unease, and they have a hard time pinpointing any specific areas. Gaining an understanding of where the discomfort exists is important to creating greater congruence. If we don't know what feels wrong, we won't know how to help make it right.

Keep in mind that discomfort alone doesn't inherently mean that your teen is transgender or non-binary. The types and levels of discomfort are important, but it is most important to listen to what

your teen is telling you about who they are. By the time they raise the
issue with you, they have likely done a lot of thinking, research, and
talking with others about who they see themselves to be.

Ask Questions

Asking questions can be a great tool for you and your teen to gain
insight. Be sure your questions are open-ended and remember—
you are listening and seeking understanding, not trying to "fix"
things. This is an exploratory process only. Here are some sample
questions:

- When you imagine your future, what do you see? What
  gender do you feel you are? How would you describe yourself?
- Do you imagine yourself as a parent? Do you see yourself
  as a mom, dad, or as something else?
- Imagine yourself happy in the future—what does this look
  like ten years from now? Imagine yourself unhappy in the
  future—what does this look like ten years from now? How
  is your gender a part of your happy future? Your unhappy
  future?
- Do you know anyone who seems to be the same gender as
  you? Which aspects of who they are do you identify with?
- Who do you compare yourself to in movies or TV shows, at
  school, and in the media? Who do you look up to in terms of
  their gender? What is it about them that you identify with?
- How comfortable are you with your gender? In which ways
  are you comfortable and which ways not?
- Do you know when you first started to question your

> gender identity? How did you begin to get a sense that your gender might be different from what I and others told you?
> - Do you feel sure now about your gender, or are you still questioning?
> - Have you shared your feelings about your gender with anyone else? How have they responded?
> - How have the changes of puberty made you feel?
> - Are there parts of your body that you feel disconnected from?
> - Do you feel that people see the real you when they look at you? If you don't feel that way, do you know what would need to happen for others to more readily see you as you experience yourself?

Gender Role Discomfort

"I am suffocating by the expectations everyone has for me. It seems like every sentence begins with 'Girls aren't supposed to'... But I'll never be a girl in the way they want me to be."

Some people feel like their assumed gender is a good fit in terms of their gender identity and their gender presentation. But they are still uncomfortable in their gender. This may be a result of gender role discomfort. It is often the expectations that others (family, culture, society) have of them that don't feel right. They may feel like these expectations are too restrictive or too prescribed. They may not like the messages they are receiving about how to experience and express their emotions, how to interact with others, what is deemed appropriate for them to do or say, or what hobbies or careers to prefer. Although these stereotypes impact everyone, for some, they are more conflicting than for others, and the pressures to conform can feel unbearable. Behaving in line with the gender role that is expected can feel like acting in a play, and fear of being discovered as a fake is common.

If your teen expresses discomfort with the expectations of them regarding gender roles, ask them to consider what it would be like if they could escape sexism or be taken more seriously while looking and/or acting in the ways that feel most natural to them. It is possible that what they are experiencing is an issue of sexism that they continually bump up against. When this is the case, it may not be gender identity that is uncomfortable but rather a desire to liberate themselves from a traditional gender role.

Discomfort regarding assumed gender roles may or may not include a transgender or non-binary identity. Those who step outside of gender role expectations are targets for varying amounts of ridicule, violence, and harassment. These teens often experience tremendous homophobia directed toward them regardless of their sexual orientation. This is especially significant for boys who feel limited by male gender roles and/or gender expression.

Gender Expression Discomfort

"I feel like I'm in drag when I wear the clothes my mom wants me to wear. I don't want to feel boxed in about what to wear. I want to wear what feels rights to me—and that changes sometimes— though it's never super feminine."

"I don't want my mom to tell me what to wear or limit my choices. My tastes change but they are still valid."

Some teens feel discomfort in the way that they present themselves to the world. They may feel like they are wearing a costume when they appear in traditionally masculine or feminine clothing. Some teens need the freedom to express themselves outside of gendered expectations in order to feel most comfortable. A teen's discomfort with their gender expression sometimes corresponds with a transgender or a non-binary gender identity, but sometimes it's just a desire to express themself.

Often, parents assume that if their teen is transgender, they will want to conform to the stereotypical gender roles and gender expression associated with their affirmed gender. Although this is the case for some teens, for other teens, it is not. As they have broken free from their assumed gender, they may also have broken free of the limitations of the gender system to a certain degree. For example, they may choose to continue with all of the same interests that they have always had regardless of gendered associations with those preferences. A teen who was assigned female at birth but identifies as a boy may choose to or continue to wear some makeup. Or a teen who was assigned male at birth but identifies as a girl may sometimes wear "men's" clothing.

Body Discomfort

Some transgender and non-binary teens feel gender-related discomfort in their body beyond what is typical for adolescents. Others feel comfortable in their body as it is. A non-binary or transgender person's relationship to their body is highly personal. Even if a teen feels discomfort in their body, they may also like many aspects of their body just as it is and decide that desired changes are possible simply through how they express themself, without a need for hormonal therapy or surgery. Others will require body modification in order to reach congruence.

When exploring body discomfort with your teen, try to stay away from assumptions that you have about their body based on your perceived, or their expressed, gender identity. Ask questions like: "Does your physical body feel right for you?" If the answer is no, then ask, "How does it not?" for clarification. These conversations do not commit you to a path of body modification; they help your teen clarify how they feel about themself. Regardless of what you decide down the road, the discussions about their comfort or discomfort in their body can create a deeper sense of connection between you and your teen and provide greater understanding of their experience at a given time.

Gender Identity Discomfort

> *"I am gender fluid. It took a really long time to figure it out because I thought there were three genders: boy, girl, and trans-gender. No one told me there were other people like me out there. And once they did, it honestly took me a while to believe them as I had never heard of gender fluidity."*

> *"I know what my gender identity is not; I'm still working to fig-ure out how to best say what it is."*

Most of us don't grow up with language for gender. Even the most common gender identity, "cisgender," wasn't added to the *Oxford English Dictionary* or *Merriam Webster Dictionary* until 2015! So it is no wonder that teens struggle to find a way to understand and find language for their gender identity. Most don't know there is a difference between sex and gender, and that gender is more than their genitals—how can we expect them to create the language for their experience when even the concept of gender hasn't been shared with them?

If your teen expresses discomfort with their gender identity, it may take some time for them to find, try on, and settle on an identity that feels right. That's OK. Just helping them to feel comfortable knowing what they're not, even if they don't have new language to put in its place, will likely be a tremendous relief to them.

Pronoun Discomfort

Pronouns can be tricky. When the American Dialect Society announced that their word of the year in 2015 was the "singular they" it became clear that language was catching up to the experience of many people, including today's youth. The importance of pronouns was put front and center of our culture's discussion regarding gender.

Pronouns make a difference. Some people are uncomfortable with the pronouns that others use to refer to them and find that another pronoun just feels better. A number of transgender teens express having had a gender epiphany when someone used the "wrong" pronoun for them and it felt so right! Many teens explore a few different pronouns before they find the one that best fits them. Some teens have a more fluid sense of gender and like their pronouns to shift with their gender shifts. And some teens feel comfortable with any pronoun and let the person interacting with them decide which pronoun to use. If your teen seems to react when people use pronouns when referring to them, ask them about it. Is there a pronoun that feels best to your teen?

Selecting a new pronoun may or may not accompany a desire to change other aspects of one's self. Finding the right pronoun may be all that is needed. For others, the pronoun change is a reflection of gender identity that requires other shifts as well. It's interesting to note that an increasing number of colleges and universities are allowing students to choose from gender-neutral pronoun options on their application and registration forms, acknowledging that gender identities and the associated pronouns are expanding.

Name Discomfort

Some people find that their given name simply does not fit them. It can feel like their name misgenders them right from the time of self-introduction. Ask your teen if they experience discomfort with their name. If they do, they can explore what name might suit them better.

You can use that name at home for a while to see if they like it. Some teens experiment with a new name in a new context (such as a volunteer situation or an afterschool activity). From there, they can decide if they would like everyone to start using this name.

Developing New Levels of Trust

As your teen explores, comes to understand, and gets comfortable with their gender, they are learning how to trust themselves, and then in turn asking those around them to trust them as well. This is a very vulnerable process, especially since no one has it all figured out right from the start.

Ultimately, your teen is the only one who can figure their gender out. That's the good news and the bad news. It can feel daunting and scary as a parent to watch your child, especially during times of struggle, knowing that you can't just hug them and make it all better (remember those days?). You can be on their team, but this is not something you can do for them no matter how much you would like to take this burden off their shoulders. Walking through this process with someone can make all the difference though. Let them know how much they mean to you and reassure them in as many ways as possible that they are not alone in this journey of self-discovery, and that you are confident in their ability to understand themself and what they need.

Chapter 8

Understanding How Minority Stress Impacts Your Teen

"It is hard to live in a world where I am told I don't exist."

THE EXPERIENCES OF TRANSGENDER AND non-binary youth can't be fully understood without looking at the impact of complex forms of oppression and stigma. It's an unfortunate reality that many of us have to deal with the daily stresses that come with being part of a stigmatized group, whether in relation to our race, gender, class, sexual orientation, physical ability, religion, or other identity. If you have had that experience, some of the strategies you have used to respond to oppression may help you understand and support your child through their gender journey. Of course, there will be substantial differences between your experiences and those of your child, and your teen may not want to hear how you can relate to what they are going through. However, you and your teen might be able to find commonalities in both of your experiences that will be helpful to one another.

What Is Stigma?

Stigma is extreme disapproval from the greater society of a person or group of people based on something about them that differs from cultural norms. A stigmatized person is seen as different, as "other." That difference is devalued and leads to the person being perceived as flawed and inferior by others. The prejudice against the stigmatized person leads to social avoidance and rejection by others. Stigma is specific to a particular time period and is created by each society based on current stereotypes, values, and ideas. Therefore, what is stigmatizing today in your culture may not be so in different cultures or subcultures, societies, or points of time. People of stigmatized identities face socially condoned exclusion, discrimination, and even violence.

For transgender and non-binary teens, being a part of a gender minority means they have to confront stigma-based ignorance, stereotypes, prejudice, victimization, and discrimination related to their gender identity and/or gender expression.

Many Forms of Discrimination

If you have not directly been subject to systemic discrimination, it may be hard to understand the degree to which constant stigma affects your child. You're certainly aware of the obvious forms of discrimination your child is confronted with, and those definitely take their toll. But the everyday slights, snubs, insults, environmental challenges, and verbal/nonverbal communications are equally difficult. These include all of the culturally acceptable ways that others communicate disdain, hostility, or disapproval of people based solely on their being part of a marginalized minority group. This often takes the unintentional and unexamined forms of discrimination that establish what is considered "normal" and contrast it with the minority experience as being less valid, inferior, and wrong. To truly begin to understand your teen's daily experience, check in with your child on this issue for a week, asking them what kinds and how many of these negative interactions they had each day. Also watch and listen as your child is out in the world, and catch examples of this as it happens: eye rolling, sarcastic remarks, questions that sound innocent but inherently challenge who they are or how they express themselves. As you mentally tally these daily experiences, you will begin understand the damaging impact on your teen.

Discrimination is often seen only as individual acts between people or groups of people. This might conjure up images of anything from mean comments, to exclusionary behavior, and even physical attacks. But if we look at these acts in isolation, we miss the ability to truly understand and address the problem. We see these aggressions as the acts of a few bad apples and miss the structural changes that need to be addressed in order to prevent these kinds of behaviors. These hurtful individual acts occur in larger contexts of oppression. If these larger systems of oppression did not exist, the interpersonal interactions that can be so obviously hurtful to your child would be less present and less accepted.

Cultural and Institutional Discrimination

"[Someone who I thought was a friend] and I got into an altercation in the (school) cafeteria and it made me mad because she was sitting there antagonizing me. I wasn't saying anything to her. I was eating my lunch. When the police officer came over, he asked us to be quiet and I said, 'No because I wasn't saying nothing to this girl and she gonna turn around and start talking to me and be stupid. I'm not gonna stand for it, I'm not. I'm eating my lunch minding my own business.' And so we go into it. But when the officer came over, he stepped toward me. I'm like 'Dude, I'm not even the one yelling, so why are you coming at

me?' And he was like, 'Well go to your subschool,' and so I went down there and I started snapping because I didn't feel like that was fair. 'Why you gonna bring me down here? She's still sitting there eating her lunch. That's not fair.' They said, 'Well we can give you a disorderly conduct ticket.'"[1]

Anyone who starts learning about and understanding the complexity of gender runs up against the power of discrimination. You begin to reflect and see with new insight the cultural messages that were conveyed to you so consistently that they became part of the air you breathe. You can recognize it in the way binary conceptions of gender are part of the language most of us grew up with: *Are you having a boy or a girl?; she's such a nice and pretty girl; he's really strong and such a great athlete; boys will be boys.* Invisibility is also part of cultural discrimination. Most of us grew up unaware of the gender diversity all around us.

If you are helping your transgender or non-binary child to navigate gendered systems in school, athletics, or in state and federal agencies (passports, driver's licenses, etc.), you've already run up against how cultural discrimination is incorporated by institutions into their systems. It becomes readily apparent how discrimination is built into our institutions. These institutional barriers create mental distress and oppressive conditions for transgender and non-binary people. It isn't an individual act of discrimination when the clerk at the DMV tells your teen to change their clothes or take off makeup in order to get their driver's license photo taken; it is institutional discrimination. The photo is just one more part of a process that began by requiring a binary gender marker on the application form. This type of discrimination is seen in all the ways that institutions and their related systems don't take into account the needs—or the existence—of transgender and non-binary people.

Why is it important to understand these levels of oppression?

Because they are the context in which your child has to navigate all the other aspects of life outside of your home. The varied forms of oppression they experience every day create extra layers of stress and hardship for your child. Once you understand this, you can help your teen learn to navigate these systems and to recognize that the struggles they experience are not about them as an individual. The more your teen understands systems of oppression and develops multiple ways to deal with the pressures, the more they can build resilience and refrain from internalizing negative messages. You can be essential in helping them with this.

We all need to be resilient. Life can be messy and difficult. The world often doesn't work as we would like for it to. But while resilience is required to live in the world as it is today, many of us are actively engaged in creating the world we want to live in, making it more inclusive of all people. While it's important to help your teen build their capacity for resilience so they are able to deal with the ways others may try to dismiss and diminish them, it is also important that they know change is possible; in fact, change is inevitable. And we all have an impact on creating the change we want to see. Your teen needs to know it is OK not to stay silent when someone tries to embarrass or belittle them, that standing up for themselves and others who are discriminated against is a part of how we make things better. Helping them to think about how to address these acts of discrimination (whether small or systemic) in advance and problem solving possible ways to effectively deal with them when they come up can be very empowering.

Let's now look at what is known about the stress stigma creates. Knowing the impact of stigma will help you understand how to proactively counteract these negative effects.

Minority Stress

"I need to know that I am loved and accepted and believed in and that life has a point and I will find it someday. That's just getting harder and harder to believe."[2]

The stress and distress attributable to a person's minority status is called minority stress. Minority stress as it relates to transgender and non-binary people has been shown to be at significant levels and to have a direct relationship to mental health conditions. Transgender and non-binary teens have significantly more negative mental health outcomes compared to cisgender youth due to this stress.

Recent studies demonstrate that when a transgender or non-binary person lives in an environment filled with gender-based external stressors such as violence, family discord, bullying, harassment, family rejection, lack of gender affirmation, social isolation, and lack of respectful, appropriate medical care, they are at risk for increased levels of psychological distress.

The higher the minority stress level, the higher the level of risk for mental health problems including substance abuse, risky sexual behavior, post-traumatic stress disorder (PTSD), anxiety, self-harm, mood disorders, distress, and virtually every other mental health disorder. Negative recurring events and interactions related to gender minority status have far-reaching, pervasive, and potentially devastating mental health outcomes. For transgender and non-binary youth, there is a direct link between the levels of minority stress and attempted suicide rates.

The Gender Minority Stress Model

The Gender Minority Stress and Resilience Measure (referred to hereafter as the Gender Minority Stress Model), was developed by Rylan

Testa Ph.D., and extends Meyer's Minority Stress Model to look at the stressors and associated mental health implications for gender minority transgender and non-binary teens.

The Gender Minority Stress Model describes how specific external stressors related to one's minority status directly lead to specific internal stressors, and how that combination in turn leads to feelings of low self-worth.

There are four areas of *external* stressors that have the greatest negative impact:

- Gender-based victimization
- Gender-based rejection
- Gender-based discrimination
- Gender identity non-affirmation

These external stressors lead to three types of *internal* stressors:

- Negative expectations for future events
- Internalized transphobia/stigma
- Concealment (nondisclosure of one's gender identity or gender history)

These stressors have been linked to an increase in a youth's perception that they are burdensome to others, and will have difficulty finding relationships and a sense of belonging, both of which are directly linked to increased suicidality and other poor mental health outcomes.

While all these stressors affect the health and well-being of your child, there are specific stressors that have a higher association with suicidality than others. Those are noted with an asterisk* below. Now let's discuss these stressors in more detail.

External Stressors

Gender-Based Verbal and Physical Victimization

Transgender and non-binary people are part of a highly stigmatized gender minority. As such, they tend to be vulnerable to threats to their safety and overall welfare. Experiences of violence and discrimination for people who are non-binary in their appearance or behaviors and those who are known or perceived to be transgender are widespread.

Transgender and non-binary teens are at greater risk of experiencing gender-based verbal and physical victimization. This may include bullying, harassment, harm to personal property, and physical or sexual violence related to their gender status. However, a safe and welcoming home and school environment can do a lot to counteract this risk.

Gender-Based Rejection*

Gender-based rejection is one of the most damaging forms of external minority stress for transgender and non-binary teens. The degree to which a teen experiences this form of rejection directly impacts how they feel about themselves. This is a very concrete area where your response as a parent has either a direct positive or negative impact on your teen's current and future health and well-being. Gender-based rejection is exactly what it sounds like: rejecting someone because of their gender. This can happen in many ways: losing friends or social opportunities because of their gender identity or gender expression; no longer being welcome, or made to feel uncomfortable at home or at family gatherings. Gender-based rejection also happens when your teen isn't allowed to play on the sports teams of their affirmed gender or join a club because of their gender identity or gender expression. Whether rejection comes from family, school, friends, romantic partners, ethnic/racial communities, or faith/religious communities, the effects are devastating. We have heard thousands of examples over the years, and they are heartbreaking.

Gender-Based Discrimination

Gender-based discrimination can be a day-to-day occurrence for many transgender and non-binary people and includes things such as difficulty getting medical care, finding a bathroom to use, getting a job, and getting identification documents.

Gender Non-Affirmation*

This occurs when others do not affirm a person's gender identity and/or gender expression. For instance, a transgirl may be asked to go to the boy's gym class, or a transboy may be referred to by his legal (girl's) name during attendance at school. If someone with a non-binary identity asks you to use a gender-neutral pronoun (e.g., they) and you continue to use pronouns associated with their assumed gender, then that is non-affirming. Non-affirmation of your teen's gender identity may occur more or less frequently depending on how their gender expression is interpreted. Non-affirmation is associated with mental distress, as well as with perceived general life stress, depression, and social anxiety.

Gender non-affirmation occurs when a person:

- has to repeatedly explain their gender identity to people;
- has to repeatedly correct the pronouns that people use;
- has difficulty being perceived as their gender;
- has to work hard for people to read their gender accurately;
- has to be "hyper-masculine/feminine" for people to accept their gender;
- has others invalidate their gender because of their appearance or body; and
- is misgendered and misunderstood because others don't see their gender as they do.

Internal Stressors

The Gender Minority Stress Model helps us see how external stressors, especially feelings of rejection and non-affirmation of their gender, can lead a non-binary or transgender teen to internalize stigma, resulting in a negative self-image and poor self-worth.

External stressors such as gender-based discrimination and victimization can contribute to a person's belief that they are a target for violence because of their gender and increase their distress even further. Research shows that students who believed they were targeted for violence or discrimination because of their identity were at higher risk for negative outcomes than someone who believes they were targeted for some other reason. In other words, how a person perceives and attributes the cause of the event partially determines the impact of it. If they think it was just a random mugging, for example, then they're stressed. But if they think they were targeted for the mugging because of their gender, then the impact of the event is compounded.

Negative Expectations for Future Events*

One result of minority stress is a hyper-vigilance that comes from beginning to *expect* rejection and victimization from other people. A stigmatized person navigates their world trying to avoid any potentially upsetting or dangerous situations. It's like having your adrenaline system always turned on, and it can be exhausting, making it difficult to fully participate in other day-to-day activities. Imagine trying to focus on a complex math problem when you are worried that the person behind you is about to shame you in front of your peers or physically attack you after school. The mathematical equation in front of you might slip into the background as you consider a host of frightening possibilities.

Hyper-vigilance can also develop as a stigmatized person develops finely tuned radar looking for allies in any given situation. This has been called scanning for safety. Young people can become masterful at finding that one adult or student in a building who uses gender-neutral language or presents in a gender-expansive manner. Finding these allies can be helpful, but even that takes extra energy.

Fear of future experiences of victimization, discrimination, or rejection manifest as the following: If I express my gender identity,

- Others won't accept me.
- I won't be hired for the jobs I want.
- People will think I am crazy or mentally ill.
- People will think I am disgusting or sinful.
- People will think less of me or look down on me.
- I could be a victim of crime or violence.
- I could be arrested or harassed.
- I could be denied medical care.

Internalized Transphobia/Stigma*

There is also danger that your teen will internalize the messages telling them that who they are and the way they experience and express their gender are wrong. Internalized stigma, sometimes called internalized transphobia, happens when a person believes the negative messages they are hearing about their gender and feels hatred, anger, or shame for who they are. When this happens, the risks are significantly increased, as it is extremely difficult to have positive gender identity consolidation when you've internalized these messages. If your teen has internalized stigma, it also increases the likelihood that they will not report negative events they experience (harassment, discrimination, violence, etc.) to authorities and others who have power to make decisions regarding their lives. Even more tragic is that due to internalized stigma, your teen may not feel safe or comfortable opening up about negative events or trauma even with you.

When a teen has internalized stigma/transphobia, they might:

- resent their gender identity or gender expression;
- feel depressed or unhappy when thinking about their gender;
- feel like an outcast because of their gender identity or gender expression;
- wonder why they aren't "normal";
- feel ashamed or embarrassed of who they are because of their gender;
- envy people who are cisgender;
- feel isolated or separate from those who share a similar gender identity/expression; and
- deny their gender.

Concealment

> *"Even though the only negative responses I have ever gotten have been from adults, I am still afraid to tell other kids my age that I am trans. I suppose it is internalized transphobia. But I always have to remind myself that people my age are so much more accepting than their parents are."*

Once you become aware of all the different stressors your child is dealing with, it's not surprising that if your child isn't visually nonconforming in their gender presentation, they (and you) may prefer to conceal their transgender or non-binary status from others. Research indicates, though, that self-concealment (intentionally hiding one's gender history/identity—not to be confused with being selectively private about whom to share this information with) further decreases self-worth, which in turn increases distress. Concealment also reduces the chances that they will connect with a transgender or non-binary community, which has been known to reduce the isolation youth experience.

Concealing their gender can leave your child isolated. This is commonly the case with teens who were supported in their gender identity and expression since childhood and may not be known to anyone as transgender or non-binary beyond their family and possibly closest friends. The isolation can build up over time. Likewise, even when a teen is embraced by friends, family, and their school, if they do not know anyone else like them or don't see themselves positively reflected in the world (community, media, etc.), they can feel alone.

When transgender and non-binary teens are afraid of others knowing their gender history, they may censor or change the way they talk about certain experiences from their past.

Most people focus on the specific acts of stigmatization (harassment, violence, etc.) when they think of minority stress; however, this framework helps us see that this is only one dimension of stress on the individual. In fact, not only are specific acts of stigmatization risk factors for suicide in their own right, but the negative self-image and feelings of low self-worth that are created within someone after these experiences also damage the overall health and well-being of the stigmatized individual.

When Your Teen Has Multiple Stigmatized Identities

"Living in Portland [Oregon], a very progressive city for LGBTQ rights, I've learned to love myself as a queer person. But Portland isn't very racially diverse or progressive. I am not VALUED here as a black man. As in the rest of the country, I am seen as DANGEROUS, as a CRIMINAL—when I have committed no crimes. Although Portland may be progressive in some ways, I still experience daily reminders that there are many people in this city who think I am dirty, unattractive, unintelligent, and inferior. I am tokenized, then criminalized, and ultimately

treated like I have no value. I don't know how to love myself as
a young, black, queer person, when the world tells me that I am
not someone who deserves to be loved. Yet, I cannot stop being
black any more than I can stop being gay, or genderqueer, or
Jamaican, nor can I designate one of those identities as more
important than the other."

Non-binary and transgender teenagers who have less privilege and/or multiple marginalized and stigmatized identities face additional pressures, discrimination, and victimization. This casual, constant, and mostly accepted form of degradation is especially difficult for teens who are just trying to get a personal handle on all aspects of their identity. Other aspects of a teen's identity such as sexual orientation, race/ethnicity, and religion can all influence and intersect with gender identity and gender expression, creating a more complex and unique experience of gender. This same intersection of identities can make it more difficult to sort through so many different messages that can erode self-worth. Because of this, non-binary and transgender youth with multiple types of minority status are at significantly increased risk and in greater need of support in order to live in a dominant culture that devalues them in so many ways.

This makes the visibility of transgender and non-binary adults and young people who share your teen's additional minority identities particularly important. For example, some teens might hear from others that being transgender is a white person's issue. If they are a person of color, this stereotype serves to further discount their experience. That's why it can be helpful for youth to know about people like African-American actress Laverne Cox; Latina and Jewish White House staffer Raffi Freedman-Gurspan; African-American writer and activist Tiq Milan; as well as other gender minority role models and leaders from other countries. It can also be reassuring for youth to learn about how their own cultural heritage may have deep roots in a more non-binary system. Much has been written about non-binary identities in cultures from around the world. Resources such as these can be found in many places, including the Gender Spectrum website.

Suicide and Minority Stress

"I didn't know how to tell my parents. I knew they'd be so disappointed in me. I thought it would be better for everyone if I just died."

All of these stressors leave transgender and non-binary teens with a feeling that they are a burden to others, including parents (perceived burdensomeness) and to an increased fear that their needs for belonging will go unmet (thwarted belongingness). Although many factors determine whether a transgender and non-binary teen contemplates suicide or attempts to take their life, research indicates that there are some predictors:

- Thwarted belongingness: isolation and a lack of connectedness
- Perceived burdensomeness
- Gender identity confusion and/or discomfort
- Low self-worth

When trying to understand the extremely high rates of suicidal ideation and suicide attempts for non-binary and transgender youth, it is valuable to examine the issue within the context of minority stress. Looking at it this way can help to put some of the alarmingly high rates of suicide into perspective and assist you in lowering these chances with your teen.

Thwarted Belongingness: Isolation and Lack of Connectedness

"I was mean to people so that they would not come near me, so they would not question, so that I would not have to answer awkward questions. I hated people for a while. But, nowadays it is um, basically stay quiet, stay safe."[3]

Transgender and non-binary teens frequently experience the strongest predictors of suicide: isolation, loneliness, social disconnectedness, and lack of support directly due to their minority gender status. Rejection and fear of rejection keep many transgender and non-binary teens isolated and disconnected from others. Thwarted belongingness is marked by an absence of support. It is also associated with loneliness, feelings of rejection, social withdrawal, and gender-based family conflict. Transgender and non-binary teens who feel a sense of connection—even with one adult—are at lower risk for suicide.

Perceived Burdensomeness

We often see teens who feel like they are a burden to their families. The teen looks at the difficulties their families have with their gender identity or gender expression and wonder if everything would just be better if they "weren't around." They might focus on financial costs (medical, therapy, legal, document change fees, clothes, etc.), time spent dealing with others (school, extra-curriculars, professionals), and complicated family dynamics (parents arguing, splits in the family, siblings being bullied) associated with their gender and determine that their world would be better off without them. It is important to remember that it is a *perceived* burdensomeness—you may not feel they are a burden, but if they think they are, then this is a significant issue and risk factor for them.

Gender Confusion and Discomfort

Research shows that one of the top reasons transgender and non-binary people attempt suicide—as identified by individuals who were unsuccessful in their suicide attempts—is related to gender confusion and discomfort. In the past, it was thought that the primary cause of increased psychological distress was the difference between a person's gender identity and their sex assigned at birth, suggesting that the distress was innate and unavoidable. However, current research shows that the feelings of distress around being transgender/non-binary (or the possibility of being so) are the most damaging and dangerous internalized forms of minority stress. The distress comes from the cultural and internalized stigma associated with having a different gender than the one assumed, having a gender identity that's stigmatized, and the feelings that your gender identity isn't congruent with your body (gender dysphoria).

Low Self-Worth

It is easy for transgender and non-binary teens to experience shame and low self-worth because of their gender minority status. We already examined how low self-worth develops from repeated exposure to discrimination and negative events. Low self-worth can also develop from internalized messages of stigma, as well as from real or perceived, rejection (or the fear of it), bullying, and other forms of gender-based victimization.

Parenting to Counteract Minority Stress

Understanding the various stressors your child deals with and the effect this will have on them throughout their lifetime, the more you can understand why parenting to support and enhance their resilience is potentially life-saving for your child. By understanding how stigma is likely to affect your teen and its potential to impact multiple areas of

their overall health and well-being, you can be on the lookout for ways
to counteract the negative impact now and in the future.

1   Maurice N. Gattis and Sara L. McKinnon, *School Experiences of Transgender and Gender Non-Conforming Students in Wisconsin,* Madison, WI: GSAFE, 2015.

2   Human Rights Campaign and Gender Spectrum, *Supporting and Caring for our Gender Expansive Youth,* [2014].

3   Maurice N. Gattis and Sara L. McKinnon, *School Experiences of Transgender and Gender Non-Conforming Students in Wisconsin,* Madison, WI: GSAFE, 2015.

Chapter 9

Professional Support and Mental Health Considerations

"I have to be honest; I began to feel like maybe I was crazy or something. I didn't know exactly what I was; I thought I must be some kind of freak. I really could have used a counselor to help me—but my mom didn't know where to find someone who would understand. She was afraid they would try to take me away from her. Once I realized I was transgender and that there are others out there like me, I felt so grateful I wasn't crazy…"

"I've never reached out for mental healthcare. I'm worried they'll be more concerned about my gender identity and sexuality (which I am fairly confident in) than they will be about my actual problems."[1]

WE NEED TO START THIS chapter by being very clear: Gender identity and gender expression do not cause mental health issues. Rather it is the impact of negative reactions to a person's gender—the harassment, discrimination, and social stigma that they face—that creates the context for mental health issues. It is easy to develop mental health issues when your friends, family, teachers, classmates, religion, and/or society at large do not accept who you are. Mental health issues for transgender and non-binary youth also arise from the struggles they may have with a body that does not match their psyche. Trying to come to terms with having a less common gender identity or expression in a society that tries to enforce conformity also has its own mental health challenges.

Some teens struggle to understand what is going on with them. At first they may not have any idea that the depression, anxiety or angst that they feel is in any way gender related. It is common to experience a lot of confusion before coming to a recognition of being transgender, non-binary, or otherwise gender-expansive. This is especially true if your teen was previously unaware of the full spectrum of gender diversity. It can create a profound sense of disequilibrium to let go of previously held notions of who they thought they were without yet having language for who they are. Some teens experience relief once they have language for the discomfort or distress they have been feeling. For other teens, their depression or anxiety actually increases once they realize that they are transgender or non-binary, particularly if they believe this will create conflict in their family or social support systems. It also isn't unusual for teens to experience depression or anxiety during the process of deciding what is needed for them to experience gender congruence and while taking steps to achieve it—a process that can take years. Of course, all transgender and non-binary youth experience a wide range of emotions when they experience rejection and discrimination. It can be difficult for these teens to navigate their world; family and professional support can be the lifelines they need to survive and ultimately thrive.

Does My Child Need Counseling/Therapy?

*"The thing my therapist keeps telling me is that even though
I may not know what exactly is me—I am going towards the
things that make me feel better and away from the things that
make me feel worse. That makes sense to me. I wish it made
sense to my mom. I really need her now."*

Your transgender or non-binary teen doesn't need therapy simply
because they have a gender identity that is something other than
cisgender. However, non-binary and transgender teens, no matter how
well adjusted, can benefit from working (individually or as part of
a group) with a therapist or other adult who is knowledgeable and
trained in both gender and adolescent issues. Therapists and counselors can be instrumental in helping your teen identify their gender
and in empowering them to feel positive about who they are. Counseling can help teens increase their resilience in the face of adversity by helping them access their inner strength, hone coping and
decision-making skills, develop support systems, and learn to accept
themselves. Your teen may also be required to see a therapist or counselor as a prerequisite to receiving certain medical/surgical services
related to their seeking congruence.

Therapists and counselors trained in working with this age group
can assist with depression, anxiety, harm reduction, school issues,
family issues, developing resilience, and bolstering self-esteem. Sometimes, a teen is willing to share things with a counselor they are not
able to share with their family.

There are many aspects of a therapeutic relationship that are bene-
ficial, perhaps none more so than affirming your teen's gender identity.
This is part of why a therapist should be more than just accepting
of gender diversity; they should also be well versed in the particular
stressors that transgender, non-binary, and gender-expansive youth

face. Counseling can often be incredibly useful in integrating the multiple identities each of us has, especially when they appear to be at odds with one another. Counseling can help all members of your family understand and value your teen's gender identity, provide a way for each person to communicate their feelings about this, and address any issues that need attention.

Role of Counseling for the Family

Whether or not your family is in crisis around your child's gender identity or gender expression, adolescence can be an important time for both individual and family counseling. Research confirms the effectiveness of family-based interventions in not only preventing future difficulties, but also addressing existing problems such as eating disorders, depression, and substance abuse. A 2011 longitudinal study of teenagers in the U.S. found that teens who felt highly valued by their family and were able to confide in family members had substantially lower risks for mental illness. A counseling setting can be the ideal context in which such understandings can be established.

Working with a counselor or other advisor capable of affirming your teen's gender, while honoring the challenges you as parents may be experiencing, can help relieve some of your family's distress. It can provide you with a place to ask questions, gather information, and sort through some of the issues you're struggling with most. A therapist can also help your family shift any patterns of communication that aren't working and help identify what each person in the family, including siblings, may need. If the connection between you and your teen is tattered, a family counselor or social worker can help to connect you once again, and assist your family in openly and productively discussing issues related to gender. If there are cultural or religious beliefs that you feel do not embrace gender diversity, a family therapist who respects your cultural values while still being affirming of your teen's gender can be invaluable. It's possible to find a peaceful place in your relationship again, where you understand one another and enjoy spending time together.

When to Seek Therapy

How do you know when your teen might need therapy? If they come to you saying that they want to see a therapist, that's a clear indicator. Absent that, as a first step, ask your teen. If they say it might help, then it's a good idea for whatever period of time they find it helpful. If they say they're not interested, but you see behaviors that indicate significant stress or other factors that indicate a lack of well-being, tell them what you're seeing and ask that they consider going, even if only a couple of times to see if there's value. Because many transgender, non-binary, and questioning teens are hypersensitive to the implication that there might be something wrong with them, it's important to reassure your teen right from the start that your suggestion regarding therapy is nothing more than a desire to provide them with as much support as possible. You might want to let them know that you understand there may be things they would like to talk about with someone other than you, and counseling will give them a safe place to do so. Depending on the maturity of your teen, you might share with them about the elements of minority stress and how easy it is to internalize negative messages about themselves; counseling can be useful way to deal with these stressors and build inner wells of resilience.

It is best for you to get help for your child regardless of their expressed desire to not go to therapy if you're seeing any of the following behaviors:

- *Significant isolation.* Withdrawal from family, friends, and other human interaction. While most teens require some separate space from family, if you see an unusual level of isolation, it is important to talk with your teen regarding what is going on with them. Many transgender and non-binary teens withdraw from family life because it is difficult for them to reconcile who they experience themselves to be with who they think their family expects them to be. They fear that sharing about themself and their gender with their family may result in rejection. Withdrawal may also indicate that your teen is dealing with social problems at school, low self-esteem issues, or is simply feeling off-kilter as they evolve into their authentic gender. Consider significant isolation or withdrawal a warning sign and take action.

- *Immobilized by self-doubt and negative self-talk.* If low self-esteem keeps your teen from pursuing interests they have, if they begin spending a significantly increased amount of time at home, or they openly say very negative things about who they are, they need to speak to someone and get help to see themselves in a healthier light.

- *Acting out dangerously.* Many transgender and non-binary teens will experience harassment, ridicule, threats of violence, violence, or abuse because of their gender. When a teen lacks the resources to address these harms and their associated pain, they may act out violently or aggressively. Take this as an indication that your teen needs help.

- *Significant shifts in behavior.* Your teen may need help if they are no longer connecting with friends, or you are seeing noticeable shifts in their behavior related to sleep, eating, amount of time spent alone, interest in school, or performance in school.

- *Significant changes in communication.* Your teen may need professional help if they shut down and are unwilling to talk with you about topics they used to discuss with you, or if they have become more aggressive in the way they speak to you.

- *Depressed, anxious, or distressed.* If your teen is experiencing any of these emotions and it is persistent and/or affecting their quality of life, then professional support can help.

- *Talking about suicide.* If your teen talks about suicide, get professional help immediately.

Check in with your teen regularly. Talk about their day with them. See if there are concerns arising for your teen; if so, feel comfortable getting more feedback. Hear what others connected to your child have to say. Sometimes, their friends, extended family, family friends, school counselor, or teacher might raise a flag if they see things that concern them and they know you value their perspective.

How Do I Choose a Mental Health Provider?

"The first time I met [my counselor] I had to tell her my legal name to get my paperwork, and so, she said, 'OK this is your legal name, what do you want to be called?' Great. I love this. And I came out to her and she, like, wanted to help me 'in whatever way I can.' I was always welcome…to talk to her about any troubles I was having."

Once you have determined that you will seek a therapist or counselor's support, you must then identify a professional who will be most appropriate for the needs of your child and family. By no means are all therapists well informed on issues of gender as they relate to children and youth. As you seek the services of professionals, ask them what their experience is working with transgender, non-binary and gender-expansive youth. The wrong therapist can do more harm than good. If you cannot find a qualified therapist in your area, consider finding someone you are comfortable with and who is open to learning; they can then consult with another therapist who has experience around issues related to gender and youth. Some families choose to work with an experienced therapist via Skype, though you should note that there may be licensing issues if the therapist is outside your state.

When a Letter Is Needed for Hormones or Surgery

In some locations and with some medical providers a letter is required from a mental health professional in order to secure insurance coverage, or for the doctor to be able to prescribe hormones or perform the desired surgical procedure. If your teen is seeking mental health support from providers out of state please be sure that they will qualify.

Ongoing monitoring of the therapy relationship is important. If the therapist is for your teen, keep the lines of communication open between you and your teen, as well as between you and the therapist. You want to make sure the environment remains supportive and affirming for your child.

If you need help finding a mental health professional who is committed to affirmative care and support of gender diverse youth, there are gender centers throughout the U.S. and in other countries that may be able to refer you to someone.

Some Questions to Ask When Choosing Professionals to Work with Your Child or Family

- Have you worked with transgender, non-binary, or questioning youth before?
- Are you willing to learn if I can connect you with some resources?

   Many practitioners will not have experience working with kids and their gender before, but if they are genuinely open-minded and willing to learn, that is the most important factor.

- What do you see as your role in a teen's gender journey?

   Be wary if a professional wants to help your child conform to more traditional gender roles or indicates that their treatment can change your child's gender identity/expression. A practitioner who gives your child negative messages about who they are, including their gender, can do more harm than good.

   You want to find professionals who recognize gender diversity as a naturally occurring aspect of humanity that crosses all lines of identity, geography, and other forms of difference.

   Look for a professional whose goal is to support your child on whatever their authentic path is in relation to their gender.

- Do you think teens are too young to determine their gender identity?
- Do you think teens can seek congruence measures, including medical options such as hormones or surgeries?

   Seek professionals who understand that children can

know their gender identity at any age, but who won't put them in any box or force them on any particular path. The idea is to follow your teen's lead, and to create a safe space for them to figure out their true identity and what they need to feel congruent.

- Are you familiar with non-binary genders?

  Try to find professionals who understand that gender is a spectrum.

  What if I am not on the same page as my partner or my child's other parent?

  Ideally, professionals will meet parents "where they are at" and reflect an understanding that parents have their own process to go through. A skilled professional can help families navigate difficult decisions when adults and kids aren't on the same page and need help understanding each other.

Principles of Gender-Affirmative Care

Professionals across various fields are calling for affirmative care and support for transgender, non-binary, and gender-expansive young people. A body of knowledge now exists about the necessary elements of such care. Increasingly, psychologists, therapists, social workers, counselors, and many others charged with supporting the healthy development of their young patients are recognizing the need to help them understand (and navigate the reactions of others to) their gender. Networks of mental health professionals are establishing a set of practices that allow for a young person's safe and healthy exploration of gender.

These practices, in turn, are informed by a number of core principles:

- Naturally occurring variations in gender exist; these variations are not inherently negative and should not be categorized as disordered.

- Gender roles and presentations are diverse and varied across societies and over time, and any attempt to analyze them must account for various cultural and historical factors.
- Authentic gender emerges from the complex interaction between one's body, gender expression, and gender identity.
- Gender is not fixed, but evolves for both individuals and cultures over time.
- Sexual orientation and gender identity are different but related aspects of identity; anyone can be at any place on each spectrum.
- Congruence of internal feelings with external presentation of gender is essential for long-term well-being.
- Stigma, prejudice, and violence affect the short- and long-term health of transgender and non-binary individuals.
- Gender identity intersects with all other identities. Having multiple minority identities increases the stigma and associated minority stress.
- Transgender and non-binary youth have the best chances for healthy lives when they have supportive families.
- Ambiguity as a temporary and/or permanent place of gender identity or expression is common.
- All gender identities and expressions deserve equal respect.
- Pathologies associated with a teen's gender most often result from the negative reactions of those surrounding, rather than from within, the individual.

These and related principles inform a growing field of gender-affirmative care and practice. Rather than being grounded in strictly binary, socially normative notions about gender, such affirming care is marked by a number of characteristics. Specifically, gender-affirmative care:

Acknowledges the individual's own perceptions of gender as being real and genuinely held.

Rather than assuming the therapist knows the correct way for the patient's gender to unfold, affirming mental health providers instead create space in which the teen's experiences of self are valued as authentic and real. This does not mean the provider does not encourage the patient to explore this aspect of self—quite the opposite, in fact. It does, however, appreciate that for such exploration to take place, the person must feel seen and heard as the expert on their own experience.

Assists the family in creating a supportive home environment.

Having working knowledge of the strong impact of family on the long-term health and well-being of non-binary, transgender, and gender-expansive youth, affirmative care providers work with the family to create a safe home. They are aware of the significant, potentially life-threatening risks facing youth without the support of family. Without compromising a family's values, the provider can assist in leading the family toward supportive parenting practices and educate them about how to avoid potentially damaging behaviors. They can help to normalize the reactions of family members and assist with family adjustment issues.

Balances the needs of all involved.

Many parents who approach a mental healthcare provider will be seeking concrete answers, desperate to know how this will all work out. Teens may be anxious to have access to the medical options for congruency that they desire. It is important to find a way to address the needs of the teen and the needs of the family, especially if they are seemingly in conflict. This may mean that the family also needs counseling. In fact depending on the situation, it may be the parents, and not the teen, who need mental health support, particularly if the teen is comfortable in their gender but the family remains distressed.

Regardless, it is critical for the mental healthcare professional to work with those around the teen to become more comfortable with the uncertainty that is inherent in the situation and to move with the appropriate speed warranted to address the health and well-being needs of the teen.

Affirms the teen's strength.
Along this same line, it is important that a transgender or non-binary teen and their family have an opportunity to perceive their child's gender in a balanced light. Despite a variety of challenges, there are also many positive aspects to be affirmed as the teen seeks to discover or insists on being seen for who they truly are.

Supports the teen and family in navigating the world around them.
Mental healthcare providers can serve as problem-solvers capable of understanding the various contexts of the teen's life, and can assist in developing various strategies for responding or adjusting to challenges as they present themselves. Whether with other family members, within the neighborhood or community, at school or places of worship, a child's gender may be seen as fair game for any manner of public comment or questioning, and perhaps outright condemnation. Helping families and teens anticipate and respond to these possibilities is a critical aspect of affirmative care and support.

Acknowledges genuine issues of safety.
Affirming providers recognize the need to protect the transgender or non-binary teen and their family. They can help the teen to identify situations in which their safety might be compromised, emotionally or physically, and to strategize effective solutions ahead of time. Mental healthcare professionals must work to help their patients recognize these situations and provide them with the tools necessary to avoid or minimize the negative effects. In the case of difficult, discriminating,

harassing or violent experiences, the provider can assist everyone in processing the impact of the event. An important mantra of gender-affirmative care is safety first, safety last; it is perhaps here that this approach can have its most important impact. When affirmed in the authenticity of their experience, young people are more likely to treat themselves more positively, and expect and insist upon the same from those around them.

Stays up to date with medical options.
Many transgender and non-binary teens will need some form of medical treatment in order to come to full congruence. Therefore, a provider's awareness of current medical options serves to assist in the process of gender confirmation. Affirmative care mental health providers are called upon to work collaboratively with a patient's medical providers when needed. Medical treatments are deemed appropriate when they lead toward congruence. Non-binary medical options are honored.

Has a strong working understanding of minority stress.
An awareness of minority stress and research-based means of bolstering resilience is an integral part of the framework for therapy. Affirmative care understands that treatment for transgender and non-binary youth is often complex due to the impact of minority stress on therapy including internalized negative attitudes and feelings of low self-worth, as well as lack of recognition or denial of the severity of the impact of discrimination, violence, and harassment. An affirmative provider is aware of the additional stressors associated with multiple oppressions and works to assist the teen in integrating all identities and consolidating a positive personal identity. They are aware of and promote resilience factors specific to transgender and non-binary youth directly and with the family as a whole when appropriate.

Dangers of Conversion Therapy

Not surprisingly, the challenges for transgender and non-binary people can seem staggering. No one wants their child to face such pain and difficulty. Tremendous fears about your child's future may well have you thinking, "How can I prevent my teen from being transgender, non-binary, or gender non-conforming so that they don't have to go through this?" For this, and a number of other reasons, some families try to help their transgender or non-binary child by taking them to therapy, camps, or other programs designed to "cure" them of their gender identity and/or what they perceive as their nonconforming gender-related behaviors. Some of the parents who choose this believe that they are acting from a place of love and support for their child. Faith leaders, or other respected members of their community may have advised them that this will help their child.

"Reparative therapy," also known as conversion therapy, refers to therapy or other actions designed to alter a person's sexual orientation or gender identity. We want to be very clear here: There is *no* clinical evidence or scientific validity for such therapy being effective. In fact, quite to the contrary, there is a wealth of evidence that it is harmful and can dangerously exacerbate the risk factors already discussed. *If you have your child in such therapy or are engaged in a program designed to "cure" them right now, we strongly urge you to stop this treatment immediately and gather more information about this approach to prevent potentially irreparable harm to your child.*

What Are the Risks Associated with Conversion Therapy?

Conversion therapy has been shown to result in greater levels of self-blame, shame, feeling dehumanized, loss of religious and/or spiritual faith, depression, guilt, despair, self-loathing, isolation, suicidality, substance abuse, increased hostility toward parents, and more.

What Do Mental Health Organizations Have to Say about Conversion Therapy?

Many leading mental and medical health organizations have publicly come forward against reparative therapy, citing the dangerous effects it can have. The American Academy of Child and Adolescent Psychiatry states that such therapy "may encourage family rejection and undermine self-esteem, connectedness and caring, important protective factors against suicidal ideation and attempts." These organizations also state that there is no scientific credibility supporting its use. The American Psychiatric Association states, "Furthermore, anecdotal reports of 'cures' are counterbalanced by anecdotal claims of psychological harm. In the last four decades, 'reparative' therapists have not produced any rigorous scientific research to substantiate their claims of cure."

What Legal Protection Is Available?

The state of California led the way in passing legislation to prohibit therapists from trying to change the gender identity of anyone under eighteen years old. Other states, including New Jersey, Oregon, Illinois, Vermont, and the District of Columbia have passed similar laws, and many more states are attempting to pass similar legislation now. In Canada, Ontario and Manitoba have also passed such legislation and Malta is moving toward a nationwide ban. These laws prohibit efforts to alter gender expression and allow for therapies that encourage coping skills, acceptance of self, identity exploration/consolidation, and self-acceptance. The law also continues to allow therapists to assist patients who wish to seek medical and social congruence measures.

In the U.S., President Obama has called for a legislative end to "transgender conversion therapy." A White House senior advisor responded in 2015 to a petition calling for a federal ban on conversion therapy by saying, "We share your concern about conversion therapy and its devastating effects on the lives of transgender as well as gay, lesbian, bisexual, and queer youth.... As part of our dedication to protecting America's youth, this administration supports efforts to ban conversion therapy for minors." In 2015, Ontario, Canada, passed Bill 77, the Affirming Sexual Orientation and Gender Identity Act. The bill prohibits healthcare providers from offering any services intended to change the gender identity of a person under eighteen. It also specifically states that providers may still engage in supportive care to facilitate coping skills, social support, and identity exploration and development. It also allows providers to continue to provide sex-reassignment surgery.

At the time of our writing, the U.N. Committee Against Torture is reviewing conversion therapy as a potential violation of the Convention Against Torture and Other Cruel, Inhuman or Degrading Treatment or Punishment—making it an issue of international human rights law.

Co-Occurring Concerns and Diagnoses

"Even though I still struggle with depression/anxiety/PTSD, since learning about gender and being able to figure out who I am and being out and open about it, there has been a drastic improvement in my life and how I interact with people and I am no longer suicidal."[2]

When a teen is exploring their gender, it can be difficult for them, you, or a therapist to uncover what exactly is going on, as there may be other mental health concerns presenting at the same time. The picture can be complex. Sometimes, these mental health or behavioral concerns will resolve or be alleviated by claiming their authentic gender and receiving the necessary alignment measures; however, sometimes the gender issues and mental health concerns are separate issues. When the coexisting concerns are serious, such as depression, self-harming behaviors, disordered eating, suicidal isolation, or substance, abuse it can be challenging for a teen, counselor or parent to know the right issue to address first. If gender dysphoria is not the leading issue treated, two things are common:

1. The mental health concern may not subside until the dysphoria is addressed, as it is the underlying factor for some teens. It is common with non-binary and transgender youth for the mental health issues to be driven by the gender issue. Once the gender issue is dealt with and congruence measures have begun, the co-occurring psychological issues often lessen or resolve.

2. Likewise, if the other clinical issues are treated first, the dysphoria can loom much larger than before because the teen may have been using that behavior (disordered eating, drug use, cutting, etc.) as a coping mechanism to downplay their dysphoria. Removing the coping mechanism can serve to highlight the underlying issue at hand.

When it comes to other co-presentations such as developmental disorders, autism spectrum conditions, or schizophrenia, it may or may not be difficult for the teen to fully explore and articulate their gender identity. It can also be difficult for people with multiple diagnoses to receive proper medical alignment measures despite the fact that the *Diagnostic and Statistical Manual of Mental Disorders* (DSM) recognizes that both gender dysphoria and other conditions can and do coexist.

Individuals with co-occurring conditions should have equal rights and access to appropriate care for their gender dysphoria. However, in many cases, a doctor will not prescribe cross hormones or perform gender alignment surgeries without a letter stating that the gender issues are not a product of the other condition or stating clearly that the co-occurring issue will not interfere with the gender-related medical treatments. Many mental health professionals are not up to date on gender issues and are unwilling to write such letters; thus coexisting diagnoses can impact access to congruence measures. However, there is no reason why one can't have a mental illness and be transgender or non-binary. They are not mutually exclusive, and generally one does not cause the other. If your teen's care providers withhold congruence measures due to coexisting conditions and you feel strongly that they are separate conditions, keep searching for care providers who will listen and provide the appropriate care and support.

Autism Spectrum Conditions

"Asperger's made it more difficult to realize that I was trans. I was unaware of most of the social aspects of gender. Until my late teens, I had a very difficult time recognizing and verbalizing what I was feeling. This made it difficult to distinguish dysphoria from any other type of bad feeling. Externally, indicators of gender dysphoria were attributed to my autism: No dresses and short hair because of sensory issues, resists bras and hides periods because change is overwhelming, doesn't relate to girls because of lack of social understanding, etc. Once I transitioned, socializing was easier, and my depression and anxiety were less

severe. I still have Asperger's of course, but the negative aspects of it are easier to handle now that I've transitioned."

"I never suspected that I was on the autism spectrum until I transitioned and dropped the mask that society wanted me to wear. When I started acting like my true self, I couldn't figure out why I was having so much difficulty being understood by some people. I started making friends, slowly, and at one point I noticed that all of my friends had Asperger's. When I said this to my partner, they said they thought it was already established that I did, too. It's really helped me out, just looking up information about the autism spectrum and tips from other aspies that help me deal with stuff."

Although there have been an increasing number of studies attempting to look at the co-occurrence of Autism Spectrum Conditions (ASC) and transgender identities, it is simply too new of a field to be able to conclusively answer many of the questions that parents and mental health professionals share. While it appears that there may be a higher co-occurrence rate of ASC with transgender youth than in the general population, more research is needed.

Parents of a teen who identifies as transgender or non-binary and is on the autism spectrum often struggle to sort out whether the gender issues are real or a symptom of their ASC. It is not always clear. This is due to many of the overlapping criteria for each, as well as the possibility that the cross-gender or non-binary identification could be a manifestation of an autism spectrum-related obsession. Unfortunately, the research is not yet very useful in helping to answer this or any of the other overarching questions.

Research seems to indicate that a higher percentage of people who are transgender or non-binary are on the autism spectrum. Research also appears to indicate that there may be a higher percentage of people on the autism spectrum who are transgender or non-binary. However, there are so many factors at play that making these correlations with certainty at this time is impossible. Sample size is certainly a factor: There are a small number of people on the autism spectrum and a small number who identify as transgender; the number of people who are both is really very small.

As a parent, it is important for you to understand that there are overlapping criteria for both gender dysphoria diagnoses and ASC diagnoses. Be cautious of new ASC diagnoses in your non-binary or transgender teen. If your teen is experiencing social difficulties and social anxiety, is not reading social cues, or is feeling isolated, this does not necessarily mean they have Asperger's or are elsewhere on the autism spectrum. Some transgender teens no longer meet the criteria for ASC after they transition, or as their symptoms dissipate with congruence. In other words, for some youth, the symptoms being observed were a byproduct of gender stress or distress and not symptomatic of being on the autism spectrum. On the other hand, some transgender and non-binary teens only get diagnosed with ASC after gender congruence is reached, as the assumption was that all the concerns were gender-related when they were really both.

There are certainly overlapping experiences for both teens and parents in these populations. For example, people with autism spectrum conditions and people with less common gender identities are each marginalized and stigmatized groups that are often misunderstood by the general population. They are also both at increased risk for depression and suicide due to stigmatization. And unfortunately, it is often the case that gender specialists are not ASC specialists and vice versa. This can make for frequent misdiagnosis and difficulty securing appropriate care—including necessary medical congruence measures for people who are transgender or non-binary.

Being on the autism spectrum and being transgender or non-binary presents a greater level of complexity when interacting in day-to-day life. For example, when social cues are absent, or not perceived, it can be more difficult to identify situations that are not safe for a transgender or non-binary person. This is something to be aware of so that your teen can receive the support that they need in order to express themselves authentically.

Professionals are trying to catch up with this double diagnosis of ASC and gender dysphoria and how to support access to desired congruence measures. For some, there is concern that informed consent may not be possible, while others discount this notion and see it as stemming from continued lack of understanding about people with ASC. People on the autism spectrum frequently have others questioning their ability to understand and advocate on behalf of themselves, doubting the authenticity of their experience and emotions. As one young person put it, *"When I told people that I was transgender, I had to deal with people doubting me and thinking that I was obsessing on gender. It is such a paternalistic viewpoint that they know better than I do about my experience."*

When it comes to supporting transgender and non-binary teens with ASC in seeking congruence, there is an increased need for different forms of support than for teens who do not have ASC. For example, teens with ASC may have more complex sexual health and safety issues to consider associated with their transition process. Because each of these groups is independently a target for harassment, abuse, and discrimination, their risk for negative and potentially dangerous interactions is increased.

Being on the autism spectrum and being transgender or non-binary presents a greater level of complexity when interacting in day-to-day life. For example, when social cues are not perceived, it can be more difficult for a transgender or non-binary person to identify situations that are unsafe. This is something to be aware of so that these teens can receive the support they need in order to express themselves authentically while keeping safe. The particular tools used to guide a transgender or non-binary teen with ASC to assess potentially risky situations and to protect themselves may differ from those for teens without ASC.

A Therapist as a Valuable Member of Your Team

Therapy can be transformative for you, your family, and your teen. It can boost everyone's self-esteem and be a vital form of affirmative support for your teen's experience of themself. It is excellent to have a mental health provider as a part of your team who can collaborate with your child and your family and advocate on behalf of your teen whenever necessary. Many therapists end up meeting with extended family members and even schools and faith organizations to help them better understand and meet the needs of your teen. If formal letters or assessments are required in order for your child to have access to medical congruence measures, this person can provide them as a natural extension of the work they are already doing with your teen.

---

1   J. Veale, E. Saewyc, H. Frohard-Dourlent, S. Dobson, B. Clark, and the Canadian Trans Youth Health Survey Research Group (2015), *Being Safe, Being Me: Results of the Canadian Trans Youth Health Survey; Stigma and Resilience Among Vulnerable Youth Centre*, School of Nursing, University of British Columbia, Vancouver, BC.

2   Veale et al.

Chapter 10

What You Can Do to Improve the Odds

"I just told my child, 'I want to support you in finding what is most comfortable and honest for you. Whether or not that includes a name change, pronoun change, identity marker change, hormone replacement therapy, or surgery, I am here for you every step of the way. Let's do this together.' I had nothing to lose by being crystal clear in my support. But I knew enough to know I had everything to lose if I showed any doubt regarding what he was telling me about his gender. By supporting him first and foremost, I created stable ground for us to explore what felt right to him together in the months to come."

WE KNOW IT CAN FEEL overwhelming to think about the grim statistics we shared in Chapter 6: "What Keeps You Up at Night," about transgender and non-binary teens. But there is hope: There are absolutely things you can do to help your child. While there are no guarantees, we know from the research that has been done and our own extensive experience working with families, that your support and affirmation of your child's gender are the most critical factors in improving your teen's odds for having a healthy and happy life into and throughout adulthood. Let's now turn our attention to what support actually looks like.

To see the effect that supportive parenting has, let's return to one of the most frightening statistics we've shared: the percentage of transgender youth who report having attempted suicide. A teen's perception of parental support dramatically decreases the chance that they will attempt to take their life. In the 2012 Transpulse study regarding transgender and non-binary teens, 35 percent of teens who felt they had strongly supportive parents considered suicide in the past year, but most did not make a suicide attempt. In contrast, 60 percent of teens who felt they did not have strongly supportive parents considered suicide in the past year, and almost every single one of them did attempt suicide. Teens who perceived that their parents supported them in regard to their gender were 93 percent less likely to attempt suicide than teens who did not perceive that they had parental support. This is perhaps the clearest indication of the tremendously positive impact that parent support can have.

Given the impact your support will play in improving your child's health and well-being, it begs the question of what support actually looks like. What are the specific things you can do? Are there certain behaviors you should avoid?

As parents, we think that loving our child is all that is needed to boost their self-esteem and protect their well-being. Unfortunately, this is not the case. Research indicates that love is not enough; rather it is the *specific ways in which our love is felt* that make the difference when it comes to the long-term health and wellbeing of transgender, non-binary, and gender-expansive teens.

Many of the specific forms of support described here come from the groundbreaking research conducted by renowned child welfare expert Dr. Caitlin Ryan and the Family Acceptance Project (FAP). A wealth of FAP data clearly indicates a direct and significant impact of specific parenting approaches on your teen's outlook on life, risk of suicide, drug use, HIV, depression, and homelessness.

Teens Need (and Want) Their Parents' Attention

Given the amount of focus on and time spent with friends, it may surprise you that family remains the cornerstone of life for teenagers. For non-binary and transgender teens, family can be a vital source of support. Positive relationships with their parent(s) can be the single most critical factor for positive outcomes for these youth. All teens are looking for a sense of validation, caring, closeness, warmth, safety, and comfort from their families, but transgender and non-binary youth especially need this in order to more favorably weather the discrimination they face outside the home.

Many Transgender and Non-Binary Teens Feel Misunderstood

The results of the 2015 Canadian survey of transgender youth, *Being Safe, Being Me*, indicated that transgender youth feel their parents care about them. However, one-third of the youth surveyed did not feel that they had an adult in their family whom they could talk to, and 70 percent of them felt that their family did not understand them. This is further indication that, as parents, our love and care are not always felt in the ways that our teens need. Affirming parenting practices have been found to be very specific, leading teens to feel understood by their families and to know that their place in the family is secure. This in turn results in better outcomes for these teens.

Making Small Changes Can Make a Big Difference

Not only does FAP research show which specific behaviors are affirming and which are not, it also demonstrates that the degree of each matters as well. High, moderate, and low levels of non-affirmation are experienced by teens as rejection and associated with significantly different levels of risk. Youth from highly rejecting families were 8.4 times more likely to have attempted suicide, whereas those from moderately rejecting families were only twice as likely to have attempted suicide. This shows that even a moderate reduction of behaviors perceived by your teen to be rejecting can have a considerable impact. That bears repeating; even if you don't feel you can 100 percent get behind what your child tells you they need at this moment, just increasing your support in as many ways as you can will make a difference.

Parents who are not accepting, ambivalent, struggling, or still coming to terms with their teen's gender do not generally want to cause their child harm. If this is the situation with your child, understanding which of your behaviors as a parent could cause long-term harm to your teen and what specific things you can do to increase your teen's health and safety is essential.

Every family is unique. Various dynamics—religion, race, culture, financial status, or immigration status—impact the choices each parent makes. Perhaps you feel that certain parenting choices you make are keeping your teen safe in an environment they have to be in. Not allowing your child to dress a certain way, or wear their hair the length and style that they wish, or openly identify in a way that is consistent with their gender identity may seem to you like you are protecting them from possible mistreatment, harassment, and even violence. If this is the case, discuss your rationale with your child. It is an important distinction for them to know that you support their affirmed gender, but worry about dangerous conditions in a particular environment, rather than that you are ashamed, embarrassed, and/or disapproving of them.

However, even in the face of such grim possibilities, you must weigh the effects of your parenting approach on your child's long-term psychological well-being. It is important to recognize that many teens would rather risk the potential consequences associated with being who they genuinely are rather than have negative feelings about themselves because they are trying to appear to be someone they are not.

In order to be able to give your teenager the support they need, you may need to find appropriate support for yourself—ideally from someone who has some understanding about transgender youth; it could be from a therapist, friend, family member, or support group.

Consider the Impact of Your Approach

While you are integrating your child's gender identity or gender expression into your established beliefs, prioritize finding ways to separate your personal feelings about your child's gender from being able to provide for their basic needs for love and safety.

Your teen will forever remember the approach you chose to take in relation to their gender. Will your teen remember that they had your love and support? That you listened as they tried to figure out what was going on for them? That they could sit close or get a hug when they needed reassurance?

In a relatively short time, your child will be going through this without your day-to-day interaction as they move toward living on their own. Set the foundation with them now so they know they are never without someone to talk things through, to share moments of rejection and celebration, to simply be loved by someone who knows and values them. When your teen gives you the gift of sharing such a personal and vulnerable aspect of who they are, you have an incredible opportunity to demonstrate your unconditional love for them. By walking hand in hand with them along this journey, you will not only help them grapple with the many challenges they will face. You will also establish a life-long connection with them that you both will be able to cherish.

As parents, we are entrusted with the well-being of our children. If your child doesn't feel that you are in this process with them (again, this does not mean that you just go along with everything they want!), then they will move on without you. Potentially dangerous to your relationship going forward, this can also jeopardize their health and well-being. As you know only too well as a parent of a teenager, your window for helping your teen move from childhood to adulthood is limited. Even in the midst of your fears, you must meet your child where they are as you assist them to ultimately stand on their own.

It can take courage to offer the kind of support your child needs. You may subconsciously feel that your child should be the one guiding you in the process, that you should take your cues from them. If your teen is depressed, withdrawn, or anxious, you may erroneously assume that they must not really know what they are feeling. You may perceive their hesitation and guardedness around you to reflect inner confusion. Because of already-existent fears, you might believe that your support might "push them" toward the "wrong gender" and thus hold it back. Or you may believe that you have expressed a level of support and that your teen's response does not measure up to some predetermined level of relief you would expect to observe in them, again causing you to hesitate in continuing to provide it.

Your support may not translate, especially at first, into a clear, positive response from your teen. You may see residual fear of your rejection. Your teen might well be testing, consciously or unconsciously, whether your support is genuine. Hang in there. Make it clear that you and your love aren't going anywhere. In most cases, if your teen feels your support and can rest in the knowledge that you love them no matter what, their confidence will grow. This will increase their safety. If they know you are there for them and that they don't have to be something they are not to win your love, they can relax and feel sustained by your love.

The Effects of Different Parenting Practices on Your Child

The information we are about to share applies to all adults in a transgender or non-binary teen's life, not just parents. You can make a significant impact even if you are not a teen's parent. Having a caring and understanding person in their life will have positive impact and will model for them that there are people who accept them just as they are. Having just one reliably nonjudgmental person to turn to can mean the world to a teen who is not feeling loved and understood at home, or perhaps is no longer even welcome at home. Your support will make a difference even if you are having only short, periodic interactions with the teen. Your accepting smile and use of the correct pronoun could be the little bit of sunshine that sustains that teen until they come across another embracing person in their life.

Supportive parenting is affirming parenting—offering support and encouragement to a teen regarding their gender. Create an environment that feels safe for your teen to be who they are without shame, judgment, or pressure to be someone else. This level of understanding and acceptance helps them feel seen and validated. It allows your teen to trust that you love them unconditionally.

What Are Potentially Damaging Parenting Behaviors?

"Consider where you want to be five years from now: in a loving relationship with your child who knows you love them, or alienated because you won't accept them.... Don't let your pride get in the way of your love. You don't have to like the situation to love and accept your child."

Non-affirming behaviors undermine a teen's self-esteem and feelings of self-worth.

Refusing to accept your child as they are and behaving in an unkind, punitive, or disrespectful manner communicates to your child that you don't value them.

Parents sometimes resent their teen for causing disruption to the household without realizing that their own behaviors are contributing to family conflict. When a family tries to change their child's gender identity, blocks their connection to other transgender and non-binary teenagers, or forces them to wear clothes that are not true to their gender, they may believe they are acting out of care for their teen. They usually want to protect their child from the harm they assume their child will experience in the world if they were to express their authentic gender. However, when a teen feels that their parent can't accept who they are, they interpret this as rejection. Family conflict around gender can escalate to a point where the teen leaves home, is removed from the home, or is forced by their family to leave. This then leaves the teen vulnerable to becoming homeless or entering the child welfare or juvenile justice systems.

As you read this next section, try to have compassion toward yourself. Most, if not all, parents have employed at least one of these behaviors at one time or another. What is important going forward is to commit to modifying any damaging behaviors and implementing the affirming parenting behaviors (based on FAP's research) we describe in the following section so that your child perceives your actions as love and support.

Damaging Parenting Practices

"I could tell I wasn't what they wanted me to be."

"I view myself as a female, personally, but because of my home life, I haven't really been able to transition into being a female. I have to wait till I'm out of my mother's house. Most of my

*friends do say 'she' and 'her,' but if people call me 'he' and 'him,'
I really can't get mad, because...I look like a boy, so what am I
supposed to do?*

Each of the following practices invalidates your child and increases
their risks of substance abuse, depression, sex work, and self-harm
(including suicide).

Physical or Verbal Abuse

One of the most damaging things you can do is verbally or physically abuse your child. It won't get them to change who they are,
and it places them at a far greater risk for running away and suicide.
Protect your child from physical and emotional abuse in your home,
including transphobic or otherwise hurtful or degrading language
and bullying.

Exclusion from Family Activities

The urge to have your teen hide or change their gender in order to
avoid feeling embarrassed by them sends a message of shame. It
implies to your child that letting go of their core identity is required in
order to be a member of the family. Insisting they "dress properly" or
"act normally" makes your child feel that the comfort of others is more
important to you than their comfort and trumps their own sense of
well-being and security.

Blocking Access to Supportive Friends or Activities

Preventing your child from seeing non-binary or transgender friends
and allies or participating in gender-diverse activities will only generate
a sense of isolation and significantly increase risk factors. Blocking
your child's access to others like themselves not only cuts them off
from a critical support system, it also stigmatizes them.

Blaming Your Child for the Discrimination They Face

Saying that your child deserves the mistreatment they encounter simply for being who they are is incredibly dangerous. It is an implicit message that your teen is to blame for any cruelty they experience.

Denigration and Ridicule

When you speak or treat your child with disrespect or allow others to, it shows them that they cannot count on you for the love and protection they desperately need. Further, it encourages negative messages from the rest of the family and others, impacting your teen's ability to love themselves.

Religious-Based Condemnation

Hearing that your parents believe you are sinful and going against the teachings of your religion sends a painful message that you believe your teen is not a good person and that you feel they do not have inherent worth. Telling a child that god will punish them greatly increases health and mental health risks, and can compromise their faith or spiritual community as a vital source of solace. Gender is a complex matter in most faith communities, and individual beliefs are often easier to come by than specific doctrine. Each of the major religions has a tremendous range of teachings; if you are worried that your religion is opposed to gender diversity, it is worth the time to explore it further. There are some excellent resources on the Internet and in literature published on the topic. If you need further assistance, the Gender Spectrum website has some resources listed as well.

Distress, Denial, and Shame

When a child sees that they are causing their parents great distress and shame, they internalize this pressure. It is damaging to openly communicate the impact their gender identity or expression is having on your own life and happiness.

Silence and Secrecy

Insisting that your child remain silent about their gender identity tells them that there is something inherently wrong with them. If you are wanting your teen to remain silent out of fear for their safety outside the home, discuss this fear with them. In the absence of doing so, they can only assume that you are ashamed or embarrassed by them and do not want others to know about who they are.

Pressure to Enforce Gender Conformity

Asking your teen to mask who they are indicates there is something wrong with them, even when motivated by a desire to protect them. Teens hear your insistence on gender conformity as rejection. While your requests may be a way of addressing your fear of what might happen to your child in the outside world, ask yourself if there are other motivations as well, including those related to any discomfort you may have talking with coworkers, extended family members, and others regarding your child's gender.

Refusing to Use Their Preferred Name and Pronouns

Refusing to call a person by their preferred name and use the pronouns that feel appropriate to them invalidates them. This is an overt way of causing conflict and communicating that you do not support your teen's sense of themself. Each time you do not use their chosen name and preferred pronoun, you communicate that you know better than they do about who they are; it serves to lower their feeling of self-worth and distances you from your teen.

Examples of What Damaging Practices Look Like in Daily Life

"They out me to people I don't even know without asking me if I'm comfortable. My mom told her whole office about me before I was even out to my closest friends. They think it's OK to out ANYONE whenever it pleases them."

It's very difficult to see your child struggling, possibly in real pain and distress directly stemming from their gender and the stigma surrounding it. As parents, we want to alleviate our child's hardships, fix whatever we can, and protect them as best we can. We hear the stories and statistics about the violence and self-harm that transgender and non-binary people are subjected to. So it's understandable if you chose any of the following in response to learning about your teen's gender identity. However, please note that *these are examples of well-meaning but damaging parenting practices.*

- Trying to convince your teen that this is a phase and postpone addressing the gender issues they have identified. This might be as simple as suggesting that they drop it for now and if they feel the same way in six months or a year, you'll talk with them about it then.
- Making a deal with your child that you will support getting them clothes, accessories, etc., to "experiment" with privately at home if they agree to drop the discussion and dress "normally" at school and elsewhere in public.
- Suggesting keeping this a "family thing," not the whole family, such as grandparents, aunts, uncles, cousins—just the family they live with. "Nobody needs to know our family's business anyway."
- Invalidating their experience. This can happen in a number of ways:

- Appearing to validate their feelings ("Everyone feels that way sometimes—don't worry, it's just part of being a teenager")
- Dismissing their feelings ("Typical teenager—doing anything to be different")
- Undermining their understanding of self ("How do you know that it isn't just because you're having a hard time with friends, relating to the other girls/boys?" or asking "What if you change your mind? Remember when you loved the color pink and we painted your room and all your clothes were pink? How is it possible you think you're a boy now?")
- Disrespecting their needs related to identity ("It's OK if you have other people use this new name, but I don't think I would ever figure that out, so I'll just use your old name" or "You can change if you want, but you'll always be my son/daughter")

These kinds of behaviors and communications are damaging to your teen and your relationship. If you read these and aren't sure why they're harmful, don't be afraid to reach out to someone to discuss further. It's important. Let's turn now to what supportive parenting looks like so that you can make choices that affirm your teen in their gender and help them to weather the challenges related to their gender identity and/or expression.

What Are Affirming Parenting Behaviors?

"My advice to other parents is to love and support your child unconditionally at home. Transgender kids are faced with so much in the outside world that they need a place to feel safe, supported, and 100 percent LOVED!"

"My advice? Love your kid. No matter what their gender expression or identity is. That's not what matters. It matters that they're your kid, they're your family, and that they know that. They need to know that you love them and they are safe to be themselves with you."

Affirming parenting behaviors strengthen a child's self-esteem and sense of self-worth. It is important to take whatever steps you can to demonstrate to your child that you are with them on this journey. Accepting families come from all backgrounds—everyone can love, support, and validate their children. When children feel valued by their parents, they learn to value themselves.

Create a Supportive Family Environment

The ability to make your home a sanctuary of security and support for your child is an important factor in promoting their lifelong health and well-being. It creates a buffer for your child from the hardships they may face outside of the home. Creating such a space may not come easily for you, particularly if you are struggling with accepting your child's gender identity or expression, but as we've learned from the FAP research, each change you make toward affirming your child can have a tremendously positive impact.

Require Respect within the Family

"I personally asked (respectfully) the few people that were uncomfortable with the concept to please try to honor his request and use the new name/pronouns. Only one person was unable to choose to change the pronoun, but was willing to use the new name."

With immediate and extended family, it is imperative that you require and accept only kindness and respect for your child. While you may not be able to change other people's opinions, you can certainly dictate how you expect others to behave and speak around you and your child. It can be scary to make this demand of family members yet many parents report that once they've taken a stand on their child's behalf, they feel a great sense of relief and empowerment.

Allow Zero Tolerance for Disrespect, Negative Comments, or Pressure

> "With people we know, we expect them to use the right name and pronouns. If they slip up once, I let it slide, but if it happens again, I say 'they.' If they refuse to use the right pronouns, I have told people that I really don't want to be around them if they can't support my child (even my own mom)."

> "I really like it when my brother says things like—hey, that's my brother you are calling a freak. My dad always tries to ignore it, but I like it when my brother stands up for me that way."

A concrete way to demonstrate ongoing support for and acceptance of your child is to tolerate absolutely no negative comments about them, from anyone, whether your child is with you or not. This means following up with the people who make such comments in a firm way that makes clear your commitment to your child's well-being. It may also mean needing to follow up with other parents or the school about the comments made by staff or students. Be a model of accepting and affirming behavior for others to follow.

Allow Your Child to Naturally Express their Gender

What does this look like? It means allowing them to choose, without pressure or unspoken messages, the clothes they wish to wear, how and with whom they wish to spend their free time (as long as it is safe and consistent with your parenting practices for your children), the accessories they favor, the manner in which they wear their hair, and the decorations and images with which they surround themselves. Clothing and personal presentation are important elements of self-expression. This does not mean that anything goes. If you believe an aspect of their expression is inappropriate and would limit it for any of your children, then set the limit. But if it is a limit only for your trans-gender or non-binary teen, then this is a signal to them that you have an issue specifically with their gender.

Support Your Teen to Make the Decisions about Their Gender That Feel Best for Them

It may be critical for your child to have their external appearance reflect their sense of themselves. We all prefer congruence. Within your family's means and ability, and consistent with the limits you've established for your other children, find ways to support your teen's gender. Use their chosen name and pronouns and help them find any gender-related care that they need—these are very clear ways of showing validation and support.

Empower Your Child To Respond Positively And Safely To Difficult Circumstances

This means helping them prepare for any negative reactions they may encounter outside the home by practicing their responses with them and making sure, when appropriate, that there is a plan or safe adult for them to turn to in case they need assistance.

Maintain Open and Honest Communication with Your Child

"This is their [your child's] journey with gender, not yours. Realize that you can be wrong, and work toward understanding."

Stay open about this journey, both your child's and your own. Share with your teen your own evolving understandings about gender. By demonstrating to them that you are a partner in this process and showing a genuine sense of inquisitiveness about how they see themselves, what they think, and what they are experiencing, you show that you are there for them. This open level of communication will also help you to better assess your child's level of stress or distress, and whether they may need additional outside support or intervention. It is important to note, however, that you should discuss any negative or conflicting feelings you are struggling with over your child's gender identity or gender expression with other adults, *not* with your child.

Preparing the Foundation for Support

In the following chapter, Nurturing Your Teen's Resilience, we suggest concrete ways to demonstrate your ongoing support as you deal with practical situations in your life. For now, let's address the work you may need to do as a parent in order to be supportive of your teen.

Explore Your Own Gender History

Perhaps the most fundamental step you can take as a parent seeking to support your transgender or non-binary teen is to examine your own gender history. Everyone has a gender. Every one of us has been raised with particular ideas about gender instilled in us from the time we were born (and maybe even before!). Your own experiences with gender impact your perceptions of your teen's gender journey.

If we make our gender histories part of our family conversations, then gender becomes about all of us, not just about the one child who is "different." At Gender Spectrum, it is our mission to create more gender-inclusive and supportive environments for all children and youth. And as part of that mission, we hope to create dialogues around how gender affects every single person—not just transgender and non-binary people.

Gender norms and expectations are different now than when you were growing up, and they will continue to change. Many teens and young adults today experience and define their genders in ways most parents didn't even know existed when they were their age. It is important for parents to accept this new gender frontier and to take the time to think about how their children's experiences relate to their own experiences growing up. What assumptions have you made about gender based on how you were raised and the messages you received? Are these the only way to think about gender? How have gender norms affected you in ways you do or don't want them to affect your kids? These areas of personal exploration help to increase understanding of your child's gender, as well as your own, which can only help you become a better parent.

Heal Any Damage Already Done

"I was watching TV with my Nana one night and there was a show about transgender kids and I said—that's like me. I hadn't expected to come out to her, but I just did! She got really angry at me and said my mother never liked to wear dresses either, but she's not that way and I'm not either. She started lecturing me about how I'm almost an adult and I need to figure out my

life. We didn't talk about this again for months, and I started to avoid her and stayed away from the house as much as I could.… Then out of nowhere one day she came home after work and said she had talked with a friend at work who said some things that she wanted to talk with me about. I guess her friend has a niece who is transgender. She started asking me questions about why I thought I was a boy and I couldn't believe we were actually talking about this! I know she doesn't really get it yet, but at least I know that she cares about me and has a little bit of an open mind now. You have no idea how much that helps!"

Although it is difficult to acknowledge that you may have done things that you now realize could have been hurtful to or unsupportive of your child, recognizing your errors can go a long way toward lessening their impact. All parents make mistakes and bad decisions. Acknowledge yours and ask for forgiveness. After you have apologized, share with your teen the actions you are taking to learn how to be a better parent to them. Let them know again how much they mean to you.

Begin to build the bridge back to your teen. If you feel brave enough and the moment is right, ask what they need from you. Do not take offense if they tell you to leave them and their gender alone. At some point, you will ask and they will tell you. Rebuilding trust may take time. Do not lose hope if your teen is withdrawn from you. Your teen needs your love and care. Have the courage to be vulnerable. Show up for your teen in as many ways as you can. Write it down for them and speak to them directly about how much they mean to you—and that you are doing all that you can to get up to speed so you can be there for them. And most important of all—walk your talk by following through on any promises or commitments you make. They'll be paying attention to what you do more than to what you say.

Confront Your Anxieties So Your Parenting Is Not Fear-Based

"I know all parents worry about the safety of their teens, but I've always felt an extra burden on this front. I gave my child a phone earlier than I normally would have. I've taught them to always be aware of their surroundings, like checking out the street signs so they know exactly where they are if they need to call someone for help. I've told them I will pick them up anytime, anywhere with no questions asked (that's a hard one but worth it)."

It is perfectly normal for parents of transgender and non-binary teens to feel afraid and worried for their teen (actually, it's normal for parents to feel fear and worry for all of their kids). However, when fear dictates our actions, it can distort the best of intentions. When fear is behind the wheel, it can quickly turn concern into control and protection into policing. If you find that your thoughts or your speech are often focused on what could go wrong, what you want to prevent, or what you want to protect your child from, you are probably parenting from fear more than you think. Learning to cope with your emotions will allow you to remain focused on the present and start working together with your teen.

No matter how hard we try, we cannot protect our children from all danger. Given this, coming to terms with your fears will allow you to shift the focus of your parenting to supporting your teen's resilience and their healthy decision-making. This does not mean that you won't try to protect them in every way that you can. But you will do so with a clear head, honoring who they are and accounting for their needs as you seek to make decisions together about their gender. Moving from fear-based parenting to connection-based parenting will not only positively impact your relationship, but will also allow you to work together as a team to help your child strengthen their skills to handle both danger and adversity. Setting limits is part of parenting; just make sure that any limits you are setting around your teen's gender expression are there for the right reasons. When you keep your fear in check, you can more effectively explore options and better prepare your child to thrive in the world.

Address Bullying and Pressure within the Home

If you or other family members have utilized humiliation, pressure, force, or ridicule as means of interacting with your gender-expansive, non-binary, or transgender teen around issues related to their gender, it is time to put an end to that behavior. This is an essential step in creating a safe home for your child and may mean that certain shaming patterns and language will need to be changed.

Family bullying can include name calling, threatening, belittling insults, sarcastic remarks, humiliation, continuous criticism, exclusion, withholding affection, and physical punishment. Parents can mistakenly try to motivate their children into gender-normative behavior by being derisive. More subtle behaviors, such as eye rolling, sighing, talking under your breath, moving to another part of the room, or leaving the room when your teen enters, further communicate disregard for your teen's very existence.

The goal of shaming a child is to have them curtail their behavior or self-expression, and it contributes to negative beliefs and feelings about themselves. Demeaning actions that evoke shame are especially damaging. If these are longstanding family patterns of interaction, you may need support and guidance from a professional to learn new approaches to parenting.

Reset the Tone

If your relationship with your teen has become a cycle of negative interactions, consider pushing the pause button. You can intentionally reset the tone of your family interactions and parenting. It is a powerful practice. Spend some time focusing on the feeling that you wish permeated your family life and then practice living "as if" that is the case; eventually it will be.

Ongoing closeness and connection are possible even in the midst of your anger, confusion, fear, and grief. How do you want your child to feel? Reach out to your teen. It does not have to be over gender—in fact, it can be helpful to regularly take the topic of gender off the table. Strengthen your bond in other ways. Strive to regain or deepen your connection. Spend time with your child doing something you both like to do together. Find ways to laugh together. Talk about something that interests them. Communicate your love for them through your actions.

For adolescents in general, and non-binary and transgender teens specifically, evidence abounds regarding risk and protective factors present within the family. Establishing a secure base, being caring, creating connectedness, showing value, providing support, and embodying a sense of belonging are all linked to positive outcomes in adolescence and continue into adulthood. Shift your focus from trying to change your child to celebrating the child you have!

Next Steps for Truly Deepening Your Understanding

Educating yourself about gender and integrating your personal beliefs and experiences around gender with this new information will do more than help your family come to terms with your teen's authentic gender. It will also transform the way that you view the world and enrich your life by deepening your understanding of diversity in its many forms.

Gather Information

A very important step for getting comfortable and familiar with gender diversity is to gather as much information as possible. By doing so, you also demonstrate to your teen your commitment to understanding what they are experiencing and supporting them along the way. Educate and familiarize yourself about gender identity, gender expression, and sexual orientation. Read everything you can about the gender spectrum.

Meet People on Less Familiar Places of the Gender Spectrum

In order to address any discomfort or lack of familiarity you may have, it is very helpful to meet a variety of people all across the gender spectrum. This discomfort usually stems from having only socially stigmatized messages and images about individuals that were generally collected over time from the media and other aspects of popular culture. Be willing to call these preconceived ideas into question.

Once you are able to spend time with non-binary and transgender people, you are likely to become more comfortable. This will help you drop biases or judgments you might have and allow you to more fully embrace your own child. Although you can certainly read many people's stories online, or watch videos of people online, it is not the same as being engaged together and having the ability to connect one on one. An easy way to achieve this is by attending a conference or participating in a local group examining gender diversity.

Meet Other Parents Who Are Raising Transgender and Non-Binary Teens

"In trying to find a community for my child, I found a community for me.... These groups have really made a difference in our lives, not just in gender issues."

"It is a slow process to find a community of support. It is hard to predict people's reactions when they learn about my child. Some people are supportive and others are not, so friendships and relationships shift and change. It is a long journey and we are not at the end, but there is hope as more people come out as transgender."

One of the most common things we hear from parents with a non-binary or transgender child is the feeling of being alone as a family. There is no need to go through this experience alone. Support is available. There is nothing like meeting other parents going through the same thing to diminish your isolation, shame, or sense of being overwhelmed. It is also sometimes the only place we can truly voice our feelings without being judged about our parenting. Because gender is an innate part of who we are, gender-diverse teens come from all walks of life. Attending a parent support group in person or online, or attending a family conference can serve to normalize your personal situation. Many families attend a conference for the first time because they feel their family is in crisis and then return in following years because it is such an incredible resource of emotional support, practical information, resources, and community. At conferences, families are able to meet transgender, non-binary, and gender-expansive adults who are thriving, and their teens are able to connect with other teens and be in an environment of support and validation. To learn more about the support services offered by Gender Spectrum, please visit our website.

Empathy Exercises

Consider the following:

- What does gender mean to you?
- Have there been expectations placed on you because of gender? Look back at all the periods of your life with this question in mind: as a kid, as a teen, as an adult?
- Do you feel that you have complete self-determination over your gender?
- If you were to describe your gender to someone else, what would you say?
- How do the children in your life regard gender? How have you had an impact on their gender experience?
- Are there areas of your life where you are not completely free to determine what you do with your body? Are there times when your gender presentation is limited? If there are, how do you feel at those times or in those contexts?

Tell Your Extended Family and Friends

"I have been surprised by who has been accepting and who has not in my family. People I thought of as conservative and rigid have said things like 'as long as she is happy, I'm happy.' Others I thought would be in our corner have disappointed us. We had to rearrange a lot of our social circles, but they are stronger than ever."

First, talk to your teen about how they would like to handle issues of disclosure. Do they want to talk to family members and close friends?

Do they want you to? Include your teen in the communication strategy. After all, it is their story.

It can be nerve-wracking and scary to bring up the topic of your child's gender with family and friends. Once your closest friends and immediate family members are aware of your child's gender expression and gender identity, it may be hard if people who you have been close to you respond in a non-supportive manner. There is not just one way to deal with this situation, of course, as all family members and friends are different.

Remember that family members and friends are at different places in their understanding of gender diversity; recognize that while you've had some time to think about this (and think about it, and think about it…), this may be completely new to them. Despite their potential ignorance on the subject, you may find that people have a lot of opinions that they do not hesitate to share with you, whether they are close to your child or not. This is a time when being very clear about your expectations for the behavior of others is essential. It is one thing to be unknowledgeable about gender; it is something else when that lack of knowledge translates into mistreatment of or disrespect for your child.

One strategy to avoid some of the potential awkwardness and judgments is to call or write to family and friends before seeing them. Before communicating with others, spend some time identifying your expectations, and then be very explicit about what you are requesting of them. Let them know about your child's gender and that you are supportive of your child. Of course, it's natural for others to have questions; let them know they are welcome to ask you anything in private, but they should not talk about it in front of your teen or your other children. Let them know that regardless of their personal feelings, you expect them to be kind and respectful to your child. Make it clear that whenever they speak about your teen and family, you expect them to avoid negative comments about hair, clothes, mannerisms, etc. On the Gender Spectrum website, we have collected some sample letters that parents/caregivers have sent to family members and friends to assist you in this communication.

It can be helpful to remind your family and friends that your child is more than just their gender, and that they should see and relate to your whole child. If they are nervous, tell them what your child's current interests are so they will have some safe topics to discuss. Direct them to the Gender Spectrum website or offer some articles or books for them to read so they can learn more about gender diversity.

The more you learn to speak with confidence and pride about your child, the easier it will be for others to accept your child and your parenting. People will take their lead from you on how to respond and react to your child. You have nothing to apologize for or be ashamed of. Remember, it's your job to take care of your child, not the needs of other adults. A desire to help other people feel comfortable is natural, but if you find yourself doing so by denying or dismissing your child's authentic self, it can be quite hurtful. Your priority is your child's well-being.

Support All of the Children in the Family

"I didn't think about the fact that my younger child might be bullied because her sister is transgender. She didn't even mention it to us when it started happening. I don't think I would have ever found out about it if she didn't have a wonderful teacher who told us what was going on. This was a wakeup call for me. Thankfully, the teacher made sure the bullying stopped at school and I made sure that I spent more time with my younger daughter."

Sometimes having a non-binary, gender-nonconforming, or transgender family member can create a sense of perpetual crisis in a family (at least in the beginning). Because of society's discomfort with gender diversity, you may find yourself unconsciously bonding with your cisgender children more than the child you perceive to be the root of the family stress. In doing so, you may inadvertently place siblings in a position of choosing loyalties within the family. Alternately, you may focus on the tremendous needs of your transgender or non-binary child, overlooking the siblings as a result.

It is very important to stay in touch with all of your kids, especially during the process of adjustment. It can be difficult being the sibling of someone who is non-binary or transgender. Therapy may be helpful for siblings who may feel like they lost their brother or sister and are grieving, or are possibly dealing with bullying at school related to their sibling's gender. Parents frequently forget the impact that this can have on the other kids in the household.

A sibling of a transgender or non-binary teen can be anything from their best ally to their worst enemy. A sibling may act out in an effort to gain attention, possibly in ways that are hurtful to their gender-expansive sibling. For example, the sibling may "out" or disclose personal information about their transgender, non-binary, or otherwise gender-expansive sibling at inappropriate times or in a disrespectful manner. That's a lot of power and responsibility to hold, and it can be difficult for young people to feel as though they're keeping a "secret." This may be too much pressure. It may be necessary to strategize together to identify safe people they can share personal information and feelings with.

Your transgender, non-binary, or gender-expansive teen may be teased and bullied outside of the home by their own siblings. Siblings may participate because they feel pressure from their peers to ostracize or be critical of their transgender, non-binary, or gender-expansive sibling. On the other hand, some siblings feel obliged to defend their transgender or non-binary sibling from bullying by others. Siblings may be teased and bullied themselves.

One strategy to avoid the division between transgender or non-binary children and their siblings is to make sure your discussions about gender relate to all people. This not only avoids treating the transgender or non-binary child as if they are the "problem," but also helps support siblings in their experiences as well. The suggested exercises of examining your own gender can be used as good dinner-time conversation for everyone in the family.

Finding a Supportive Religious or Faith Community

"The other thing I did that I think helped was that I spoke to the pastor directly to make sure he would be behind the issue before asking his staff (i.e., youth group leaders) to change names/pronouns. Knowing I had his support before I potentially could have unwittingly created a division paved the way for the journey."

Acceptance of gender diversity can vary tremendously across different religious communities. If you belong to a religious community, it can be helpful to take stock of the degree of support you can find there as a family. You may want to reflect and create a list of the overt messages about gender that you hear from faith leaders and laypeople. You might identify people whom you perceive as "safe" to discuss what is needed for your family to be a welcome part of a religious community.

With sensitive exploration, you may find people in your religious community who are more tolerant than others. Some people find that they can educate their present religious community about gender diversity. Other families find they need to seek new religious communities that are more welcoming. In the process of supporting your child, you may well lose important people in your life, but more than likely, you will also gain some important new people to replace them. It is best if you can find ways to reconcile your faith with your love and support of your child. This will lessen the internal burden you carry and give you and your child the solace that faith can bring.

Moving Forward from Here

There are quite a few things that you can do to help increase the safety of the non-binary or transgender teen in your life. It is powerful to know that your choices can have a direct impact on their overall health and well-being. While fear can paralyze us, the ability to take meaningful action can mobilize us. The steps you start taking now will help guide you in the weeks, months, and years to come. Many parents of non-binary and transgender teens continue to work in the world to support wider understanding of gender diversity even after their own child has left home. It is a way of continuing to make the world a safer place for your child and all children.

When parents support their child, their child begins to blossom and bloom. Your support can directly increase their safety. Parents are often encouraged by the positive changes they see in their child as they begin to express their support more openly.

Insist on Safety at School

Be prepared to advocate on behalf of your child in their school setting. It is important that your child attend a school that will affirm their gender identity and gender expression.

It will be important to work with the school to ensure correct use of name and pronouns, your teen's privacy, bathroom and locker room options, grooming freedom, and dress code. If need be, you may need to challenge restrictive policies to allow your child to be able to be themselves at school. You may also need to insist that gender identity and gender expression clauses be added to their nondiscrimination policy and advocate for school-wide education on issues of gender diversity.

We have worked directly with hundreds of middle and high schools in the U.S. and other countries. We are more than confident in saying that when training and education take place, transgender, non-binary, and other gender-expansive students not only experience less harassment, but also find increased acceptance and understanding from their peers. The school climate itself undergoes a transformation, allowing greater safety for all students to express themselves. Schools we have worked with become more capable of responding to gender issues in general and those specific to particular students. Occasionally, a school is unwilling to engage in gender diversity training, is resistant to actively supporting its gender-expansive students, or is unwelcoming to the idea of your teen undergoing a gender transition at school. This can be incredibly frustrating and deflating, but know that you have a variety of tools at your disposal. Your family may decide to homeschool for a period of time or transfer your child to another school. However, do not assume that your child will not be safe at school.

Ensure That Your Child's Medical and Mental Healthcare Providers are Supportive

Although you may need to advocate for your child in the healthcare system, keep searching until you are able to locate compassionate and affirming providers. You will want to find someone who does not try to suppress your child's gender expression or gender journey and recognizes that gender diversity is a naturally occurring aspect of humanity. Together with these providers, you can safely explore regular health and mental health issues and also concerns directly related to gender. By supporting your child in finding knowledgeable healthcare providers willing to provide them with appropriate healthcare services, you will be decreasing the chances of your teen resorting to buying hormones over the Internet or on the street and from engaging in dangerous activities to procure them. Affirming providers can be found anywhere—you do not need to go to a specialty gender clinic or a healthcare professional who identifies as a gender specialist in order to find proper care for your child. Instead, focus on the degree to which a care provider is affirming in their interactions with you and your teen. There is a growing body of gender specialists to whom they can turn for consultation about the technical aspects of care, if needed.

Finding a Knowledgeable Primary Care Provider

Your family needs a primary care provider who is familiar with and comfortable working with transgender and non-binary youth. At the very least, you need a care provider who is fully accepting and willing to continue to educate themselves on pertinent healthcare issues related to gender. If your care provider does not fit this description, then ask them for a referral to a provider who is or seek a referral elsewhere.

Bias in the medical establishment is widespread when it comes to transgender and non-binary patients. Unfortunately, many transgender and non-binary people report harassment, disrespect, and discrimination from care providers. Sometimes, they are even turned away from services due to their gender identity or gender expression. Cisgender people usually do not risk these factors when seeking healthcare.

Your teen's primary healthcare provider can refer your family to gender specialists; they should also coordinate with all of your teen's specialists to ensure that appropriate collaboration occurs when needed. That way, when one provider initiates or adjusts a medication, such as hormones, all other medicines can be adjusted or monitored accordingly.

Search Out Role Models and Mentors

All youth need positive role models and mentors for their healthy development. It allows them to be inspired and to see a positive future for themselves. Depending on where you live, you may need to put some effort into seeking out such mentors. If you do not find any in your community, seriously consider traveling to a conference or gathering in support of gender diversity.

Welcome Your Child's Non-Binary, Transgender, and Gender-Expansive Friends into Your Home

When you welcome people of all gender identities and expressions into your home, you make a clear communication that gender diversity is OK with you. You also communicate your support for your teen getting to know other transgender and non-binary youth. Consider attending events together that focus on gender or transgender issues where you both will learn more about gender and meet gender-diverse people.

When Parents Begin to Relax (It Happens!)

For many parents, the shift comes when they start to be able to truly envision a happy future for their child. This may be the result of seeing your child come out of their shell as they move forward with your support. Maybe they are smiling a bit more, or their curiosity has returned. It may come from meeting gender-diverse adults who have happy marriages, children, and successful jobs. It may come from seeing positive images of transgender characters on major TV shows, or from the realization that the Pentagon has lifted the prohibition on openly transgender people serving in the military, then acceptance is coming from all areas of our society. As education, awareness, and understanding of gender diversity increase, discrimination and

violence naturally decrease. Over time, you will begin to have faith
that it will all work out for your child, and you'll begin to sleep again
at night.

Imagine Joy

It's important to keep the challenges your child faces in mind so that
you don't forget how important it is to provide them with the necessary support. But it is only one part of the story. Most transgender and
non-binary adolescents successfully move into adulthood and create
fulfilling lives for themselves, including loving relationships with partners, children, and communities of faith. Imagining the possibilities
that may ensue as a result of a happier, healthier teen is really important. Consider for a moment your teen feeling fully seen and loved by
those closest to them.

Your child is navigating their path toward a happier life. They
know what it looks like better than anyone else. You can play a critical
role in making this future a reality. Something great can arise from
this journey.

> "Having a transgender child has enriched my life in ways that
> I didn't know were possible; from the people I have met to the
> stripping away of years of stereotyping and misinformation. I
> discovered myself to be a vocal ally for my child and those like
> her with an ease I didn't think possible. Every day is a challenge
> and brings questions—and every day I feel like I am a better
> person because my daughter is who she is."

Chapter 11

Nurturing Your Teen's Resilience

"This will be a lifelong process. Just support and love your child through it all. It makes a world of difference to them."

"It is crazy hard some days, but I remind myself that my family loves me. I can get through this."

DESPITE THE CURRENT PROGRESS BEING made in society to increase awareness of gender diversity in today's youth, the world remains a difficult and sometimes hostile place for transgender and non-binary teens. Nonetheless, there are many transgender and non-binary teens and adults who exhibit clear signs of resilience. They have a good self-image, thriving relationships with family and friends, and a strong sense of belonging and connectedness. The great news is that as a parent there are very specific things that you can do to help your child survive and thrive in the world we live in.

Your role in the life of your teen is very powerful. You may not be able to prevent all hardship, bias, discrimination, and other painful life experiences they may encounter, but your love and encouragement will go a long way. Through resilience-based parenting approaches, you can actively nurture and nourish their resilience every day, fostering their capacity to cope and handle the stressors in their lives.

What Is Resilience?

Resilience is a person's ability to withstand and recover from stress and daily challenges. It requires an ability to adapt to changing circumstances and continue going in the face of adversity. A resilient person is able to thrive despite the setbacks and difficulties experienced in day-to-day living.

Some people are more naturally resilient than others. In fact, research indicates that people may come into the world with varying levels of resilience to meet life's stressors. However, this baseline can be boosted; there are things you can do to help your teen increase their capacity to be resilient.

How well any child copes with stress, uncertainty, and change is directly related to what they believe about themselves and the level of connectedness and sense of belonging that they feel. As we explored previously, lack of connectedness and belonging, as well as perceived burdensomeness, are some of the highest predictors of depression and suicidality. So, when you strengthen your bond with your children, you strengthen their resilience. Resilience in the face of harassment, discrimination, and stigma is of particular importance, as the risk factors associated with these stressors for transgender and non-binary youth are high.

The biggest building block in fortifying resilience in transgender and non-binary teens is solidifying a positive gender identity.

Having a strong, positive, and integrated identity requires the following:

- Embracing self-worth
- Defining one's own identity
- Having a positive sense of the future

The key components that support these goals are:

- Family acceptance
- Social support (peers, community, and professionals)
- Identity pride

You can help your teen with all of these, most importantly by enhancing their self-esteem, affirming their gender, and doing everything you can to increase their sense of belonging and connectedness.

Ideally, actively fostering resilience should begin when your child is young and continue throughout their life. However, it is never too late to begin. Even if the connection between you and your child has been damaged, there are things you can do now to repair and rebuild your connection and foster resilience.

Specific Conditions that Build Resilience in Transgender and Non-Binary Youth

Protective factors are conditions or characteristics in individuals, families, and communities that build resilience, promote healthy development, and help prevent unhealthy behaviors, thereby reducing the negative effects of stigma. They include specific strengths, skills, coping strategies, and resources. They can be internal qualities, such as the ability to be reflective and recognize personal strengths, or conditions related to the external environment, such as a safe and welcoming religious community or a supportive family. These protective elements allow a person to thrive in the face of known challenges.

Each of these protective factors should be considered within the cultural contexts of your family. Families express love and support differently. Some are more likely to use verbal expressions (e.g., saying "I love you"), while others may use physical contact such as hugs, or communicate love and support through actions and doing special things together. Most use some combination of these. As you read through the following suggestions, consider how they are right for your family and what your child seems to respond most positively to.

So what are the specific protective factors and strategies to help reduce risks? The information we will share with you comes from both research and our experience working with thousands of families. Resilience-based parenting focuses on intentionally incorporating these protective factors and strategies into your day-to-day parenting. Doing so will help you support your child and provide them with as great a chance of success for true self-acceptance as possible.

The protective factors we will focus on are organized into six areas:

- Create a base of family love and acceptance
- Support your teen's gender journey
- Develop positive self-esteem
- Maintain physical health
- Increase affirmative social support and gender pride
- Strengthen your teen's ability to withstand and recover from adversity

Your love, when directed in these ways, is protective. We could summarize the entire chapter in these words: Accept your teen for who they are and make sure they know that you love, accept, and value them.

Increasing Parental Resilience

Just as it is important to foster resilience in your teen, it is valuable to foster resilience in yourself. The journey of parenting a non-binary or transgender teen can require you, at times, to dig deep. You want to have a renewable well of inner strength to draw on. You need to be able to bounce back from the unexpected challenges. You may want to take an inventory of your personal coping skills. Do you respond to stress in a healthy way? There is always room for improvement when it comes to self-care. This is especially so if you find yourself turning to old habits in times of stress such as unhealthy or disordered eating, substance use/abuse, and suboptimal communication patterns. Connect with a community of other parents raising transgender and non-binary children. This will help you gain perspective, as well as gain support from others who understand what you are going through. Create a network of support for yourself. Take the time to identify who in your life is supportive of your teen and understands their gender, people who can be there for you without judging you or your child. This may be friends, family members, community elders, or religious or spiritual leaders. Consider whether this may be a good time for personal or couples counseling.

Strengthening Your Partnership

If you are raising your child with a partner, managing the issues related to your child's gender will be stressful for all involved. In the beginning, you may find that you have time for little else. There may be discussions with friends and family, medical and therapy appointments, meetings at school, etc. When you get a moment alone with your partner, you spend your time bringing each other up to date and discussing where to go next. If you have other children, you're trying to stay connected with them as well, worried that they may get lost in all that is going on in the family. Before you know it, your relationship with your partner goes from stressed to fraying, and you struggle to find the comfort and support you once provided to one another. Try to take time out to care for and nurture your partnership along the way. Consider setting regular date nights when you agree not to talk about the kids. Find whatever ways work for you to continue to grow and strengthen your connection to one another.

Continue Moving Forward, Even in Grief

There are times when we simply think we can't possibly bear what's happening. It is too much for us to adjust to. It is too much to see our children have to suffer, too much worry, too little sleep. It is overwhelming. This is grief. Grief comes in waves. You can be long past the initial adjustment, feel at peace and complete acceptance of who your child is, and yet something will trigger the feelings of pain, loss, or injustice and it all comes back again. Ride the waves of grief. They too will pass. And tomorrow, get up again and find the strength to fight another day in support of your child.

Adapting to Changing Circumstances

Being resilient includes the ability to adapt to changing circumstances; as a parent, that includes continual learning to enhance your parenting skills. Assess your areas of strength and areas where you would like to improve as a parent. If you identify gaps in your skills, or have an interest in building a stronger base of knowledge in an area, don't hesitate to take classes, listen to podcasts, watch videos, talk to friends and colleagues about issues—anything that helps you feel confident and capable about the parenting skills that matter most.

Create a Base of Family Love and Acceptance

"I heard her crying one night and I went in there and hugged her and kept asking what was wrong. She sobbed, 'I feel like a boy' and just kept crying and crying. I reassured her that everything was going to be OK and that we loved her no matter what."

Transgender and non-binary teens who experience unconditional love from their immediate and extended families tend to thrive and are linked with higher self-esteem, greater resilience, better long-term health, and increased success in adult relationships. The love and support your teen receives from family will help them to achieve a healthy sense of self. By encouraging your teen to develop their own identity within a nurturing home, you are providing them with the greatest opportunity for long-term success. When you actively encourage your teen to become who they are (and not who you imagined them to be), you provide an invaluable service to them. This requires an ever-changing balance of setting boundaries and being flexible, holding on and letting go, and protecting while allowing room for them to learn from their mistakes.

"I was born Mexican within the matriarchal system where there is no space for the nontraditional or unconventional. Despite loving us so much, my family could not understand [my transgender daughter] and condemned what was happening. I thought that we would have to live far from my family, that I would have to lose the love and respect of everyone, so I pleaded with my mother to attend the annual Gender Spectrum Conference. Gender Spectrum assigned my mother a translator since I did not want to be with her in fear of her judgments.

I was scared to talk to her at the end of the conference. My mother hugged me and cried for a long time in the lobby of the hotel, surrounded by all the parents, teenagers, and children who attended the last day of workshops. She apologized to me for not understanding before and told me about the families who she had met and spoken to through the translators of both languages, a family from Japan, another one from China, Germany, and several families from Latin America and she told me their stories and information she had learned. She told me it was difficult for her to understand all of it but that she would continue trying to understand and learn more.

Two nights later I received a call from my brothers. My mom, using her matriarchal rights, had spoken with everyone by phone and explained what she had seen and learned at the conference and told them that they had apparently made a mistake in judging and that everyone should read the information that I had sent to them. My brothers apologized and said that they would try to learn, that they loved us and were waiting for us again for Christmas in order to meet their new niece. This event gave light to my life. I had recovered my family thanks to the transformation that education had inspired in my mom!"

Dedicate Time to Your Relationship

Your teen needs you to spend time with them, to be available, to listen and guide them. While it may take time for you to absorb and integrate your teen's gender identity or authentic self-expression, do all that you can to remain a reliable parent. If you take the time to listen and respond with care and sensitivity to your child, you increase the chances of bringing your family together in a deeper and more meaningful way.

Pursue your child's interests together as a way of investing in your connection. Meet them in their world; do not think they should always join you in yours. You can also invite your teen to join you in something they know is important to you, as long as you are not pressuring them to like the same things you enjoy. Find shared interests. Take a class together; learn a new hobby together; have a shared TV show or game. Ask your teen to introduce you to their music or show you how to play their favorite game. It can become a vehicle for connection and a self-esteem builder as your teen becomes the teacher and you the learner.

Be Persistent Even When You're Getting Mixed Messages
Adolescence is a time when your support should be available and accessible, even as you learn to give your teen more personal space. It's not easy: Back off too far, and they may experience it as rejection; not far enough, and they may feel like you are smothering them. Let them know what you're doing and why so they see it as an expression of your love and understand that you're trying to provide the right balance for their needs. Stay involved and available with your time, listening ears, and hugs. You may need to find new ways to foster connection as they continue to individuate and define who they are. Keep trying, even if they don't always seem interested and even if they have pushed you away in the past. Ask them for feedback on what kinds of connection feel best to them, what they would like more of and what they would like less of.

Parent with Empathy
Empathy, the ability to be aware of and sensitively respond to another, is the key to connected parenting. When a person is parented with empathy, there is less room for loneliness and the accompanying fear, depression, anxiety, and despair. This helps a teen feel safe and loved, which directly relates to being able to envision a positive future.

Communicate Your Love
Do everything you can to consistently communicate to your teen that they are wanted, unconditionally loved, valued, and cherished.

When you feel good about your teen, take the time to acknowledge it to them directly. Speak highly of your teen to others in their presence. Remember to show your love in ways that they experience as being loved and that feel right in the context of your family.

Show Appreciation

Show appreciation for your teen. It's easy to focus on the things that aren't being done—the messy room, the dirty dishes, the missing homework assignment—and forget to acknowledge everything that's going well. Notice the small things: "I love that you carry in the groceries. It is very helpful to me. Thank you." Appreciation is an act of recognition. Your teen will feel connected as a valued family member when you express appreciation for both the good they do and the bad they don't do.

Share with your teen what you are enjoying about them as they mature. Notice their positive character development and let them know that you like to see it. Show respect for their feelings. Make room for their point of view; this will aid you both in the transition to an adult relationship.

Actively Listen

If you want your teen to share with you what is important to them, be accessible. Put aside electronic (and other) diversions when you talk. Of course, finding time to talk can be difficult with teens because if you're not available when they want to talk, the moment may pass and they may no longer be in the mood. Do your best to take opportunities when they arise. Invite your teen to tell you about what they are thinking and feeling. Our experience is that active listening skills are most effective with teens (and probably with the rest of us too). Ask open-ended questions. Spend more time listening than talking. Try not to interrupt, "solve" their problems, or judge what they're saying. Repeat back to your teen what you heard them say; this will help them feel heard and encourage them to explain further or keep going. Active listening does not mean that you agree: You are simply understanding and respecting their perspective.

Support Your Teen's Gender Journey

Family support helps your teen develop a strong, integrated, and positive identity. Through your connected and supportive family relationships, you can help foster the development of your teen's sense of self, and your family will serve as a stabilizing force in your teen's life.

Express Overt Acceptance of Your Teen

One of the best things you can do for your child is to value their individuality. Encourage their self-expression and honor their uniqueness. Resist any urge to tell your teen how to think or feel—especially in regard to issues connected to their gender. This can interfere with healthy development and cause shame. When your teen feels accepted and affirmed by you, their own self-acceptance and overall feeling of self-respect improve.

Let Them Know That You Think They Can Do This

Your teen needs to know that you believe in them and their ability to navigate the gender journey they are on. Your belief will help them believe in themselves.

Affirm Your Teen's Gender

Everyone wants to be seen and recognized for who they are. Being fully accepted is part of feeling a sense of belonging. Being accepted for who they are and treated by others as they see themselves are important for transgender and non-binary teenagers, and they increase feelings of happiness, belonging, and self-worth and decrease levels of distress. You affirm their gender when you proudly reinforce to others how much you love and support your child.

Support Your Child's Journey to Congruence

Feeling congruent is a crucial element of self-acceptance and positive identity integration. Every person's journey to align these different parts of their gender is unique. Your teen will need your support in aligning their identity with their body and external presentation.

Decisions around congruence are very personal; there are often many layers involved in aligning one's outer appearance with one's gender identity. Teens who are supported in creating congruence between their inner experience of their gender and their socially expressed gender, whether through clothing, medical, and/or legal means, experience deeper peace with themselves, greater contentment with life, and more meaning in their relationships with others.

Research shows that for transgender and non-binary people, living as one's authentic self leads to greater confidence, personal comfort, and connectedness with others. Alignment also leads to reduced anxiety and is directly related to lowered rates of depression as well as a reduction in suicidal thoughts and attempts.

This is a delicate time in your relationship. Navigate it carefully, but know that you are not alone. There are support groups (in person and online) and other resources to help you sort through the feelings that may come up for you. Reach out—support is available.

Medical Congruence

A 2016 study by Jaclyn White Hughto and Sari Reisner from Harvard and Yale found that hormone therapy for transgender people leads to significantly improved psychological functioning after three to six months. After twelve months on hormone therapy, quality of life is improved. If your teen and their healthcare providers believe hormones are important for your teen, seeing hormone therapy as a medically necessary, rather than elective, treatment for the health of your child may help you come to terms with them.

Gender Dysphoria

Gender dysphoria is something commonly experienced by transgender and non-binary youth. It is the experience of feeling discomfort or distress with parts of their body, specifically in the ways they feel it doesn't accurately reflect their experience of their gender. Lots of different things can make some one feel dysphoric, including their genitals, hair growth (or lack of it), breast size, voice pitch, etc.

Not all non-binary and transgender people have dysphoria. And for those who do, every person experiences it in their own way. The remedy for dysphoria depends on the severity of the feeling. For some, this feeling is unbearable and can lead to hopelessness, self-loathing, severe depression, and suicidality. For others, it is something that comes and goes, but isn't a serious or significant issue. Dysphoria is an important matter to acknowledge and discuss with your child on an ongoing basis, even if they are already utilizing various means to address congruence needs.

Identify Positive Aspects of Being Transgender or Non-Binary

> *"I find that living beyond the binary allows me to see things more clearly. I am not concerned so much with what other people think. I get to spend that same energy elsewhere in my life. I feel more free than most people I know!"*

> *"I feel like I really know myself. My friends who haven't had to struggle with their gender haven't really had to look in the mirror and ask 'Who am I?' until they find the answer. I think that makes me more sure of myself."*

> *"Being trans has deepened my inner well of compassion. I feel like I can empathize with anyone going through personal struggles, anyone who feels alone, and anyone who experiences prejudice."*

As adults, we know that it is always possible to see a positive side to almost any situation if you look for it; it's helpful to start sharing this perspective with your teen. Learning to view the gifts in our challenges is a life skill that serves everyone. It boosts confidence and creates meaning, both of which help us to create the life we desire, even when it seems the world around us isn't helping. Positive narratives of identity encourage authenticity as they reduce shame and replace it with pride. So it's useful to frame your child's gender experience as positively as possible. Focus on the positive aspects of being transgender or non-binary such as the ability to explore who they truly are in a way that many cisgender people do not. Encourage your teen to share with you any positive experiences or attributes they find related to being transgender or non-binary.

Research indicates that just inquiring about a teen's positive experiences actually helps. Many come to find that they have greater empathy, inner strength, and higher levels of self-awareness from the experience of claiming their gender and having met and overcome so many challenges.

Develop Positive Self-Esteem

"I am profoundly impressed with my (trans) son. He knows himself so deeply and is so self-reflective. The other day, he explained to me that he feels like he is an overachiever in life because of the fact that he is transgender and feels inside of himself a deep need to prove himself. He expressed that although this is not ideal, and he is working on deepening his self-worth, he is choosing to use his achievements to propel him into a career of medicine."

Resilience is closely connected to positive self-esteem and self-confidence. Self-esteem is the belief that you are a worthwhile person who is capable of meeting life as it comes. Healthy self-esteem exists when a person believes that they are competent to meet life's challenges and are worthy of being loved and accepted. Parents, more than anyone else, can enhance their child's self-esteem. Your positive love and attention have a great impact on how your child feels about themself.

A teen with high self-esteem will be able to:

- feel a sense of self-worth and value,
- enjoy healthy relationships,
- tolerate frustration,
- handle their emotions responsibly (most of the time),
- step into roles of responsibility,
- have a sense of what they want or need,

- be comfortable with change, and
- accept challenges and take calculated risks.

On the other hand, a teen with low self-esteem will:

- feel unloved and unwanted,
- feel they have little or no inherent value,
- be easily influenced by others,
- avoid trying new things,
- blame others for their own shortcomings,
- feel burdensome,
- have little ability to tolerate frustration, and
- devalue their own talents and abilities.

Part of self-esteem comes from being treated with love and respect. Being around positive role models also enhances self-esteem. Self-esteem and self-worth can be built; it requires intentional and mindful effort to build or rebuild self-esteem in your teen. If you're not sure how to help your child in this way or would like feedback on what you're doing to try and help your child, don't hesitate to reach out to others for help. Whether it is a friend, family member, faith leader, or therapist/counselor, it can be helpful to get an outside perspective.

Self-Esteem Is Linked to Confidence

Self-esteem and self-confidence both help us face the challenges of life. People who feel good about themselves experience greater ease, which leads to feeling confident about their place in the world. When someone's self-esteem is high, they can see their strengths and positive qualities, which give them the confidence to try new things and take greater risks. If things don't work out as hoped, a person with high self-esteem and high self-confidence will view it as an exception rather than the rule and an opportunity to learn from.

On the other hand, low self-esteem reduces confidence; when self-worth is low, self-doubt takes over. When you don't respect yourself, confidence is diminished. It is easy to feel uncertain and less secure in adolescence for all teens, but this potential is dramatically increased if a teen is struggling with elements of their identity or if they are facing rejection due to their identity.

The physical changes of adolescence often impact a teen's confidence by making them feel self-conscious. Add to this the possible dysphoria of feeling like their body is betraying them, or other gender related body issues, and your teen's confidence can really be undermined. When teens feel self-conscious about their bodies, it impacts their overall confidence and how they feel about themselves. This can make them especially anxious in new situations as where typical teenage insecurities are often exacerbated.

If you notice that your teen is isolating, not participating in group activities, or giving up easily on interests they pursued before, they may be struggling with their confidence. It will help them to talk about it, especially if they feel that you are really listening to them. Your teen may not be seeing areas they are managing competently; helping them to see other areas of their life that they are managing effectively, and how they have done so in the past, will help your child to see themself more clearly. Your child has strengths and capabilities—like the rest of us, they may just need to be reminded what they are.

Confidence is an important element for all teenagers in making healthy, informed decisions. Confident teens are able to know and accept both their strengths and their limitations without relying on the opinions of those around them. Confidence allows a teen to avoid situations that are not right for them and to find ones that are. Confidence encourages growth as it allows teens to try new things and take more risks. Increased confidence also communicates to others that they are comfortable with themselves and aren't looking for anyone else's approval; this naturally leads to greater social acceptance.

Self-Esteem and Emotional Intelligence

Emotional intelligence is the ability to identify, understand, and manage your emotions. Supporting your teen in learning to recognize and control their emotions and resolve conflict amicably will serve them throughout their lives. These necessary life skills help tremendously in bolstering self-confidence and self-esteem. They also create a pathway to greater connectedness and resilience. Talk with your teen about the ways in which you work (and sometimes stumble) with your own emotional intelligence. It helps them to know they're not alone and that in fact we all work on this throughout our lives.

Positive emotions, good health, and strong social connections all influence each other; improving one of these areas helps improve the others and increases overall happiness and well being. According to a 2014 study by the American Psychological Association, adolescent stress levels are surpassing those of adults. Another study, conducted in 2013 of more than 123,000 college students (not transgender or non-binary specifically) from over one hundred fifty colleges, showed that more than one-third of the college students surveyed experienced intense depression, and more than one-half experienced overwhelming anxiety. Stress levels coupled with a lack of emotional intelligence are creating a significant crisis for many youth today.

Studies show that emotional intelligence can be learned and directly leads to stronger friendships, improved conflict resolution skills, greater academic achievement, and less stress. In fact, Lady Gaga's Born This Way Foundation and the Yale Center for Emotional Intelligence teamed up to bring awareness to the pivotal role that emotions play in successful development for youth in the Emotion Revolution Summit. Yale Center for Emotional Intelligence has also partnered with Facebook to create Inspired, an online resource center for teens and educators to foster social and emotional learning. Boosting your teen's emotional intelligence can not only act as a buffer against hopelessness, depression, and suicide—it can positively affect their overall health and well-being.

Teach Your Teen About Affirmations

One way to enhance self-esteem and self-awareness is to reduce the amount of negative thoughts your teen has on a daily basis. Negative self-talk can be very powerful because we tend to believe what we tell ourselves, especially when we repeat it frequently. Self-esteem naturally increases as a person moves away from negative thinking. We can teach our teens how to talk to themselves differently and show them the positive impact that can have on their daily lives.

An affirmation can help replace a negative thought with a more helpful positive one. Affirmations are repeated phrases that focus on what someone wants out of life. They are stated in the first person and are positive and concise. You may have learned to use affirmations to reach the goals you have set for yourself in your life. For many people, they are effective for a positive focus or helpful in attaining a specific goal. Affirmations can be related to anything your child is working on. Examples include "I am beautiful just the way I am," "I am capable of knowing myself and what I need," "I am worthy of love and respect," and "My uniqueness is my strength." Teaching your teen the power of these spoken, sung, or written words is a tool they can use to turn around negative thinking and instill positive thoughts. In the same way, when your teen has a thought like "I'm never going to be loved and accepted for who I am," have them practice consciously interrupting it with "I am surrounding myself with people who love and accept me." Eventually, the negative self-talk will lessen.

One way you can help your teen get a boost of self-esteem and show them the power of affirmations firsthand is to create an affirmations jar. Write some great things about your child in a jar and leave it in a central place. They can take one out every day. There are affirmation apps for teens available that they can download onto their phones with the focus of supporting healthy self-esteem. Repetition is key when building new habits. If your teen thinks this sounds cheesy, tell them that any negative self-talk they have today is also a repetition of what they have been saying to themselves. It's about time we put that repetition to good use and say something positive to ourselves!

Introduce the Power of "Yet"

If you hear your teen declaring that they can't do something, encourage them to add a "yet" to the end of the statement. "No matter how hard I try, I can't shoot a three-point shot." You add, "It is true, you can't shoot a three-point shot yet. Keep trying!" Carol Dweck has written an excellent book that you and your teen can read entitled *Mindset* that explores concrete ways of altering the way you think about things in order to achieve greater success.

Encourage Your Teen to Share Their Feelings

Part of why some teens fail to develop emotional intelligence is because they keep their deepest emotions to themselves. Encourage your teen to share their feelings with you. Let them know that it is common to have more than one feeling simultaneously. Help your teen learn to identify and name their feelings. Just being able to label one's emotions can bring a heightened level of clarity and self-awareness. Improved emotional intelligence can result in widespread benefits for your teen including better moods, increased resilience, and more overall enjoyment of life.

Teach Your Teen to Recognize and Address Stress

It is best to address stress with your teenager immediately. Listen, be open, and be ready to advocate on their behalf, seeking support when needed. Stress is contagious; monitor your own stress levels so your stress does not spill over onto them (and vice versa). If your teen is just learning to be emotionally aware, they may not realize when they are stressed. If you notice their stress level is on the rise, gently and respectfully point this out. This will help them to recognize the same feeling and connect it to stress the next time it occurs.

Teach the Art of Managing Emotions

Once your teen is able to recognize and identify their own emotions, the next step is to learn how to control them. This is a difficult but important step. Learning to be appropriately expressive with one's emotions is a tall order that takes practice and patience (and acceptance that you're not always going to get it right). Central to resilience is the development of coping skills to restore emotional equilibrium following an overwhelming emotion or negative event. Coping skills help to dissipate overwhelming feelings. Teaching teens that they have the power to manage their feelings helps them know they can do something to gain control of how they feel and shift it.

Help Your Teen Learn Mindfulness

Emotional awareness can naturally lead to emotional stability. Teach your teen to practice staying in the moment and trying to be aware of exactly what they are feeling and thinking. Just recognizing what's going on for them emotionally and physically, instead of just feeling overwhelmed by emotion, is an important step toward emotional stability. Many teens find meditation practices helpful as well. There are courses and books targeted specifically at teens.

Help Your Teen Choose Emotionally Stable Friends

Emotional drama can be contagious. If your teen is surrounded by emotionally unstable friends or people who have frequent and dramatic mood swings, it may be a good time to encourage opportunities to meet new people. Supporting new opportunities is different from suggesting that your teen no longer hang out with their friends. Your teen will resent you if they feel you are judging their friends or trying to limit their time with friends. However, they may enjoy new activities that expose them to new people, and friendships may organically form out of those contexts.

Develop Conflict-Management Skills

An important element of emotional maturity is learning how to resolve conflicts amicably rather than acting out impulsively and getting into trouble. Share with your teen that conflict is inevitable and healthy. They can't ignore a conflict, but it is best to share their feelings and really listen to the other person. In the moment, it can feel as though the most important thing is to be right or to win an argument, but negotiating a solution to a problem is the win in the long term.

Maintaining Boundaries and Expectations Is (Still) Important

> "After he came out, we were kind of lax about enforcing our rules, like curfews and screen time. Then his brother called us on it. 'Just cause he's a guy now doesn't mean he gets to do whatever he wants, does it?' We realized we still had to parent our kid!"

It's easy to get off-track sometimes in our parenting. Shifts in family dynamics, changes that a family member is going through, or even a modification in schedules like the transition from school year to summer can throw our regular boundaries, routines, and expectations off-kilter for awhile. If you realize this is the case in your family, that enforcing boundaries has taken a back seat to focusing on your child's gender issues, it may be important to get back to "regular life." Your teen still needs you to uphold family rules and values, and any other children you may have need to know that while some things are changing, they can count on many things to remain the same. Likewise, respectful, loving limits are positively correlated with decreased depression, moral development, impulse control, and healthy peer choices. You may all find comfort in the familiarity of the normal life.

Be Involved and Aware

It is still very important to be involved in your teen's day-to-day life and activities. Teenagers need your support in learning how to manage their world on their own. Stay in touch with your child's life and let them know you are involved and aware. Let them feel your interest in their life: grades, hobbies, work life, after-school activities, friends, and what they do for fun. By staying involved, you help your teen know that you care and that their life is important to you, but it also makes it less likely they will explore with risky or unhealthy behaviors.

Maintain Physical Health

Physical well-being can be just as important as emotional well-being for your child, especially if they are feeling a disconnection between who they know themselves to be and their physical body.

Identify opportunities for exercise

Exercise releases endorphins, powerful chemicals that energize us and lift our moods. Teach your teen that if they are in a funk or over-whelmed by emotions, a healthy response is to exercise. Be careful not to try and force your child to do activities that they dislike or might make them feel even worse about themselves. Transgender and non-binary teens may have body issues that make them feel uncomfortable in specific physical activities. Work with your teen to find an activity that they want to do—whether long walks by themself or pick-up basketball games with supportive friends in your neighborhood.

Teach Healthy Eating Habits

Nutritional needs during adolescence increase because of the increased rate of growth. While there is a significant increase in the energy expended in adolescence and the accompanying nutrient requirements to meet those needs, other factors come into play that may negatively affect any adolescent's food intake and nutritional status. For many transgender and non-binary teens, eating sufficiently can be a very complicated issue.

Focus on helping your child establish healthy eating habits while simultaneously keeping a vigilant eye out for restricted eating, excessive exercise, and disordered eating.

Teens as a whole tend to be concerned about:

- having energy to do what they want and need to do,
- looking good,
- doing well in school, and
- optimizing athletic performance.

Transgender and non-binary teens have additional concerns of wanting to be perceived as the gender they experience themselves to be and may try to manipulate their shape to increase this likelihood. You can help to address all of their concerns by helping them to understand that healthy food is what gives them energy, feeds their brain function, helps them perform academically, and keeps them looking (and feeling) good. If they're not sure what foods are healthy choices, this can be a nice opportunity to make some food together that they can eat during the week.

Eating Issues Are Common for Transgender and Non-Binary Teens

A great many transgender teens and non-binary youth who are not yet on hormone replacement therapy use food to help gain or lose weight in order to accentuate or suppress parts of their body related to gender perception. If your teen doesn't see themself reflected in the mirror as they want to be seen, they may try many approaches, including disordered and restricted eating and excessive exercise, to alter their shape. For some of these teens, this is a temporary means of expressing their gender that fades away once hormone replacement therapy has begun to make the desired shifts. For others, the obsessive quality of this drive leads to formal eating disorders.

Starting in puberty, male and female bodies distribute weight differently. They have different body shapes, and although some of that difference is related to bones and muscles, most of it is actually related to fat distribution; where a body stores fat is directly related to hormonal levels. Testosterone-driven bodies store fat in their middles, whereas estrogen-driven bodies store it in their buttocks, hips, and thighs. This natural distribution of weight is one of the primary contributors to shape, and shape is one of the most instinctual gender signifiers.

Losing fat allows the overall body shape to change and be less gendered in appearance. The shape becomes more androgynous. For transgender and non-binary teens, extreme weight loss can be a means of regulating the gendered impression of their body. Because teens are rapidly growing, extreme weight loss is dangerous not only in the short term but also in the long term. Their bones are still forming, and malnourishment can permanently stunt growth. So, if you are concerned about your teen's eating or see significant weight changes, you may want to talk with your teen and their doctor about what you've noticed and see if they are trying to create congruence through their eating. If this is the case, you may want to discuss initiating medical alignment measures in order to end the disordered eating behaviors.

If your teen begins hormone therapy, any weight they gain migrates to the desired places, and fat becomes less of a gender signifier. As a result, after starting hormone replacement therapy, many transgender and non-binary teens who became thin for gender reasons allow themselves to return to a more natural weight as extra weight does not alter as much the way that others perceive their gender. Hormones allow their shape to be more congruous with their experienced gender.

For teens assigned male at birth who are now presenting as female, there may be new pressures due to cultural obsessions with thinness. If these teens first went through at least some of their natal puberty, they were immersed in the male adolescent culture of eating voraciously. Their hormones require and society reinforces that it is good, healthy, and masculine to eat a lot in adolescence. For adolescent girls, on the other hand, puberty often brings an expectation of dieting and restricted eating. Some transgirls will binge eat and then vomit as a way of meeting the new eating expectations. For many this distorted eating pattern does not persist once they learn how to regulate their food intake. For others, it transforms into a full-blown eating disorder.

Increase Affirmative Social Support and Gender Identity Pride

"My son does not feel a connection with other transgender or non-binary teens. In fact, it is more of an aversion. But when he meets other transgender and non-binary adults, he feels like he has met long-lost family members."

"Find a tribe. It doesn't have to be focused around gender identity; it can simply be around a shared interest, a hobby, a game.

> *But find a tribe of people who accept you and your child for the*
> *awesome kid they are and make them into family."*

Affirmative social support is a protective factor for tansgender, non-binary, and gender-expansive youth. Studies indicate that being able to name your gender identity/expression and to express it to others is important for positive identity integration. It is important for transgender and non-binary teens to have social contexts outside of their home, where their gender is accepted and affirmed. Having their gender affirmed, not just in transgender or non-binary communities, but also in cisgender communities, can act as a source of strength and connectedness in the face of larger societal stigma. When teens are supported in their gender identity and gender expression, they have better mental and physical health and overall well-being.

It is believed that our needs for connectedness are hardwired. Isolation is dangerous for healthy self-esteem. People who feel included in their communities, connected to their social networks, and engaged in community life have better health outcomes and are better at withstanding and adapting to change.

As parents, one of the ways that you can promote resilience in your teen is to promote the importance of connections to community. You can work with your teen to identify ways they can break out of their fear of rejection and find peer support and develop relationships outside of the family. Peer support can be instrumental in buffering the effects of stigma. Work together with your teen to identify organizations like local youth groups (religious or community-based), sports teams inside or outside of school, and volunteer organizations to see if any of them have or would be interested in creating a gender-inclusive environment. Be willing to make these calls yourself, but engage your teen in the process, so this becomes something they have an interest and investment in as well.

Recognize and Support Group-Level Coping

*"Me finding my own identity was when I learned one could iden-
tify as non-binary and I was like, 'Yep, that's me,' and it was
great. Also when I saw people like Jeffree Star or Marylin Man-
son—people who were coded as androgynous—and I saw them
and knew I wanted to look 'more like them,' not yet knowing I
craved gender ambiguity."*

A sense of empowerment develops from belonging to a group.
Minority groups often utilize group coping skills in response to
prejudice and stigma. Group identity encourages a connection that
protects its members from the negative impact of discrimination.
One way that this is accomplished is by creating a group identity
that is outside of the dominant culture where their experiences are
normalized and even celebrated, rather than marginalized. This leads
to a sense of collective self-esteem and positive social identification.
Strengthening social identity is a key component of healthy, positive
overall identity.

Knowing Others Who Share Your Identity Makes a Big Difference

When transgender and non-binary youth are able to make
connections with other people in the trans* community, they are
able to develop stronger positive group identity, which improves
self-esteem and a sense of belongingness. They are also able to
learn about resources, expanded options for self-identification
and expression, and share strategies for coping with prejudice,
discrimination, harassment, and violence directed toward them.

Just being with other youth and adults like them bolsters self-esteem and reduces the negative effects of stigma.

Straight transgender and non-binary people often do not feel they are part of the LGBQ community and when people add the "T" to LGBTQ, they do not feel that references them. You may need to assist your teen in finding other youth they can connect with outside of the LGBQ community. The Gender Spectrum Lounge has online groups for teens, and there are a number of organizations that provide both in-person and online support and common interest groups for youth who identify across the gender spectrum.

Assist Your Teen in Meeting Others with a Similar Gender

Your teen may need help learning to safely navigate ways to meet others like them. They may be concerned that through open connections with other gender-diverse people, their privacy will be compromised. If this is the case, finding safe venues may entail traveling to national conferences and finding online support groups, YouTube channels, and online forums. It is uniquely empowering to meet other transgender and non-binary people. It may take a few tries to find a community forum that feels like a good match, so keep trying!

The idea of establishing a group identity can be met with resistance if your teen has internalized transphobia. Internalized stigma/transphobia can unwittingly create a deeper level of unrecognized internalized shame and isolation as they cut themselves off from the community because of negative views of transgender people. We also see a decreased desire to connect with the transgender and non-binary communities in teens who socially transitioned when they were young. These teens may not identify as transgender or may believe they are somehow different from other transgender people, and therefore not have a desire to be a part of a "transgender group." Others who transitioned when young may feel that their gender is no longer a primary identity they are thinking about and don't have an interest in gender-related groups and events. The challenge in all of these situations is that these youth remain isolated and miss the opportunity to find kinship with others who share an understanding of their life in important ways. You may be able to influence your teen to find a connection to a gender community that feels right for them. If so, there is likely a real benefit in doing so for your child.

Finding Communities that Affirm All of Your Child's Key Identities

Being connected to the communities of one's identities, including religious, cultural, or physical ability, is vital to establishing a healthy sense of self. However, if some of those identities are transphobic, it can result in internal conflict and complicate the process of self-acceptance and healthy gender identity consolidation. Finding gender-affirming communities of intersecting identities can be important in self-development. Sometimes these can only be found online or within larger transgender and non-binary focused communities. Many teens report using social media to connect with sub-communities such as deaf trans teens, trans youth of color, or non-binary teens with Asperger's. By making connections between their identities, transgender and non-binary teens can often learn about and access resources outside of their local area. These connections can help reduce isolation and increase the positive association of having multiple identities. By connecting with others with the same overlapping identities, they are able to learn new strategies for dealing with the prejudice they face as members of multiple minority groups.

Gender Pride

As we mentioned before, finding pride in one's gender is an important part of developing a positive relationship with one's less common gender identity. One common way for this to occur is to feel a part of a greater social movement. Thus, shame, internalized stigma, and isolation can be replaced with a sense of belonging and pride. Being positively associated with others like you and a movement of social justice allows for a feeling of solidarity with others who are also fighting for gender equity issues.

When a transgender or non-binary person feels pride around their gender, they are less concerned about the responses of others and less likely to anticipate negative reactions. You can use Dr. Rylan Testa's list of pride markers to help assess whether your teen feels pride in their gender. People who experience pride in their gender feel like:

- My gender makes me feel special/unique.
- It's OK for people to know my gender is different from my sex assigned at birth.
- I have no problem speaking about my gender identity and history to almost anyone.
- It is a gift that my gender identity is different from my sex assigned at birth.
- I am like others.
- I am proud to have my gender.
- I'd rather have people know everything and accept me with my gender history.

Consider how you may help your child nurture gender pride.

Find Mentors and Role Models for Your Teen

"My son has been living as a boy for the majority of his life. We tend to forget that he is trans. It is not a big issue in our life anymore. But I see how important it is for him to meet adult transmen. Every time he has the opportunity, it is like he comes alive! He has so many questions and feels an automatic kinship."

When adolescents have mentors, they have a higher sense of self-worth, are more likely to challenge themselves, and are more likely to take positive risks. Any adult who serves in the role of mentor to a teen has a profound guiding impact. Studies show that teens with mentors feel more positive about their identity, are able to make stronger, more empowered decisions about their life, and have increased feelings of happiness and overall well-being. If we combine this research with the fact that transgender and non-binary teens have limited access to positive role models, it's exciting to think about what a wonderful impact a transgender or non-binary mentor could have in reducing isolation, helping your teen cope with stigma, and developing personal pride in their gender. If you know anyone who might serve as a mentor to your child, we encourage you to talk with them about this possibility.

Strengthen Your Teen's Ability to Withstand and Recover From Adversity

"There are still many challenges to be faced and overcome, but feeling confident in being out and generally having people be receptive to my explanations of gender (and lots of folks respecting my request for neutral pronouns even if it is a challenge), and

being able to inspire others to feel safe in being out, has had a very positive impact on my life."[1]

"Luz explained why learning martial arts made her feel more secure: 'I will not put my hands on nobody if I do not have to. If it's not a life or death situation, I will walk away from you. I'll let you piss me off because there is just so much you can say. But, it's a good investment. It can keep you safe because if someone knows you know how to kickbox and fight and judo throw somebody...they're not going to mess with you.'"[2]

Teens gradually gain new abilities in adolescence. They are able to think ahead, consider alternatives, predict consequences, dream about the future, perceive subtleties, and identify their personal values. Parents who give their teens appropriate autonomy provide them with self-esteem-enhancing advantages: the experience of making their own choices; pride stemming from having made good choices; and opportunities to accept and learn from their mistakes. In this section, we're going to focus on how to help your teen strengthen their core resilience muscles, leaving them in a stronger position to withstand and recover from any setbacks and difficulties experienced in their day-to-day living.

Teens Develop Positive Attributes through Experience

Teens need experiences in order to learn how to integrate higher thinking skills and develop social skills—both of which are critical for developing a positive identity. These attributes are developed through experience and practice. Providing opportunities to think about or even role-play how to respond to inappropriate and unwelcome questions and asserting needs related to their gender are important in building the foundation needed for adulthood.

Provide your teen with experiences where they can be successful.

Walk them through how you go about doing something you are unfamiliar with and how to ask for help.

Praise Effort and Progress, and Celebrate Success

Verbally acknowledge and praise the positive effort or progress your teen makes. This demonstrates not only that you notice their efforts but that you value them.

Foster Independence

As your child ages, your role shifts from direct supervision into being a part of a network of observers. As you are stepping back, it will still be useful to stay connected with other adults in your teen's life: Communicate with teachers, coaches, parents, and your teen about their world. You want to foster your teen's independence while still supporting and guiding them.

Encourage Persistence

Encourage your teen not to give up when they experience resistance or failure. Resiliency is the ability to bounce back. Find examples in your own life when you failed or needed to keep trying in order to succeed at something. Let your teen see when you try something new and what you will be doing to try to succeed at it. If it does not work out as planned, model resilience and share with them what you will do next to keep trying or what you now realize you could have tried this time.

Allow for Their Differing Opinions and Handle Them with Respect

Listen to your teen and value their perspective and opinions. Take the time to explore their viewpoints on things. Engage them in conversations about family concerns, political topics, social issues, and more. Be prepared to expand your own thinking. Take their viewpoints seriously, and remember that tolerance is a quality that can be learned.

Their dramatic forms of communication are age-appropriate as they learn to express differing opinions in conversations.

Encourage Your Teen to Be a Mentor or Role Model for Others

"Every time I present to a church group or a school, people come up to me so grateful to have met me. They tell me I am inspiration to them. They say listening to me they see areas of their own life where they need to have more courage to express themselves more honestly. It is really rewarding."

Once your teen has a strong sense of self, it can be incredibly empowering for them to be able to become an inspiration to other kids and teens struggling with their own gender, and to families needing to see that there is hope at the end of the tunnel for their child. For many, engaging in activism and the education of others around issues of gender equity is an important step in strengthening their pride in their gender. It is a powerful way to dispel stereotypes and misconceptions. To educate and inspire others with who you are and how you live your life is a way to take pride in your identity.

Model for Your Teen How to Self-Advocate

"My child stands up for her right to be different, and for the most part is accepted for doing so. It helps that she is intelligent, confident, well spoken, and accepting of differences in others."

Although the world may not be as welcoming and understanding of your teen's needs as you would like it to be, you can teach your teen how to recognize and address their needs in the larger world. As you advocate for their rights in school, share with them what you are doing and why it is important not just for them, but for all students.

As they get older and more confident, strategize together about ways that they can advocate for themselves in school. As you search for affirming healthcare providers, share with your teen what qualities you are looking for and what you do to find such providers. As they get more comfortable with their gender-specific medical desires, support them in navigating their healthcare appointments from start to finish, using you as needed for support and as their ally and advocate. As you make legal changes, share the process with them. Show them that they matter and how to go about finding support in their expanding world. These are life skills that they need to learn.

In each context, you can go over with your child ahead of time what your goal is, what questions you have, and how you will approach getting this achieved. Watching you go through the process is not only instructional, but it is also affirming that their needs are important. Collaborate with your teen around the specific challenges that they face and guide them in how to find the resources and support they need. Show them tenacity and determination, as well as how to not personalize ignorance in the search for equity. This helps to prepare them for greater levels of independence. From there, you can strategize together about other current and future situations in their life, such as how to identify local programs and resources at college and the work-place, issues of disclosure, how to locate sensitive medical providers in a new area, etc.

Support Healthy Decision-Making Skills

As adults, we can teach our teens how to make safer choices in their day-to-day lives. It can be very useful to walk through specific areas of their lives and brainstorm together how to make wise choices. Confidence is a key component in healthy decision-making for teens. Research indicates that confidence is a key quality of teens who are better able to navigate circumstances and people that are not as safe for them—and to have the ability to seek out those that are right for them.

You can teach how to make healthy decisions by example and through dialogue. Ask your teen open-ended questions that pinpoint their take on a situation and what may need to be changed. Help your teen to understand how emotions can influence their thinking and behaviors. Help your teen to see that there are multiple choices in each situation. You can assist your teen in weighing their options and considering the consequences of each one. Likewise, when your teen makes a decision that was not so wise, take the time to explore together in a non-judgmental fashion what happened and possible tactics that they might utilize in the future to make a decision that will create more of the results they desire.

Prepare Yourself

This is a transition you must make—moving from making all important decisions for your children to supporting them in making decisions on their own. Which decisions around their gender are you able to support them in making on their own? How will you handle it if they make a decision you would not make for them? Be clear ahead of time, if you can, about what is in their hands, what you will decide collaboratively, and what decisions you feel you have the right to make on their behalf.

Encourage Your Teen to Think Through the Options for Each Topic

You can help your child develop their critical thinking skills as well as their ability to self-reflect by teaching them to think through their options. Although you want your teen to come up with their lists of options, identifying the pros and cons of each one on their own, let them know that you are available as a sounding board. Try to keep your judgments out of the process; allow it to be their own. Remember that younger teens may need more guidance in this part of the process as they are still gaining these skills.

Making Decisions

As parents of teens, one of the tasks at hand is to support them in making their own decisions. Practice the following steps with as many topics as you can from as young an age as possible so that you both gain experience with the process. That way, when it comes to the decisions specifically pertaining to their gender, you both will have greater confidence. Be sure your teen knows that emotions can cloud judgment and to always make decisions when they are calm and centered. Encourage them to take time when making important decisions. However, know that for a teen, the time it takes to make a strong and healthy decision may be much shorter than it is for an adult. In some ways, their perspective is clearer. Also realize that the way your teen approaches decision-making may be different from the way you do; being young, they are less burdened and may be more creative in their decision-making process.

Let Your Teen Know Which Decisions Are in Their Hands

Letting your teen know explicitly which decisions are in their hands is important. Even if you encourage your teen to share their thoughts with you, they may still assume that you will be the one deciding. Give your child verbal permission to decide on the issues you feel are theirs. You can let them know that you are available to work collaboratively with them on these decisions, or you can let them know at what age you feel they can make these decisions independently, and how decisions on these subjects will be made in the meantime.

Final Thoughts on Becoming a Trusted Guide and Advisor

Your values and perspective remain influential for your teen. Be a sounding board for them; continue to influence how they see and perceive the world and themself. You're a role model—your teen is paying close attention to what you say and do. If you feel you need to strengthen your skills or expand your knowledge in a specific area, ask if they would like to take a class or read a book on the subject together. It is valuable to model recognizing personal areas that need growth and how to go about becoming a better person.

The key is to engage in respectful and positive dialogue on issues such as plans for the future, social issues of our times, and meaningful life questions. Be someone they can count on. Offer frameworks for how to understand negative experiences based on gender, race, or other stigmatized, marginalized, or misunderstood identities.

When you have your teen's trust, they will want and value your input about the direction of their lives. Your role becomes one of a guide or counselor who listens to them and helps them find the right course for themself as an individual.

The best way to support the resilience of your teen is to love and support them and to maintain a sense of connectedness with them. This will build their resilience and the resilience of your family, providing much-needed protection for all of you in the face of the various stressors that come your way. Beyond this, the best protection for your teen and future generations is to promote social change to reduce the negative effects of gender-based stigma and fight for gender equity. It is up to us to create a more fair and equitable world for our children and their children.

---

1   Veale et al.

2   Maurice N. Gattis and Sara L McKinnon, *School Experiences of Transgender and Gender Non-Conforming Students in Wisconsin*, Madison, WI: GSAFE, 2015.

Chapter 12

Conclusion

"Gender is the poetry each of us makes out of the language we are taught."

—LESLIE FEINBERG

WE WROTE THIS BOOK TO help you gain an understanding of gender in all its beautiful complexity in the hope that you can meet the teen in your life where they are on their gender journey. Your teen needs you. Your love, affirmation, and support can make all the difference.

Together, we can create gender-sensitive and inclusive environments for everyone. We can create a safer, better world to grow up in, where transgender, non-binary, and otherwise gender-expansive people aren't stigmatized for the simple desire to live authentically. Imagine the creativity we could liberate by allowing all children to be who they are without asking them to fit within the confines of our two narrow gender boxes right from the start. Imagine the possibilities if we stopped asking them to conceal who they are for the comfort of others.

The price of conformity is too high. We are losing children to self-harm and violence at horrific rates. We pay an enormous price—and for what benefit?

There is real reason for hope. Youth today are reimagining gender. Once they know of the true diversity of gender, they naturally believe that people of all genders deserve to be visible, supported, represented, and acknowledged. They expect inclusive environments marked by an atmosphere in which all people feel valued and respected and have access to the same opportunities. This isn't about political correctness—it's about substantively empowering everyone to be their authentic selves.

Celebrating and valuing gender diversity acknowledges that each of us has our own gender journey. Regardless of how you see, experience, name, or express your gender, there is a place for you. You belong.

> *"We need to encourage members of this next generation to become all that they can become, not try to force them to become what we want them to become.... You and I can't even begin to dream the dreams this next generation is going to dream, or answer the questions that will be put to them."*
>
> —BARBARA COLOROSO

A sea change is underway. When Stephanie first started Gender Spectrum more than ten years ago, every school training she did was in support of the one non-binary or transgender student who was trying to be themself and hoping to find understanding and respect from their fellow students. At that time, no one at the schools, adults and students alike, had heard of the possibility of transgender children or teens, and no one had heard of non-binary identities at all. Flash forward a decade and the majority of trainings we do are inspired by schools that want their cultures to be a warm and inclusive environments for *all* students. They want to set up their systems and environment to be welcoming to students of all gender identities and expressions.

An inclusive society is not a dream—it's an attainable reality. This can easily be achieved through home and school-based educational opportunities, as well as expanded options in our social environments. For example, all public spaces can provide gender-neutral bathrooms and locker rooms, even if they choose to maintain segregated ones. Sports and athletic opportunities can be divided by classifications other than gender. Registration forms can be expanded to include more gender-identity options. Rather than making assumptions, we can ask one another not only for names, but also what our preferred pronouns are. We can make school uniforms available for all students to pick and choose from. We can call out limited notions of gender whenever and wherever we see them and ask for more options. We can insist on inclusion for everyone.

Now it is rare to find a person in schools who has not heard of transgender and non-binary youth, and students easily understand and embrace information about gender diversity!

> *"Our Gender Spectrum class completely fascinated me. It was like realizing our world has color instead of black and white. It now seems so obvious to me, and I can't believe that before this class I had thought there were only two genders. I love the idea of telling this to people and let them realize this too!"*

> *"I want to spread the reality of the gender spectrum around so hopefully we can work toward changing society's ways to offer complete acceptance and equality to everyone. I would really like to see a world where it is fine to be who you are."*

> *"I am angry! Why didn't anyone tell me all of this before? I have been so ignorant and judgmental of other people without*

understanding that I had been taught such an overly simplified
definition of gender. This needs to be taught to all of us before we
reach preschool. Not for the first time in high school!"

There are other things we can make happen with little effort. Since research shows that transgender and non-binary people fare better in the long run if they have met other gender-expansive individuals before their gender self-identification, it is essential to make transgender and non-binary people visible. Media needs to cover the lives of gender-diverse people, not just stories of suicides and violence. As transgender and non-binary individuals become increasingly represented in the media, not just for their gender but as people living their lives like everyone else, then they will know that there is a place for them. In turn, as gender diversity becomes more acceptable and less stigmatized, transgender and non-binary people will feel more comfortable being visible in their own lives. It will be at that point when everyone will recognize just how much diversity of gender they have always been surrounded by without even knowing it.

"I had attended the educational evening wary about what would
be taught in my child's school. I came out of the talk realizing
that I am non-binary myself. So much just clicked for me! I am
forty-seven years old and have just learned words to describe
who I am and my experience of life."

We honor the steps you have taken to support the transgender or non-binary teen in your life. We know the strength that it takes at this point in history—it is not an easy path for either of you. Yet together, you, your teen, and all of the other people out there expanding the binary gender system are making a better world for everyone.

Stephanie Brill and Lisa Kenney

Glossary

Commonly Used Terms

Assigned sex at birth: The designation made by medical professionals of a person's sex based on a visual examination of a child's genitals at birth. If the genitals are ambiguous, further examinations and tests may be conducted. Sex designation is often incorrectly conflated with one's gender identity in our society.

Assumed gender: Assumed gender is the gender identity we presume individuals have based on their sex assigned at birth. For example, a person who was assigned male at birth is likely to have the assumed gender of a boy/man. A person who was assigned female at birth is likely to have the assumed gender of a girl/woman.

Cisgender: Refers to people whose gender identity aligns with their assigned sex at birth (*cis-* from Latin, meaning, "on the same side [as]" or "on this side [of]", in contrast to *trans-*, from the Latin root meaning "across", "beyond", or "on the opposite side [of]").

Congruence: The experience of having all dimensions of a person's gender aligned.

Gender binary/binary: A system that constructs gender according to two discrete and opposite categories—male and female. Binary gender identities include boy/man, and girl/woman. It is important to recognize that both cisgender and transgender people can have a gender identity that is binary. For example, someone may identify as a trans-woman, while another person may identify as a cisgender woman.

Gender-expansive: An umbrella term used for individuals who broaden their own culture's commonly held definitions of gender, including expectations for its expression, identities, roles, and/or other perceived gender norms. Gender-expansive individuals may include those with transgender and non-binary gender identities, as well as those whose gender in some way is seen to be stretching society's notions of gender.

Gender: The complex interrelationship between: the body (our experience of our bodies, as well as how society genders our bodies and interacts with us based on our bodies and perceived sex); identity (internal sense of self as male, female, neither, a blend of both, or something else; who we privately know ourselves to be); and expression (how we present our gender to others, and how society, culture, community and family perceive, interact with, and try to shape our gender). The interaction of these three elements comprises one's gender. Gender roles, expectations, and norms change over time and are different between cultures.

Non-binary gender: An umbrella term for gender identities and expressions that are not exclusively male or female. People who identify their gender as non-binary can feel that they are both male and female, neither male nor female, or something else altogether. Non-binary identities are recognized in many non-Western cultures around the world. Although it is an imperfect umbrella term, for the purposes of this book we use non-binary to communicate the experience of people whose genders cannot be defined purely in terms of the binary system of exclusively female or male.

Sex: Refers to a person's biological status (male, female, intersex). Indicators of sex include sex chromosomes, gonads, internal reproductive organs and external genitalia.

Sexual orientation: Part of our identity that is romantically and/or sexually attracted to others. Our sexual orientation and our gender are separate, though related, parts of our overall identity.

The gender spectrum: Rather than a binary, gender is viewed as a spectrum of multiple, intersecting dimensions.

Transgender/trans/trans*: All three of these terms can be used as umbrella terms to describe an individual whose gender identity differs from their assigned sex at birth. The terms trans and transgender are sometimes used interchangeably to describe all gender identities that are not cisgender. The asterisk in trans* is used to signify the inclusion of all non-binary gender identities. Transgender can also be used to refer to people who experience deep feelings of incongruence with their assigned sex and associated sex characteristics, and feel alignment with what many often think of as the "opposite sex." Being trans or transgender does not imply any specific sexual orientation.

Health and Wellness

Conversion therapy: Also known as "reparative therapy," this term refers to therapy or other actions designed to alter a person's gender or sexual orientation.

Gender affirmative practice: Medical, mental health, legal, or other professional practice/practitioner who supports and accepts an individual's self-articulated gender identity and gender expression.

Internalized stigma/stigmatization: Internal shame or self-hatred related to a culturally stigmatized aspect of one's self.

Internalized transphobia: Internalized stigma about being trans*/ transgender.

Minority stress: The stress and distress attributable to a person's minority status.

Resilience: Resilience is a person's ability to withstand and recover from the insults, setbacks, and difficulties experienced in day-to-day living. It requires an ability to adapt to changing circumstances and to continue going on in the face of adversity.

Gender Identity & Gender Identities

Agender, neutrois, gender neutral, genderfree, non-gendered, genderless: These are all commonly used identity terms that people who do not feel that they have a gender (or that their gender is neutral) use. Some of them feel a connection to the concept of gender, but feel they do not have one. Others cannot even understand what gender is as they do not experience it within themselves.

Androgyne/androgynous: Androgynes are typically simultaneously masculine and feminine—although not necessarily in equal parts. They frequently have both female and male gender characteristics. Some feel they are a blended gender, neither masculine nor feminine. This inner androgyny may or may not be reflected in their appearance.

Bigender, multigender: A bigender person identifies as two genders. It does not necessarily mean they identify as a man and a woman, just that there are two distinct genders with which they identify. They may identify as both at the same time, flow between genders, or feel they are a blend.

Butch: Can be a lesbian or queer masculine gender identity, gender expression, or gender role. The word butch has different meanings for different people. It is generally associated with queer identified individuals whose gender expression is perceived as masculine. For some, it is related to more traditionally masculine gender roles, while others may use it as a gender identity.

Demigender, demifluid, demiflux: Someone who identifies as demigender identifies partially with one (or more) gender(s). For example, a demiguy or demiboy identifies partially as a boy/man/masculine, but not entirely. Demigender can be a subset of bigender or multigender, but does not have to be. A demigender person may identify as demifluid or demiflux; this indicates that a part of one's identity remains stable while the other part or parts are fluid. Often, a demiflux person feels that the stable part of their identity is gender neutral or nonbinary.

Femme: A term that can be used to describe a lesbian, trans, queer feminine gender expression, gender identity, or gender role. For example, one can be a genderqueer femme or a gender fluid femme.

FTM/affirmed male/transboy: A child or adult who was assigned a female sex at birth but has a male gender identity.

Gender fluid and agender fluid: People that are gender fluid have a gender or genders that change. Gender fluid people move between genders—not necessarily masculine and feminine genders. Gender fluid people tend to experience their gender as something dynamic and changing, rather than static. They might have multiple distinct sides of their gender, and often their gender presentation shifts accordingly. Gender fluid people may have a fluid sense of gender or experience themselves as having lots of different genders.

Gender flux: Gender flux can be an identity similar to gender fluid, but usually indicates a movement between specific genders rather than fluidity. Often, but not always, one of the genders is non-binary or agender, or possibly one gender identity is fixed and the other part or parts are in flux. It also can describe the experience of gender fluid people as in: "I experience the most gender flux when I move from school to work."

Gender identity: A person's innermost core concept of self which can include male, female, a blend of both, neither, and many more. Gender identity is how individuals perceive themselves and what they call themselves. One's gender identity can be the same or different from their sex assigned at birth. Gender identity can evolve and shift over time.

Genderqueer: Genderqueer is an umbrella term to describe non-normative gender experiences. Genderqueer is often a combined gender identity, gender expression, and sexual orientation. Genderqueer individuals typically reject static categories of gender and sexual orientation. For some, genderqueer is a non-binary identification, and for others it is not. Genderqueer can often include an element of challenging the construction of gender.

Intergender: A term for those who experience their gender identity to be a combination or blend of genders, or an identity that is between genders.

Masculine of center: Some people call themselves masculine of center as a way of describing where they see themselves in the masculine and feminine continuum. According to Brown Boi Project, "Masculine of Center (MoC), in its evolving definition, recognizes the cultural breadth and depth of identity for lesbian/queer womyn and gender-nonconforming/trans people who tilt toward the masculine side of the gender spectrum".

MtF/affirmed female/transgirl: A child or adult who was assigned a male sex at birth but has a female gender identity.

Pangender: This is an identity that reflects multiple gender identities and gender expressions. Some people use it to indicate that they are all genders.

Stud: Someone assigned female at birth who identifies as masculine physically, mentally, and/or emotionally. This word is most frequently used within black and Latina lesbian and queer communities. A stud can identify as any gender.

Third gender: This term refers to the existence of more than two genders. Nepali, Thai, and some First Nation cultures are examples of just a few (of many) that acknowledge a third gender. Increasingly, there are a number of countries that include a third gender option for use on birth certificates and other government documents.

Transfeminine: This is someone who was assigned male at birth, but identifies as more feminine than masculine. This is often a subset of a genderqueer identity. Some people will describe themselves as feminine of center as a way of describing where they see themselves in the masculine and feminine continuum.

Transmasculine: This is someone who was assigned female at birth, but identifies as more masculine than feminine. This is often a subset of a genderqueer identity.

Two spirit: A non-binary gender identity specifically associated with Native American and First Nation cultures.

Sexual Orientation

Asexual: Someone who does not experience sexual attraction.

Bisexual: An umbrella term for people who experience sexual and/or romantic attraction to more than one gender.

Gay: A term used to describe anyone who is sexually and/or romantically attracted to someone of the same sex.

Lesbian: A woman who is sexually and romantically attracted to other women.

Pansexual: A term that describes someone who experiences attraction to multiple genders, or any gender. This term is often used by those who want to acknowledge that gender and attraction are not binary.

Queer: A general term for people who identify their gender and/or sexual orientation as something other than cisgender and/or heterosexual. Queer is a term used to identify oneself as outside society's norms, without having to state a specific identity.

Questioning: Describes someone who is questioning and/or exploring their romantic and sexual attraction to others.

Congruence Terminology

Alignment (gender alignment, living in alignment): The process by which someone brings the different dimensions of their gender into agreement so that they feel whole.

Congruence measures: Actions that lead to a sense of alignment with the dimensions of one's gender (body, identity and expression)

Gender congruence: A state reached when a person has accepted their gender identity and feels satisfied with how they physically and socially express their gender.

Gender dysphoria: Anxiety, distress, or discomfort regarding one's gender and/or sex assigned at birth.

Gender transition: The process of changing outwardly from one gender to another. Transition is the term used to include all of the steps a transgender or non-binary person take in order to present themself consistently with their gender identity. Transition can occur in any or all of the following ways: *social transition* through changes of social identifiers such as clothing, hairstyle, name and/or pronouns; *medical transition* through the use of medicines such as hormone "blockers" or cross hormones to promote gender-based body changes; *surgical transition* in which an individual's body is modified through the addition or removal of gender-related physical traits; and *legal transition* through changing identification documents such as one's birth certificate, driver's license, and passport.

Hormone suppressants/puberty suppressants/hormone blockers/ GNRH analogs: These medical interventions are used to pause natal puberty and the development of secondary sex characteristics.

Hormone therapy: Sometimes referred to as cross-sex hormone therapy, hormone therapy (estrogens in male-bodied people and androgens in female-bodied people) is a congruence measure used to induce and maintain the physical and psychological secondary sex characteristics that best match the person's gender identity.

Personal gender: Each dimension of gender is informed by the unique intersection of identities, experience, and personal characteristics that each of us contains. We are all more than our body, identity, and expression; we are also our race, ethnicity, class, faith community, sense of geographic place, family history, community's gender roles, expectations, etc. Our gender is personal because while we share some of these aspects of self with others, the way that all of these identities, influences, and characteristics come together is unique to each of us.

Physical congruence (appearance congruence): Physical congruence is one's effort to align one's gender identity and physical appearance. Physical appearance congruence may just include a gender expression shift, or it may include medical intervention such as surgery or hormones.

Social congruence: Social congruence is one's effort to align their gender identity and social identifiers such as name, pronoun, and gender/sex marker on identity documents.

Gender Expression and Gender Roles

Gender expression: This is our "public" gender. How we present our gender in the world through behavior, clothing, hairstyle, voice, mannerisms, and other forms of presentation, and how society, culture, community, and family perceive, interact with, and try to shape our gender. Expression is also related to gender roles and how society uses them to try to enforce conformity to current gender norms.

Gender non-conforming: Gender that doesn't comply with societal, cultural, communal, and/or familial expectations of gender.

Gender roles: This is the set of functions, activities, and behaviors commonly expected of females and males by society.

Gender socialization: The process by which a society or culture communicates and reinforces its gender expectations, norms, and roles.

Gender stereotypes: Generalizations of characteristics, differences, and attributes of a certain group based on gender. Most often these are negatively perceived generalizations, but positive gender stereotypes exist as well.

Visually gender non-conforming: This term refers to an individual whose appearance doesn't comply with what is expected of their gender, generally because it is inconsistent with their sex assigned at birth.

Gender and Bodies

Body (as a dimension of gender): A person's experience of their body, as well as how society genders bodies and interacts with us based on our body and our perceived sex.

Gender affirming surgery: Physical procedures that help a person feel more aligned in their gender. This can include genital reassignment surgery, breast surgery, facial surgery, and a variety of other surgical procedures.

Gender dysphoria: A feeling of disconnection between one's gender and the sex they were assigned at birth.

Natal puberty: Natal puberty refers to the changes one's body goes through absent any medical interventions.

Partial natal puberty: Puberty that starts without medical intervention and then is interrupted by the use of hormone suppressants and/or cross hormones.

Gender Identity Development

Ambiguous gender: A gender that cannot easily be classified within the existing binary structures.

Authentic gender: This term refers to the gender an individual self-identifies as, the gender someone knows themself to be based on how they feel inside.

Coherence: A state of feeling unified and whole. One can feel a sense of inner coherence related to their gender identity when the various dimensions of their gender come together and the person feels comfortable.

Gender identity consolidation: The creation of a healthy and coherent sense of one's gender.

Gender self-identification: An individual's ability to determine and assert their gender identity.

Gender stability: An understanding of one's gender that remains consistent over time.

Identity integration: The process by which a young person comes to know, understand, and accept parts of their identity.

Stigma (stigmatized identity): Disapproval or lack of respect for a person or group of people based on behaviors or characteristics society doesn't approve of.

Gender and Society

Assumed gender: A term used to describe the gender that is assumed of a person based on their sex assigned at birth.

Cisgender privilege: The unearned advantages of individuals who identify as cisgender.

Gender diversity: A term used to describe and call attention to the naturally occurring variety and differences related to gender that exist in our world.

Gender justice: The notion that individuals of all genders are deserving of equal protections and rights.

Gender minority: An umbrella term used to describe individuals whose gender identity is anything other than cisgender.

Gender policing: The act of regulating or placing constraints on one's gender expression or identification. Telling someone who identifies as a girl that she cannot have short hair because short hair is for "boys" is an example of gender policing.

Transphobia: Fear, dislike of, and prejudice against transgender people.

Gender Affirmation

Affirmed gender: The term for an individual's gender self-identification, rather than the sex they were assigned at birth.

Gender pronouns: A word or phrase that may be substituted for a noun that indicates the gender of the object. She/her/hers are common feminine pronouns, while he/him/his are common masculine pronouns. They/them, xe/xir, and ze/hir are some common gender-neutral pronouns.

Misgender: The act of incorrectly labeling a person's gender.

Preferred pronoun: The gender pronoun(s) an individual feels most comfortable using. Some people choose preferred pronouns based on gender identity while others choose pronouns based on gender expression. One's preferred pronoun can also change based on the environment or situation. It is also important to note that one person may assert one preferred pronoun (such as he/him), while another may have more than one pronoun they feel comfortable using (such as he/him or they/them).

References

Chapter 2: Understanding Gender and the Gender Spectrum

Correll, J. 1/f noise and effort on implicit measures of bias. *Journal of Personality and Social Psychology*, 2008; 94, 48–59.

Fausto-Sterling, A. The dynamic variability of gender variability. *Journal of Homosexuality*, 2012; 59, 398–421.

Fausto-Sterling, A., Coll, C.G., & Lamarre, M. Sexing the baby: Part 1—What do we really know about sex differentiation in the first year of life? *Social Science and Medicine,* 2012a; 74, 1684–1692.

Fausto-Sterling, A., Coll, C.G., & Lamarre, M. Sexing the baby: Part 2—Applying dynamic systems theory to the emergences of sex-related differences in infants and toddlers. *Social Science and Medicine,* 2012a; 74, 1693–1702.

Grossman, A.H., & D'Augelli, A.R. Transgender youth: invisible and vulnerable. *Journal of Homosexuality*, 2006; 51(1): 111–128.

Harris, A. *Gender as Soft Assembly.* New York: Routelage, Taylor & Francis Group (2009).

Lewis, M.D., & Granic, I. (Eds.) *Emotion, development and self-organization: Dynamic systems approaches to emotional development.* New York: Cambridge University Press (2000).

Martin, C.L., & Ruble, D.N. Patterns of Gender Development. *Annual Review of Psychology*, 2010; 61: 353–381. doi: 10.1146/annurev.psych.093008.100511.

Nowak, M.A., Plotkin, J.B., & Jansen, V.A. The evolution of syntactic communication. *Nature* 404 (2000): 495.

Pereira, M.D.M. "Doing Gender in the Playground: The Negotiation of Gender and Sexuality in Schools," University of Warwick, Department of Sociology, 2014.

Russell, S.T., Ryan, C., Toomey, R.B., Diaz, R.M., & Sanchez, J. Lesbian, gay, bisexual, and transgender adolescent school victimization: implications for young adult health and adjustment. *Journal of School Health*, 2011; 81: 223–230.

Smith L.B., & Thelen, E. Development as a dynamic system. *Trends in Cognitive Sciences* 7, 2003: 343–348.

Thelen, E., & Bates, E. Connectionism and dynamic systems: are they really different? *Developmental Science* 6:4 (2003): 378–391.

Van Geert, P., & Steenbeek, H. A complexity and dynamic systems approach to developmental assessment, modeling and research. In A.M. Battro, K.W. Fischer & P. Léna (Eds.), *The educated brain: essays in neuro-education.* Cambridge, UK: Cambridge University Press (2008) (71–94).

Van Geert, P., & Steenbeek, H. Brains and the dynamics of "wants" and "cans"; a commentary on Immordino-Yang's A tale of two cases. *Mind, Brain and Education*, 2(2), 2008; 62–66.

Van Orden, G.C., Holden, J.G., & Turvey, M.T. Self-organization of cognitive performance. *Journal of Experimental Psychology*, 2003; 132: 331–350.

Chapter 3: Embracing the Complexity

Byne, W., Bradley, S. J., Coleman, E., Eyler, A. E., Green, R., Menvielle, E. J., . . . American Psychiatric Association Task Force on Treatment of Gender Identity Disorder. (2012). Report of the American Psychiatric Association Task Force on Treatment of Gender Identity Disorder. Archives of Sexual Behavior

Carroll, R. (1999). Outcomes of treatment for gender dysphoria. Journal of Sex Education & Therapy, 24, 128 –136. Case, K. A., & Meier, S. C. (2014).

Cohen-Kettenis, P. T., Delemarre-van de Waal, H. A., & Gooren, L. J. G. (2008). The treatment of adolescent transsexuals: Changing insights. Journal of Sexual Medicine, 5, 1892–1897. http://dx.doi.org/10.1111/j .1743-6109.2008.00870.x

Coleman E, Bockting W, Botzer M, et al. Standards of care for the health of transsexual, transgender, and gender-nonconforming people, version 7. *Int J Transgenderism.* 2012; 13(4):165–232.

Colizzi M, Costa R, Todarello O. Transsexual patients' psychiatric comorbidity and positive effect of cross-sex hormonal treatment on mental health: results from a longitudinal study. *Psychoneuroendocrinology.* 2014;39:65–73pmid:24275005.

Davis, S. A., & Meier, S. C. (2014). Effects of testosterone treatment and chest reconstruction surgery on mental health and sexuality in female-to-male transgender people. International Journal of Sexual Health, 26, 113–128. http://dx.doi.org/10.1080/19317611.2013.833152.

De Cuypere, G., Elaut, E., Heylens, G., Van Maele, G., Selvaggi, G., T'Sjoen, G.,... Monstrey, S. (2006). Long-term follow-up: Psychosocial outcomes of Belgian transsexuals after sex reassignment surgery. Sexologies, 15, 126 –133. http://dx.doi.org/10.1016/j.sexol.2006.04.002.

De Vries, A, McGuire, J, Steensma, T, Wagenaar, E, Doreleiiers, T, Cohen-Kettenis, P. "Young adult psychological outcome after puberty suppression and gender reassignment." US National Library of Medicine National Institutes of Health (2014 Oct): 696-704. http://www.ncbi.nlm.nih.gov/pubmed/25201798

De Vries, A, Steensma, T, Doreleiiers, T, Cohen-Kettenis, P. "Puberty suppression in adolescents with gender identity disorder: a prospective follow-up study." US National Library of Medicine National Institutes of Health (2011 August): 2276-2283. http://www.ncbi.nlm.nih.gov/pubmed/20646177

Gooren, L. J., Giltay, E. J., Bunck, M. C. (2008). Long-term treatment of trans-sexuals with cross-sex hormones: Extensive personal experience. Journal of Clinical Endocrinology & Metabolism: Clinical and Experimental, 93, 19 –25. http://dx.doi.org/10.1210/jc.2007-1809

Kuhn, A., Brodmer, C., Stadlmayer, W., Kuhn, P., Mueller, M. D., & Birkhauser, M. (2009). Quality of life 15 years after sex reassignment surgery for trans-sexualism. Fertility and Sterility, 92, 1685–1689. http:// dx.doi.org/10.1016/j.fertnstet.2008.08.126

Murad, M. H., Elamin, M. B., Garcia, M. Z., Mullan, R. J., Murad, A., Erwin, P. J., & Montori, V. M. (2010). Hormonal therapy and sex reassignment: A systemic review and meta-analysis of quality of life and psychosocial outcomes. Clinical Endocrinology, 72, 214 –231. http:// dx.doi.org/10.1111/j.1365-2265.2009.03625.x

Chapter 4: Achieving Gender Consolidation

Bockting, W.O., & Coleman, E. Developmental stages of the transgender coming out process: Toward an integrated identity, in Principles of Transgender Medicine and Surgery. Randi Ettner Haworth Press Inc. (2007).

Clifford, C., & Orford, J. The experience of social power in the lives of trans people, in V. Clarke & E. Peel (Eds.), Out in psychology: Lesbian, gay, bisexual, trans and queer perspectives (195–216). West Sussex, UK: John Wiley (2008).

Devor, A.H., & Matte, N.; ONE Inc. & Reed Erickson. The Uneasy Collaboration of Gay and Trans Activism, 1964–2003. *GLQ: A Journal of Gay and Lesbian Studies*, 10(2), 179–209.

Ericha, S., Tittsworth, J., Meier, S.L.C., & Lermana, T. Transsexuals of Color: Perceptions of Discrimination Based on Transsexual Status and Race/ Ethnicity Status. *Journal of GLBT Family Studies*. Vol. 6, Issue 3, 2010.

Finnegan, D., & Mcnally, E. *Counseling Lesbian, Gay, Bisexual, and Transgender Substance Abusers: Dual Identities*. New York: Routledge (2002).

Koyama, E. The transfeminist manifesto, in R. Dicker & A. Piepmeier (Eds.), *Catching a wave: Reclaiming feminism for the twenty-first century* (244–261). Boston: Northeastern University Press (2003).

Kozee, H.B., Tylka, T.L., & Bauerband, L.A. Measuring Transgender Individuals' Comfort with Gender Identity and Appearance: Development and Validation of the Transgender Congruence Scale. *Psychology of Women Quarterly*, April 2012.

Lev, A.I. *Transgender Emergence: Counseling Gender-Variant People and their Families*. New York: Taylor and Francis (2004).

Levitt, H.M., & Ippolito, M.R. Being Transgender: Navigating Minority Stressors and Developing Authentic Self-Presentation. *Psychology of Women Quarterly*, March 2014, 38: 46–64.

Riggle, E.D.B., Rostosky, S.S., McCants, L.E., & Pascale-Hague, D. The positive aspects of a transgender self-identification. *Psychology & Sexuality*, February 2011.

Skidmore, W.C., Linsenmeier, J.A.W., & Bailey, J.M. *Archives of Sexual Behavior*, Vol. 35(6), 2006, 685–697.

Vanderburgh, R. *Transition and beyond: Observations on gender identity*. Portland, OR: Q Press (2007).

Chapter 5: Goals of Adolescent Development

American Psychological Association. *A Reference for Professionals: Developing Adolescents* (2002).

Casey B.J., Kosofsky B.E., & Bhide, P.G. *Teenage Brains: Think Different?* Karger Medical and Science Publishers (2014).

Lebel, C., & Beaulieu, C. Longitudinal development of human brain wiring continues from childhood into adulthood. *Journal of Neuroscience*, 2011; 31(30): 10937–10947. doi: 10.1523/JNEUROSCI.5302-10.2011.

McNeely, C., & Blanchard, J. *The Teen Years Explained: A Guide to Healthy Adolescent Development.* Center for Adolescent Health, Johns Hopkins Bloomberg School of Public Health (2009).

National Institute of Mental Health. *The Teen Brain: Still Under Construction.* http://www.nimh.nih.gov/health/publications/the-teen-brain-still-under-construction/index.shtml.

Simpson, A.R. *Raising Teens: A Synthesis of Research and a Foundation for Action.* Boston: Center for Health Communication, Harvard School of Public Health (2001).

Steinberg, L. A social neuroscience perspective on adolescent risk-taking. *Developmental Review*, 28: 78–106, 2008.

Steinberg, L., & Morris, A.S. Adolescent Development. *Annual Review of Psychology*, 2001.

Chapter 6: What Keeps You Up at Night

American Academy of Child and Adolescent Psychiatry, Practice Parameter on Gay, Lesbian, or bisexual Sexual Orientation, Gender Nonconformity, and Gender Discordance in Children and Adolescents, 51 *Journal of the American Academy of Child & Adolescent Psychiatry* 957, 2012. http://www.guideline.gov/content.aspx?id=38417#Section420.

American Psychiatric Association, Position Statement on Therapies Focused on Attempts to Change Sexual Orientation (Reparative or Conversion Therapies) (2000). http://www.psychiatry.org/File%20Library/Advocacy%20and%20Newsroom/Position%20Statements/ps2000_ReparativeTherapy.pdf.

Bullying Among Middle School and High School Students—Massachusetts, 2009, CDC. http://www.cdc.gov/mmwr/preview/mmwrhtml/mm6015a1.htm.

Cole, C.M., O'Boyle, M., Emory L.E., & Meyer, W.J. Comorbidity of gender dysphoria and other major psychiatric diagnoses. *Archchives of Sexual Behavior*, 1997; 26(1): 13–26.

Davidson, C. National Health Care for the Homeless Council (August 2014). Gender Minority & Homelessness: Transgender Population. *Focus: A Quarterly Research Review of the National HCH Council*, 3:1. www.nhchc.org.

Colizzi, M., Costa, R., & Todarello, O. Transsexual patients' psychiatric comorbidity and positive effect of cross-sex hormonal treatment on mental health: results from a longitudinal study. *Psychoneuroendocrinology,* 2014; 39: 65–73. doi: 10.1016/j.psyneuen.2013.09.029.

Empire State Coalition of Youth and Family Services, *A Count of Homeless Youth in New York City,* March 2008.

Goldblum, P., Testa, Rylan, J., Pflum, S., Hendricks, M.L., Bradford, J., & Bongar, B. The relationship between gender-based victimization and suicide attempts in transgender people. *Professional Psychology: Research and Practice,* Vol. 43(5), 2012, 468–475. http://dx.doi.org/10.1037/a0029605.

Gonzalez, C.A., Bockting, W.O., Beckman, L., & Durán, R.E. Agency and communion: Their role in depression and resilience among transgender women. *Sex Roles: A Journal of Research,* 2012.

Grant, J.M., Mottet, L.A., Tanis, J., Harrison, J., Herman, J.L., & Keisling, M. *Injustice at Every Turn: A Report of the National Transgender Discrimination Survey.* Washington, DC: National Center for Transgender Equality and National Gay and Lesbian Task Force (2011).

Haas, A.P., Rodgers, P.L., & Herman, J.L. *Suicide Attempts Among Transgender and Gender Non-Conforming Adults,* January 2014, at http://williamsinstitute.law. ucla.edu/research/suicide-attempts-among-transgender-and-gender-non-conforming-adults/#sthash.YIXxqhrj.dpuf.

Heylens, G., Verroken, C., De Cock, S., T'Sjoen, G., & De Cuypere, G. Effects of Different Steps in Gender Reassignment Therapy on Psychopathology: A Prospective Study of Persons with a Gender Identity Disorder. *Journal of Sexual Medicine,* 2014, 11: 119–126. doi: 10.1111/jsm.12363.

Hoshiai, M., Matsumoto, Y., Sato, T., Ohnishi, M., Okabe, N., Kishimoto, Y., Terada, S., & Kuroda, S. (2010), Psychiatric comorbidity among patients with gender identity disorder. *Psychiatry and Clinical Neurosciences,* 64: 514–519. doi: 10.1111/j.1440-1819.2010.02118.

Kenagy, G.P., & Bostwick, W.B. Health and social service needs of transgender people in Chicago. *International Journal of Transgenderism,* 2005, 3(2/3), 57–66.

Kosciw, J.G., Greytak, E.A., Palmer, N.A., & Boesen, M.J. The 2013 National School Climate Survey: The experiences of lesbian, gay, bisexual and transgender youth in our nation's schools. New York: GLSEN (2014).

Lesbian, Gay, Bisexual, Transgender, Queer, and HIV-Affected Hate Violence In 2014: A Report from the National Coalition Of Anti-Violence Programs, http://www.avp.org/storage/documents/Reports/2014_HV_Report-Final.pdf

Marksamer, J.A. *Place of Respect—A Guide for Group Care Facilities Serving Transgender and Gender Nonconforming Youth.* 2011.

Davidson, C. National Health Care for the Homeless Council (August 2014). Gender Minority & Homelessness: Transgender Population. *Focus: A Quarterly Research Review of the National HCH Council,* 3:1. www.nhchc.org.

Sifra Quintana, N., Rosenthal, J., & Krehely, J. *On the Streets: The Federal Response to Gay and Transgender Homeless Youth.* Center for American Progress 2010.

Veale, J., Saewyc, E., Frohard-Dourlent, H., Dobson, S., Clark, B., & the Canadian Trans Youth Health Survey Research Group. *Being Safe, Being Me: Results of the Canadian Trans Youth Health Survey.* Vancouver, BC: School of Nursing, University of British Columbia (2015).

Chapter 8: Understanding How Minority Stress Impacts Your Teen

Bauer, G.R., Pyne, J., Francino, R., & Hammond, M.C. Suicidality among trans people in Ontario: Implications for social work and social justice. *Service Social* 59 (1), 2013.

Bockting, W.O., Miner, M.H., Romine, R.E.S., Hamilton, A., Coleman, E. Stigma, mental health, and resilience in an online sample of the U.S. transgender population. *American Journal of Public Health*, 103(5), 2013. doi: 10.2105/AJPH.2013.301241

Boza, C., & Nicholson Perry, K. Gender-related victimization, perceived social support, and predictors of depression among transgender Australians. *International Journal of Transgenderism,* 15(1), 2014. doi: 10.1080/15532739.2014.890558.

Bradford, J., Reisner, S.L., Honnold, J.A., & Xavier, J. Experiences of transgender-related discrimination and implications for health: Results from the Virginia transgender health initiative study. *American Journal of Public Health,* 103(10). 2013. doi: 10.2105/AJPH.2012.300796.

Davidson, C. National Health Care for the Homeless Council (August 2014). Gender Minority & Homelessness: Transgender Population. *Focus: A Quarterly Research Review of the National HCH Council,* 3:1. www.nhchc.org.

Gattis, M.N., & McKinnon, S.L. *School Experiences of Transgender and Gender Non-Conforming Students in Wisconsin*. Madison, WI: GSAFE (2015).

Goldblum, P., Testa, R., Pflum, S., Hendricks, M.L., & Bradford, J.B. The Relationship Between Gender-Based Victimization and Suicide Attempts in Transgender People. *Professional Psychology Research and Practice*, 10/2012; 43(5): 468. doi: 10.1037/a0029605.

Grant, J.M., Mottet, L.A., Tanis, J., Harrison, J., Herman, J.L., & Keisling, M. *Injustice at every turn: A report of the National Transgender Discrimination Survey*. Washington, DC: National Center for Transgender Equality and National Gay and Lesbian Task Force (2011).

Grossman, A.H., & D'Augelli, A.R. Transgender youth and life-threatening behaviors. *Suicide & Life-Threatening Behavior*, 37(5), 2007; 527-537. doi: 10.1521/suli.2007.37.5.527

Hendricks, M.L., & Testa, R.J. A conceptual framework for clinical work with transgender and gender nonconforming clients: An adaptation of the Minority Stress Model. *Professional Psychology: Research and Practice*, Vol. 43(5), 2012, 460–467. http://dx.doi.org/10.1037/a0029597

Joiner, T. *Why people die by suicide*. Cambridge, MA: Harvard University Press (2005).

Meyer, I.H. Prejudice, social stress, and mental health in lesbian, gay, and bisexual populations: Conceptual issues and research evidence. *Psychological Bulletin*, 129(5), 2003. doi: 10.1037/0033-2909.129.5.674

Plöderl, M., Sellmeier, M., Fartacek, C., Pichler, E., Fartacek, R., & Kralovec, K. Explaining the suicide risk of sexual minority individuals by contrasting the minority stress model with suicide models. *Archives of Sexual Behavior*, 2014. doi: 10.1007/s10508-014-0268-4.

Sevelius, J.M. Gender affirmation: A framework for conceptualizing risk behavior among transgender women of color. *Sex Roles*, 68 (11–12), 2013.
Supporting and Caring for our Gender-expansive Youth. Written by Gender Spectrum and the Human Rights Campaign Foundation. 2013. Available at https://www.genderspectrum.org/youth/

Testa, R.J., Habarth, J., Peta, J., Balsam, K., & Bockting, W. Development of the Gender Minority Stress and Resilience Measure. *Psychology of Sexual Orientation and Gender Diversity*, 2014. http://dx.doi.org/10.1037/sgd0000081

Testa, R.J., Sciacca, L.M., Wang, F., Hendricks, M.L., Goldblum, P., Bradford, J., & Bongar, B. Effects of violence on transgender people. *Professional Psychology: Research and Practice*, 43(5), 2012. doi: 10.1037/a0029604.

Toomey, R.B., Ryan, C., Diaz, R., Card, M., Russell, N.A., & Stephen, T. Gender-Nonconforming Lesbian, Gay, Bisexual, and Transgender Youth: School Victimization and Young Adult Psychosocial Adjustment. *Developmental Psychology*, Vol. 46, No. 6, 2010.

Van Orden, K.A., Lynam, M.E., Hollar, D., & Joiner, T.E. Perceived burdensomeness as an indicator of suicidal symptoms. *Cognitive Therapy and Research*, 30(4), 2006. doi:10.1007/s10608-006-9057-2.

Van Orden, K.A., Witte, T.K., Cukrowicz, K.C., Braithwaite, S.R., Selby, E.A., & Joiner, T.E. The interpersonal theory of suicide. *Psychological Review*, Vol. 117(2), 2010, 575–600. http://dx.doi.org/10.1037/a0018697.

Van Orden, K.A., Witte, T.K., Gordon, K.H., Bender, T.W., & Joiner, T.E. Suicidal desire and the capability for suicide: Tests of the interpersonal-psychological theory of suicidal behavior among adults. *Journal of Consulting and Clinical Psychology*, 76(1), 2008. doi: 10.1037/0022-006X.76.1.72.

Xavier, J., Bobbin, M., Singer, B., & Budd, E. A needs assessment of transgendered people of color living in Washington, D.C. *International Journal of Transgenderism*, 8(2–3), 2005. doi:10.1300/ J485v08n02_04.

Chapter 9: Professional Support and Mental Health Considerations

American Academy of Child and Adolescent Psychiatry, *Practice Parameter on Gay, Lesbian, or bisexual Sexual Orientation, Gender Nonconformity, and Gender Discordance in Children and Adolescents*, 51 J. Am. Acad. Child & Adolescent Psychiatry 957 (2012), available at http://www.guideline.gov/content.aspx?id=38417#Section420.

Bess, J.A., & Stabb, S.D. The Experiences of Transgendered Persons in Psychotherapy: Voices and Recommendations. *Journal of Mental Health Counseling*, Vol. 31, No. 3, 2009.

Burnes, T.R., & Chen, M.M. The multiple identities of transgender individuals: Incorporating a framework of intersectionality to gender crossing, in R. Josselson & M. Harway (Eds.), *Navigating multiple identities: Race, gender, culture, nationality, and roles* (113–128). New York: Oxford University Press (2012). http://dx.doi.org/ 10.1093/acprof:oso/9780199732074.003.0007.

Child Adolesc Ment Health. 2011 Feb; 16(1): 30–37.
    doi: 10.1111/j.1475-3588.2010.00577.x
    Adolescent Family Factors Promoting Healthy Adult Functioning: A
    Longitudinal Community Study. Angela D. Paradis,1,2 Rose M. Giaconia,1
    Helen Z. Reinherz,1 William R. Beardslee,3 Kirsten E. Ward,1 and
    Garrett M. Fitzmaurice4,5

De Vries, A.L.C., Noens, I.L.J., Cohen Kettenis, P.T., van Berckelaer-Onnes, I.A.,
    & Doreleijers, T.A. Autism spectrum disorders in gender dysphoric children
    and adolescents. *Journal of Autism and Developmental Disorders*, 40 (8), 2010,
    930–936. http://dx.doi.org/10.1007/ s10803-010-0935-9

Garofalo, R., Deleon, J., Osmer, E., Doll, M., & Harper, G.W. Overlooked, misun-
    derstood and at-risk: Exploring the lives and HIV risk of ethnic minority
    male-to-female transgender youth. *Journal of Adolescent Health*, 2006; 38(3):
    230–236.

Gattis, Maurice N. and McKinnon, Sara L. , School Experiences of Transgender
    and Gender Non-Conforming Students in Wisconsin, Madison, WI: GSAFE,
    2015.

Hendricks, M.L., & Testa, R.J. A conceptual framework for clinical work with
    transgender and gender nonconforming clients: An adaptation of the Minority
    Stress Model. *Professional Psychology: Research and Practice*, Vol. 43(5), 2012,
    460–467.

Lgars, M., Alanko, K., Santtila, P., & Sandnabba, N.K. (). Disordered eating and
    gender identity disorder: a qualitative study. *Eating disorders* 20(4), 2012,
    300–311.

Jones, R.M., Wheelwright, S., Farrell, K., Martin, E., Green, R., Di Ceglie, D., &
    Baron-Cohen, S. 2011 Brief report: Female-to male transsexual people and
    autistic traits.

Liu, R.T., & Mustanski, B. Suicidal ideation and self-harm in lesbian, gay,
    bisexual, and transgender youth. *American Journal of Preventive Medicine*,
    2012, 42(3): 221–228. doi: 10.1016/j.amepre.2011.10.023.

Murray, S.B., Boon, E., & Touyz, S.W. Diverging eating psychopathology in
    transgendered eating disorder patients: a report of two cases. *Eating Disor-
    ders*, 2013; 21(1): 70–74. doi: 10.1080/10640266.2013.741989.

Mustanski, B.S., Garofalo, R., & Emerson, E.M. Mental health disorders, psycho-
    logical distress, and suicidality in a diverse sample of lesbian, gay, bisexual,
    and transgender youths. *American Journal of Public Health*, 2010, 100(12):
    2426–2432. doi: 10.2105/AJPH.2009.178319.

Rachlin, K. Transgender Individuals' Experiences of Psychotherapy. *I.J.T.*, Vol. 6, No. 1, January–March 2002.

Rajkumar, R.P. Gender Identity Disorder and Schizophrenia: Neurodevelopmental Disorders with Common Causal Mechanisms? *Schizophrenia Research and Treatment*, 2014, http://dx.doi.org/10.1155/2014/463757.

Riggle, E.D.B., Rostosky, S.S., McCants, L.E., & Pascale-Hague, D. The positive aspects of a transgender self-identification. *Psychology & Sexuality*, February 2011.

Singh, A.A., Hays, D.G., & Watson, L.S. Strength in the face of adversity: Resilience strategies of transgender individuals. *Journal of Counseling & Development*, 89, 2011; 20–27. http://dx.doi.org/10.1002/j.1556-6678.2011.tb00057.x.

Tateno, M., Ikeda, H., & Saito, T. Gender dysphoria in pervasive developmental disorders. *Seishin Shinkeigaku Zasshi.*, 2011; 113(12): 1173–1183.

Chapter 10: What You Can Do to Improve the Odds

Bauer, G.R., Scheim, A.I., Pyne, J., Travers, R., & Hammond, R. Intervenable factors associated with suicide risk in transgender persons: a respondent driven sampling study in Ontario, Canada. *BMC Public Health*, 2015; 15: 525.

E. Brodsky, 2015, The Year We Thought About Love (documentary) www.theyearwethoughtaboutlove.com.

Luthar, S.S. Resilience in development: A synthesis of research across five decades, in Cicchetti, D., & Cohen, D.J. (Eds.), *Developmental Psychopathology: Risk, Disorder, and Adaptation*. New York: Wiley (2006).

Paradis et al., 2011. *Adolescent Family Factors Promoting Healthy Adult Functioning: A Longitudinal Community Study.*

Rayner, M., & Montague, M. (2000). *Resilient children and young people*. Melbourne, AU: Deakin University, Policy and Practice Unit.

Veale, J., Saewyc, E., Frohard-Dourlent, H., Dobson, S., Clark, B., & the Canadian Trans Youth Health Survey Research Group. *Being Safe, Being Me: Results of the Canadian Trans Youth Health Survey*. Vancouver, BC: School of Nursing, University of British Columbia (2015).

Chapter 11: Nurturing Your Teen's Resilience

American College Health Association. 2013 Reference Group Summary. http://

www.acha-ncha.org/docs/ACHA-NCHA-II_ReferenceGroup_Execu-
tiveSummary_Spring2013.pdf.

American Psychological Association. *A Reference for Professionals: Developing Adolescents* (2002).

American Psychological Association. *Stress in America: Paying With Our Health* (2014).

Bauer, G.R., Pyne, J., Francino, M.C., & Hammond, R. Suicidality among trans people in Ontario: Implications for social work and social justice. *Service Social*, 59, 35–62, 2013. http://dx.doi.org/10.7202/ 1017478ar.

Bauer, G.R., Scheim, A.I., Pyne, J., Travers, R., & Hammond, R. Intervenable factors associated with suicide risk in transgender persons: A respondent driven sampling study in Ontario, Canada. *BMC Public Health*, 15, 525–540, 2015. http://dx.doi.org/10.1186/s12889-015-1867-2.

Lasser, J., & Tharinger, D. Visibility management in school and beyond: a qualitative study of gay, lesbian, bisexual youth. *Journal of Adolescence,* Vol. 26, No. 2, 2003, 233–244..

Moody, C., Fuks, N., Peláez, S., & Smith, N.G. Without this, I would for sure already be dead: A qualitative inquiry regarding suicide protective factors among trans adults. *Psychology of Sexual Orientation and Gender Diversity*, 2(3), 266–280, 2015. http://dx.doi.org/10.1037/sgd0000130.

Morrow, D.F. Social Work Practice with Gay, Lesbian, Bisexual, and Transgender Adolescents, *Family in Society*, January–March, 2004, 91.

Riggle, E.D.B., & Mohr, J.J. A proposed multi factor measure of positive identity for transgender identified individuals. *Psychology of Sexual Orientation and Gender Diversity*, Vol. 2(1), 2015, 78–85.

Riggle, E.D.B., Rostosky, S.S., McCants, L.E., & Pascale-Hague, D. The positive aspects of a transgender self-identification. *Psychology & Sexuality*, February 2011.

Sanchez, F.J., & Vilain, E. Collective Self-Esteem as a Coping Resource for Male-to-Female Transsexuals. *Journal of Counseling Psychology*, Vol. 56(1), 2009, 202–209.

Singh, A.A., Hays, D.G., & Watson, L.S. Strength in the face of adversity: Resilience strategies of transgender individuals. *Journal of Counseling & Development*, 89, 20–27, 2011. http://dx.doi.org/10.1002/j .1556-6678.2011.tb00057.x.

Singh, A.A., & McKleroy, V.S. Just getting out of bed is a revolutionary act: The resilience of transgender people of color who have survived traumatic life events. *Traumatology* 17, 34–44, 2011. http://dx .doi.org/10.1177/1534765610369261.

Testa, R.J., Sciacca, L.M., Wang, F., Hendricks, M.L., Goldblum, P., Bradford, J., & Bongar, B. Effects of violence on transgender people. *Professional Psychology: Research and Practice,* 43, 452–459, 2012.

Travers, R., Bauer, G., Pyne, J., Bradley, K., Gale, L., & Papadimitriou, M. Impacts of strong parental support for trans youth: A report prepared for Children's Aid Society of Toronto and Delisle Youth Services. http://transpulseproject. ca/wp-content/uploads/2012/10/Impacts-of-Strong-Parental-Support-for-Trans-Y outh-vFINAL .pdf.

Testa, R.J., Jimenez, C.L., & Rankin, S. Risk and Resilience During Transgender Identity Development: The Effects of Awareness and Engagement with Other Transgender People on Affect. *Journal of Gay & Lesbian Mental Health,* 18: 31–46, 2014.

Testa, R.J., Habarth, J., Peta, J., Balsam, K., & Bockting, W. Development of the Gender Minority Stress and Resilience. *Psychology of Sexual Orientation and Gender Diversity,* Vol. 2(1), 2015, 65–77.

White Hughto, J.M., & Reisner, S.L. A Systematic Review of the Effects of Hormone Therapy on Psychological Functioning and Quality of Life in Transgender Individuals. *Transgender Health,* January 2016, 1(1): 21–31. doi:10.1089/trgh.2015.0008.

Additional Resources

To access a range of resources related to the information in *The Transgender Teen*, visit www.genderspectrum.org. You will find information related to a variety of topics including:

- How to access support for parents and youth.
- Current research on parenting transgender and non-binary youth.
- Gender diversity in faith-based contexts.
- Gender and the child welfare system.
- Gender diversity and the autism spectrum.
- How to support non-gender-expansive siblings.
- Biographies of transgender and other gender-expansive individuals.
- Legal issues facing transgender and non-binary youth.

You will also discover a great variety of helpful handouts, tools, and sources of support on the Gender Spectrum website. Whether you are seeking information to share with family members or friends, ideas for working with camps and other organizations, or the insights of youth sharing their own gender journeys, the Gender Spectrum website will serve as a great way to continue building your own understanding about your teen's gender.

Finally, through the website, you will be able to access the Gender Spectrum Lounge, an online community that connects individuals from all over the world seeking to learn more, share their experiences,

or ask questions about gender. With groups for teens, parents, professionals, and a host of others, the Gender Spectrum Lounge is an
incredible community designed to help adults and youth alike navigate the world of gender.

Acknowledgements

This book would not be in your hands today if it were not for the pioneering families who gathered together to support their children in the early 2000s. Not knowing if their children were transgender, non-binary or otherwise gender expansive we met at the support group I (Stephanie) was running, with Dr. Herb Schreier, at Children's Hospital Oakland. Although I had already been providing trainings around the San Francisco Bay Area on issues of gender diversity for preschools, elementary schools, religious schools, and city and county organizations, it is truly that original support group that propelled me to start Gender Spectrum. Those core families, their love, their struggles, and their incredible children are the true inspiration for all that Gender Spectrum does. I will not mention any of you by name to protect privacy; you know who you are and I will never forget any of you. Every single one of the children from those early potluck days can know with certainty that they have changed the world and helped to make it a better place for everyone.

We would also like to acknowledge the thousands of youth and their families we have worked with since then, as well as the brave and forward thinking healthcare providers, mental health providers, social workers, faith leaders, teachers and administrators, school boards, lawyers, and others who are all striving to create a world where everyone is seen and valued for who they are.

There are a number of people we owe a tremendous debt of gratitude. To the amazing staff at Gender Spectrum, especially Joel Baum, Kim Westheimer, Pamela Wool, and Mere Abrams—thank you, thank you, thank you. Your tireless efforts on top of already demanding workloads are deeply appreciated; the book is better because of you. We would also like to offer our appreciation to the following people who contributed to our writing of this book: Aarezu Rezai, Asaf Orr, Esq., Diane Ehrensaft, Ph.D. and everyone at Cleis Press. A special thanks to the many parents who reviewed chapters and provided feedback throughout our writing process. Your perspective and voice are invaluable.

And lastly, this book wouldn't be here at all without the incredible love and support of our own families. Thank you for allowing us to take the time needed in order to write this book. We couldn't have done this without you. You serve as our deepest inspiration and any difference this book makes in the world is yours too.

About the Authors

STEPHANIE BRILL is a leading expert on a broad range of topics related to gender diversity. She is the author of landmark books including *The Transgender Child* with Rachel Pepper (Cleis Press, 2008). She is the founder and Board Chair of Gender Spectrum, an organization at the forefront of work related to children, youth and gender. Her work has been featured on 20/20, The Huffington Post, San Francisco Chronicle, All Things Considered, and The New York Times.

LISA KENNEY is the Executive Director of Gender Spectrum. She's a featured speaker at conferences and a consultant to organizations and corporations on the changing understanding of gender and the implications this has for parents and families, social institutions and corporations. She co-produced the film *Creating Gender Inclusive Schools* with Jonathan Skurnik and Joel Baum and provides workshops and other events for parents and caregivers on gender. *The Transgender Teen* is Lisa's first book.